INTRODUCTION

Throughout our lives, we constantly change and adapt to new circumstances, but the transition retirement represents, is for most people, a big shift. Not the easy shift we expect that comes from not having to go to work every day, but, according to Holmes-Rahe Life Stress Inventory, a shift big enough to rank as the tenth most stressful event in a person's life.

Sounds strange, right? Unless one is retired or about to retire, most people wouldn't think of retirement as a stressful event. In fact, most people in the thick of their careers would love to retire now! Viewing the plethora of ads and commercials depicting a happily-ever-after life in retirement, you wouldn't think retirement could be stressful. You've seen these ads – a tanned couple holding hands walking on a sunlit beach in Tahiti, sailing in the crystal-clear smooth waters of the Caribbean, and whopping it up with friends (all good-looking, of course) while biking from vineyard to vineyard through France's wine country.

The reality for most people is a bit more nuanced. I've found most people do look forward to retiring from their full-time careers, but as the day approaches, doubt and anxiety start creeping in. Not for everybody, of course, but for many people, especially if they have put their heart and soul into their working lives. Retirement today doesn't look like anything in the past. Our families have changed. The economy has changed. Societal norms and expectations have changed. The old model of "stop working at age sixty-five, move somewhere warm, and pursue a life of leisure with a bunch of fellow retirees" applies only to a minority.

People realize things will be different, but they don't know how they'll be different. Retirement in the twenty-first century is a lot more complex than the retirement of our parents and grandparents. Everybody understands we live in an era of rapid technological change. What is often less apparent is how much the norms, practicalities, and choices for our retirement have changed in the last decades.

What is retirement today? According to *The Merriam-Webster Dictionary*, it's the "withdrawal from one's position or occupation or from active working life" But you already knew that. You know retirement represents an ending to a chapter in your life, but what you're most interested in is what happens next. What happens between the end of your primary career and the beginning of your new life? How do you feel about this change? Do you know what to do next? Do you know how you want the next phase of your life to look?

Looking at your parents' retirement is not much help. For starters, few people can still rely on a pension plan. Moreover, it is no longer guaranteed that your job will even be there for as long as you want. Also, people live longer now and could spend as many years retired as they did working. The family structure has drastically changed as people have become geographically scattered, and an increasing number of retirees will be single or divorced.

You can see change all around us, but the biggest change that we often don't talk about is internal. Our expectations for what we want out of life are different from previous generations. We see more possibilities, but we also face more pitfalls and hurdles. We want to not only live longer but live better. We want to enjoy today but must prepare for many tomorrows. We don't want our lives to stop now that our careers no longer define us and provide structure to our day. We feel capable of doing so many things with our time and life experience. We don't see why we should not keep pushing ahead by learning and experiencing new things and challenging ourselves to keep growing, rather than just wilting away with diminished expectations.

REIMAGINING RETIREMENT

9 KEYS TO TRUE WEALTH

ERIC J. WEIGEL

Copyright © 2022 by Eric J. Weigel

All rights reserved.

No part of this book may be reproduced in any form or by any electronic or mechanical means, including information storage and retrieval systems, without written permission from the author, except for the use of brief quotations in a book review.

Paperback ISBN: 979-8-218-05864-7

CONTENTS

Introduction	1
1. Reinvention	13
2. Designing Your Future Self	26
3. Your NEST	53
4. Earning a Sustainable Living	69
5. Getting a Return on Your Time	101
6. Work	120
7. Emotional Energy	132
8. Achievements	152
9. Learning	172
10. Tribe	186
11. Health	202
12. Acting On Your Plan	219
13. Getting Unstuck from the Messy Middle	234
14. A Retirement Full of Possibilities	245
Acknowledgments	259
About The Author	261
Bibliography	263

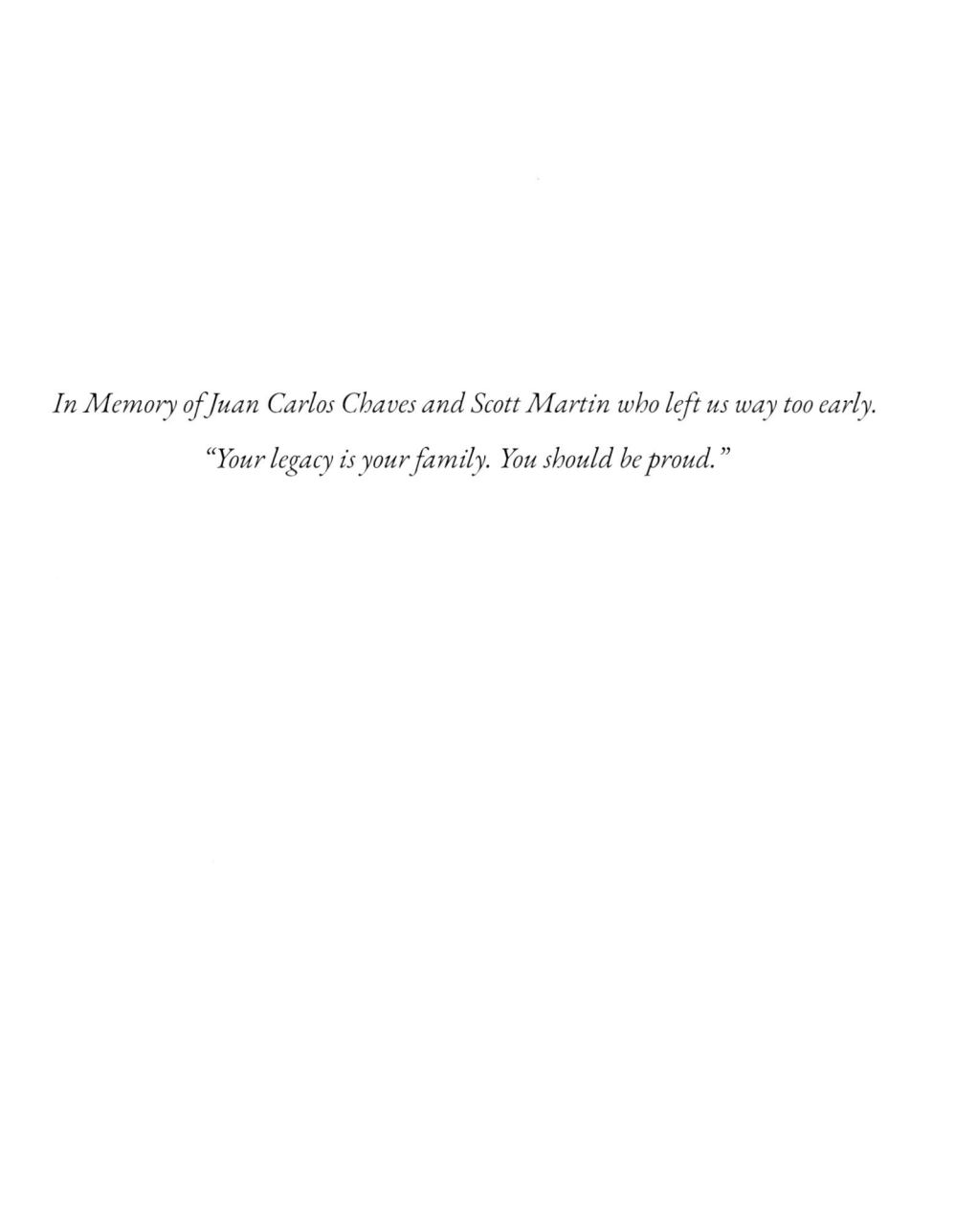

In Memory of Juan Carlos Chaves and Scott Martin who left us way too early.

"Your legacy is your family. You should be proud."

WE LIVE IN AN ERA OF CHOICE AND COMPLEXITY

The possibilities for what we want to do in this next phase in life are endless—in fact, we are cursed by what Dr. Barry Schwartz calls the paradox of choice. As our choices have expanded, we are often left more confused and stressed. On the surface, having more choices would seem good, but, more choices also mean making more decisions and living with the possibility of not always choosing well. More choices imply more responsibility. Making the best choice possible becomes more challenging as our range of opportunities expands. Schwartz's research shows that many times this leaves people frustrated and stressed.

For better or worse, we live in an era of customization. What you want is not necessarily what I want, yet we both have the same expansive choices. We can't default to antiquated models. We must make our own choices and take responsibility for our retirement. To overcome the paradox of choice we all face, we must narrow our choices to reflect what we want out of life. To do this, we must become part thinker/philosopher, part planner/decision-maker, and part doer.

FOCUSING ON SHORTCUT SOLUTIONS GIVES YOU AN INCOMPLETE PICTURE

Everybody loves a shortcut, right? Wouldn't you love to follow a recipe that promises to deliver the most satisfying life in retirement without too much thought?

People are out there who are willing to show you the "magic" recipe. Just watch all the retirement ads and make an appointment with a well-dressed, smooth-talking financial representative. The implied promise is that all your dreams will come true if you follow this well-trodden path.

Unfortunately, this shortcut doesn't work for most people. It will work if you already have millions in savings, know precisely what you want out of life, and have a plan to make your dreams a reality. You're lucky if this person is you, but you're the needle in a haystack.

Most of us will need to make decisions and choices where a cookie-cutter approach won't work. We will need to make informed decisions and tradeoffs. There are no shortcuts or recipes to follow because we often struggle to figure out what we want from life. We don't have the faintest idea of how to prepare for this next phase in life. We don't have unlimited financial resources to outsource all the details to somebody else. Even if we did have all the money in the world, what good would that do us if we didn't know how to use it to create a happy and fulfilling life?

THE GOAL OF A HAPPY AND FULFILLING LIFE IN RETIREMENT REQUIRES MORE THAN MONEY

Money can buy comfort and relieve us of financial worry, but it can't buy us most of the things we crave—love, companionship, health, a sense of meaning, and peace of mind.

The beauty of living in an era of many choices and possibilities is that we don't have to borrow someone else's definition of happiness and fulfillment. We can make up our own definitions and create our own journey.

Eleanor Roosevelt once said, "In the long run, we shape our lives, and we shape ourselves. The process never ends until we die. And the choices we make are ultimately our responsibility."

We alone are responsible for our choices of how we live, who we associate with, what we value, and how we spend our time. Having lots of money isn't going to make our job easier or give us a pass on thinking for ourselves.

A happy and fulfilling retirement requires focusing on all aspects of your life —financial and non-financial. Think about it: Can you be happy or fulfilled if your health falls apart? Or if your relationships with family and friends are stressed?

Successful retirement life is about more than how much money you have. It's about enjoying the money you do have to live well. To live well, you need money for the ride, but you also need close social connections, physical health, emotional balance, meaningful pursuits, and a lifestyle consistent with your values and beliefs.

A VISION FOR YOUR FUTURE SELF

My goal for writing this book is that you accept the challenge of designing the life you want to lead during your retirement years. Anytime you accept responsibility for an outcome, you go from observer to planner to doer, whether you're contemplating or already are in the thick of this next phase in life.

I believe that much of what you hear today about retirement planning is well-intentioned but severely lacking. Too much retirement planning is focused on money without giving much thought to where you want to go in your journey and what would make your life successful. Much of the financial advice boils down to unrelatable financial projections. You get a lot of nice-looking charts, but what does it all mean?

I feel the same way about much of the self-improvement industry. The advice sounds good on the surface, but it often fails to deliver meaningful or lasting results. It's usually geared at growing your pie instead of enjoying the fruits of your labor.

I wrote this book both for myself and all of you embarking on a new phase of life. While I'm a baby boomer, I think that the concepts and ideas presented throughout the book will be of value to all generations. Everybody faces questions such as:

- Where will I live?
- What kind of lifestyle will I have?
- How will I manage my finances?
- Will I run out of money?
- What will I do with my time?

Like most people, my life has had its ups and downs. I've been forced to look deep within and think beyond career and family.

Before the Great Recession, I thought I was well on my way to retirement after my working days as an investment manager were over. Well, as they say, life has funny ways of intervening, and my life turned upside down.

My long-term marriage ended; I moved out of our newly remodeled house and lost my job. Not exactly the type of change I expected. Within one year, I experienced three of the top ten most stressful life events, according to the Holmes-Rahe Life Stress Inventory.

But I realized that I was not alone. Several of my friends were going through similar situations. The details varied, but midlife presented many of us with challenges we hadn't foreseen, testing our equilibrium, and we needed ways to cope even before we reached the tenth life stressor: retirement.

Few of us lead linear, predictable lives. We have all seen once-solid marriages fall apart, stellar careers disintegrate overnight, retirement accounts plummet in the blink of an eye, friends die suddenly, and social connections crumble with a change in status or simply distance.

As I slowly untangled myself over the next decade from the fog of confusion, I began to understand that a magical event wouldn't miraculously fall out of the sky and turn my life around. As one of my professors used to say, I couldn't wait for the gods to descend from the heavens and show me the way. I had to figure out what kind of life I wanted and how to make it happen. Most importantly, I had to look within myself for the answers to issues beyond the standard retirement questions.

These internal questions were much harder to tackle, and I often found myself disoriented and lacking structure in my search for answers. I didn't find anything useful in the retirement planning space or, for that matter, in books supposedly targeted at high-achieving professionals still looking to grow and thrive beyond their primary occupation. The books I managed to find were all about budgets and investment strategy or identifying the best places to retire.

Given my background in finance and my life-long interest in real estate, I was lucky that I didn't need much help in those areas, but I did need help with everything else that makes for a happy and fulfilled life. Where to begin searching for answers?

I also realized how totally unprepared most of my friends and acquaintances were to figure out what they would do once their primary careers were over.

Most of them were super busy with their jobs and families and juggling multiple, expanding responsibilities.

The type of questions that seemed important to me, but weren't getting any airtime, no matter where I looked, were along the lines of:

- Who will I be for the rest of my life without the cover of a title and company name?
- What values and behaviors do I want to live by, and how do I want to be remembered?
- What gives me meaning and brings joy to my life?
- How will I keep growing spiritually, emotionally, and intellectually?
- What do I still aspire to achieve?
- How will I stay engaged with the lives of family and friends?
- How can I share my knowledge and experience with others?
- How will I deal with setbacks and unexpected challenges?
- How will I stay physically, mentally, and emotionally healthy?

These deep internal questions seemed just as important as, if not more than, the more typical retirement issues discussed in the media. There were already many resources and skilled professionals available to answer all the typical retirement questions—be they about money matters, lifestyle choices, or places to live—but for the deeper, more personal issues, there was much less guidance and fewer resources to help.

Upon reflection and further research into positive psychology, I realized that the answer to my questions already lay within me, but first, I had to peel the onion before I got to anything useful. My outside layers inevitably had a ton of socially accepted built-in norms, but the more I peeled the layers back, the more I found my version of values and beliefs. I realized that there were no right or wrong answers. I realized that it was up to me to visualize what type of life I wanted. I had to come up with my destination before I embarked on the journey. All the tools and advice in the marketplace helped with the mechanics of retirement, but they didn't help me figure out where I wanted to go with my life. It felt like putting the cart before the horse. The traditional process felt backward from the way it should be.

The solution to finding joy and fulfillment in the sea of complexity and confusion that characterizes today's retirement world is to start with what you want and then work backward. It involves becoming completely clear about your vision for your Future Self—who you want to be, what you aspire to, and what type of life you want to lead, all in alignment with your core values and beliefs.

I will lead you to find your life of joy and fulfillment by helping you design your Future Self and give you the system and tools necessary to keep your life journey on track.

The clearer you are about your Future Self, the less distracted you'll be with today's complex and endless options. You'll know where you want to go and plan accordingly. You'll deal with today's complexity and vast range of choices by, ironically, rejecting the majority of possible paths you could take. Your focus will be your strength.

There will be no doubt, no detours in your journey, but you won't succumb to the fear, anxiety, and confusion of those who haven't taken the time to design and clarify their vision for their Future Self. Instead, you'll be pulled forward to your ultimate destination despite the obstacles. You'll be in control of your destiny. Wouldn't you rather have that than living day by day wondering what is next and constantly reacting to the shifting winds of change?

WHO IS THIS BOOK FOR?

This book is for those busy living and working hard in their careers and are getting ready for or are in the early stages of retirement.

It's for those who believe it's their responsibility to control their destinies. It's for those who don't mind doing the homework to figure out what they really want out of life and how to make it happen.

It's for those who understand that taking action is necessary to create the life they want, even if they're pushed beyond their comfort zone.

It's for those who want to squeeze as much meaning and enjoyment out of their lives as possible and not be constrained by outdated beliefs and models.

This book borrows heavily from my retirement coaching experience working with couples and singles preparing for the day when they leave their primary careers behind. It also borrows from my quest for answers and practical approaches for figuring out what I desire out of life in retirement, focusing on what matters to me, and how to make it all happen from a financial and non-financial perspective.

Lastly, as a lifetime research nerd, many of the perspectives and insights throughout the book have been shaped by behavioral economics, positive psychology, and personal growth studies.

While I have spent thirty years as an investment manager and researcher of global capital markets, the focus of this book is squarely on a holistic view of all the elements necessary for living your version of a happy and fulfilled time in retirement.

This book is not about how to maximize your after-tax portfolio returns or beat inflation. It's not yet another book focused on budgets and clever ways to maximize your pension. My focus when discussing financial matters will be more on the more significant issues you need to be aware of in making wise decisions geared at providing adequate income to fund your lifestyle. I'll leave the discussion of in-depth financial matters to those books solely focused on this space.

I believe that before you pursue in-depth knowledge in any one area of your retirement life, you should first understand how all the pieces fit together and the importance of designing a life consistent with your aspirations, values, and beliefs. No amount of money or fuel will leave you satisfied if you do not know where you are going.

HOW WILL THIS BOOK HELP YOU ACHIEVE A HAPPIER AND MORE FULFILLED LIFE IN RETIREMENT?

Many people have a warped sense of how their retirement life will look. Some people cling to outmoded retirement ideas. All they see is leisure time, fun, and games, but they don't realize how boring and unsatisfying that can become year after year.

Others simply don't know or care to find out. They are too busy to take the time to think. They believe that everything will take care of itself down the road. They fail to see that it is up to each of us to figure things out in this time of choice.

Others are downright pessimistic about what their life will be like in retirement. Their financial resources may be far from where they've been told they should be, and all they can think about is survival. They have assumed that money is everything but fail to realize that happiness and fulfillment are as much, if not more, driven by meaningful relationships and activities, health, and your outlook in life.

And then some people don't want to accept the status quo and blindly follow cookie-cutter solutions. Rather than just surviving, they want to thrive and enjoy life on their terms. You are my tribe.

I hope you join me in this journey and that this book helps you discover the necessary insight and motivation to design and live a life that brings you happiness and fulfillment.

If you feel that your retirement is off-track, please don't despair. I sincerely believe that there is always time to change for the better. I don't believe that you can't teach an old dog new tricks. Everybody can change, especially if it's in their best interest. As noted author and organization psychologist Dr. Benjamin Hardy says, personality is not fixed; it's fluid.

YOU DEFINE YOUR FUTURE SELF.

Whether you feel unprepared to retire because you don't have millions stashed away or haven't taken the time to think about what you want, reading this book will benefit you. At the very least, you'll be reminded that to have a successful retirement, you must find balance in all aspects of your life—financially and non-financially.

I hope that reading this book triggers you to move from thinking to planning and taking action.

Sometimes all you need is an aha moment that nudges you. A little spark, if you will. Maybe it's a new way to think about an issue, an emotional reaction, or perhaps something that brings out a thought buried deep inside you. Don't only go for home runs. The singles and doubles of insight and self-awareness often prove more meaningful and lasting.

This book will help you turn lack of clarity, indecision, and uncertainty into a vision for your life and give you actionable steps for finding happiness and fulfillment.

You'll feel more in control of your life, be more intentional in your actions, and be better prepared to deal with the inevitable roadblocks and detours everybody faces.

You'll understand why you need to become, in equal measure, part thinker/philosopher, part planner, and part doer. The book is organized along these roles.

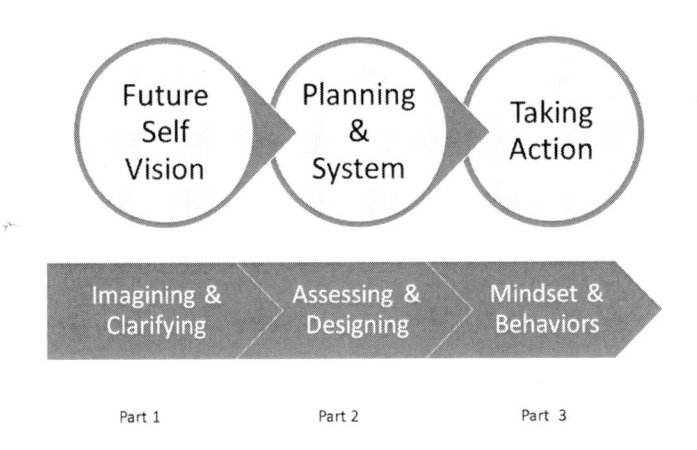

Part 1	Part 2	Part 3
Future Self Vision	Planning & System	Taking Action
Imagining & Clarifying	Assessing & Designing	Mindset & Behaviors

In part one, I lay the foundation for what retirement means today, what makes for a happy and fulfilled life, and why focusing only on money isn't enough. Hopefully, this material opens your eyes to all the possibilities in front of you. I then guide you as you explore how to turn complexity and endless choices into a crystal-clear vision of your Future Self to move you forward in your journey.

In part two, the focus changes from thinker/philosopher to planner. You move away from big goals and your innermost values and beliefs to look at the areas in your life that comprise your real wealth. I introduce you to the

NET WEALTH system that, when followed precisely, helps you focus and structure your next phase in life.

In part three, I explain how to go from planner to doer. All the planning in the world won't help if it stays in your head. Progress requires following a plan and acting on that plan. Planning comes naturally to most people, but where most of us get stuck putting that plan into action. Taking the necessary action often feels uncomfortable, and we have many creative ways to lose momentum, sticking to what we have always done and falling into old patterns. Developing ways to become action-oriented and not succumbing to what is easy and expedient is a key skill in seeking happiness and fulfillment in retirement.

CHAPTER 1
REINVENTION

> Today, retirement is more about personal transformation than money.

THE UNITED NATIONS (UN) ESTIMATES THAT BY 2050, PEOPLE sixty-five years or older will comprise 22 percent of the total US population. That is up from 15 percent in 2015. These numbers tell us that people are living longer, and the population growth rate is slowing, resulting in an aging population.

Some people retiring throughout this time will live out a traditional retirement life of leisure and comfort. But most won't—either by necessity or by design.

Sometimes, retirement is viewed as a cataclysmic event where the retiree rides off into the sunset, never to be seen or heard from again. In many ways, society, especially younger generations, looks at it this way—out of sight, out of mind.

Maybe in the old days, this made sense, as life expectancy barely exceeded retirement age. But today's environment is different, as many people can potentially spend up to thirty years in retirement.

Not only is the proportion of people sixty-five years and older steadily increasing worldwide, but personal expectations for how to maximize one's longer life span best are increasing.

The old standard of retiring at sixty-five doesn't apply today. Many people are retiring from full-time work much younger. Some are part of the Financial Independence, Retire Early (F.I.R.E) movement; others value lifestyle quality more than moving up the corporate ladder, while others would like to work longer but can't because of failing health, care-taking commitments, and age discrimination in the workplace.

And then there are many, like elder actors Rita Moreno, Judy Dench, and William Shatner, who never want to stop working. Retirement is a dirty word to them. Working until they drop is part of their life plan. Work gives them the satisfaction that they can't find anywhere else.

Some people keep working for financial reasons. Many people don't have the resources to fund their lifestyle over an extended lifespan, especially given the lack of guaranteed pension programs.

Financial considerations are, however, only part of the mindset shift. In survey after survey of personal attitudes toward retirement-age people, the overwhelming desire is to keep living an active lifestyle that includes leisure and contribution. The overall theme is one of reinvention.

In short, the word retirement has lost its old meaning. Transition and personal transformation is a more accurate representation of what is happening to millions of baby boomers and members of the F.I.R.E community worldwide.

People are coming to realize that retirement is about much more than money. Today, retirement is about having the freedom to pursue a happy and fulfilled life.

The opportunity to focus on what really matters and find fulfillment is available to all of us—rich or poor, young or old.

ISN'T MONEY IMPORTANT?

Adolf Merckle once ranked among the one hundred wealthiest people in the world, with an estimated net worth north of ten billion dollars. He was the wealthiest man in Germany. In the 1960s, he inherited a small family business that he nurtured into an empire of 120 companies with over forty billion dollars in annual sales. In January of 2009, he committed suicide. His business empire was under extreme stress, and his net worth plummeted to seven billion dollars, making him the fourth-wealthiest person in Germany (still an exceptional amount of wealth by most people's standards). His suicide note only read: sorry. It's speculated that he couldn't accept not being the wealthiest person in Germany anymore. His pride wouldn't allow such humiliation. So, he chose death because of his money troubles.

Like Adolf Merckle, Charles "Chuck" Feeney was also once a billionaire. Mr. Feeney became wealthy as the co-founder of a series of duty-free shops in major airports worldwide. Unlike Adolf Merckle, he sought to stay anonymous and kept his name off the wealthiest people's lists. He is, however, no longer a billionaire. By all measures, he lives happily in a San Francisco apartment. His business empire continues to thrive, but several decades ago, he anonymously donated nearly his entire net worth, estimated north of eight billion dollars, to charity.

The stories of Merckle and Feeney demonstrate how people react very differently to money. In the case of Merckle, money controlled him, and he used money as a yardstick of success. In the case of Feeney, he gave away his fortune for the satisfaction of helping others.

Money meant very different things to these two men. Both were billionaires at some point. One committed suicide because he couldn't bear losing his capital and status; the other lives a simple life and watches his charitable contributions help countless people in need.

Most people relate to money somewhere between these two extremes. When it comes to retirement planning, they focus on how much money they have. The exercise becomes nothing more than a numbers game, and little thought is given to any non-financial issues.

It's been drilled into people's heads that there is a certain number that you need to have saved by your retirement date, and as long as you have that number, all will be well. You'll have a great retirement. If you haven't reached that certain number? Well, good luck to you!

But there is a lot more to life than just money. Money is necessary to fuel your lifestyle, but so is your health, your relationships, and how you spend your time.

Your "number" bears no relationship to someone else's "number." A portfolio worth one million dollars can be a lot of money to one person, but it may mean very little to another person. That person might be extremely wealthy, or they could never conceive of having that much money in the first place.

HOW MUCH MONEY DO YOU REALLY NEED?

The more money you have, the better lifestyle you can afford, right? More money gives you the best health care, more time with family and friends, a grander home, exotic adventures, fine dining opportunities, and the chance to play golf at Pebble Beach (rather than at the municipal course), right? Generally speaking, the more money you have, the more options you get.

Many people believe that if you have money, you're all set. You can solve any problem that comes your way by buying your way out of it. And, in theory, they should be correct. More money should lead to a better life, but Nobel Prize winner Daniel Kahneman's research shows there's a weak relationship between more money and happiness.

The research shows that beyond a base income level of seventy-five thousand dollars, making more money doesn't translate to significantly higher happiness levels.

We all need money for our living expenses. Without it, we would be miserable, but if we have enough to pay for the basics, money hardly influences how happy or fulfilled we feel.

Let's assume you have enough money. Do you feel that your health, social connections, and spending time on enjoyable pursuits matter more than money? Do you believe leading a life consistent with your values, beliefs and aspirations is more important to your happiness and sense of fulfillment? Retirement gives you the freedom to become your Future Self, regardless of your number. You don't have to be rich to be happy and fulfilled in your next phase in life, but you must be open to possibilities and intentionally design what you want out of life. For example, the mother of a former co-worker of mine chose to help the poor in Haiti. It was her driving force during her retirement years. She chose to leave the comfort of living in the US to live in very humble and, at times, difficult conditions.

You don't have to have such grandiose aspirations, but regardless of what matters to you, the journey won't always be smooth. While seemingly easy at first glance, transitioning into retirement can be difficult for many people.

RETIREMENT IS A SIGNIFICANT CHANGE

When people start thinking of retiring, there's usually a sense of anticipation and overall good feelings. It's time. Right? But as retirement day comes closer, worry starts hanging around. What am I going to do without a paycheck? Who will I have lunch with when I'm not working? Will people miss me? Will I miss my role at work? The reality of stepping away starts sinking in. Retiring after three or four decades of working is not as straightforward as the commercials and glossy magazines have led you to believe. You start to realize that what you've become accustomed to will significantly change once you retire.

Even if you've been eagerly awaiting this day, something has changed, and for most people, that change is primarily out of view. It's not only the external stuff such as no longer getting a paycheck or commuting to work. More importantly, your identity has changed. Who you are has changed. What you now want out of life has likely changed. These new feelings and aspirations form the basis of your Future Self.

In the beginning, the details of your future life will probably be murky. You know that change is never easy. It takes time, and we all go through phases before finding clarity and a better sense of direction.

According to best-selling author William Baldwin, all change involves the following:

- An **Ending,** such as leaving a job, getting a divorce, the kids moving out, moving to a new community, getting rid of a long-held belief or attitude, etc.
- A **Messy Middle** or **Neutral Zone**, a period of introspection and uncertainty frequently followed by false starts, eventually culminating in clarity and personal growth.
- A **New Beginning**, a new way of being or belief system, a period of excitement about the possibilities, and living in a way that agrees with the vision of your Future Self.

Phases of Change

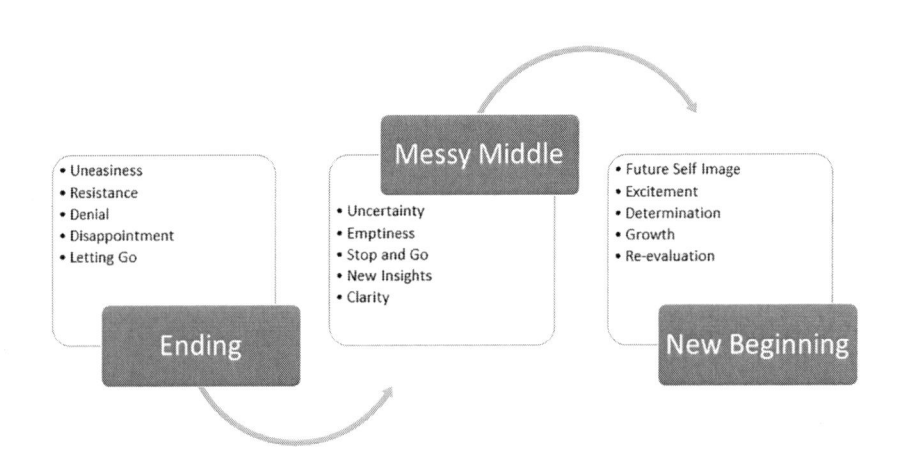

Ending
- Uneasiness
- Resistance
- Denial
- Disappointment
- Letting Go

Messy Middle
- Uncertainty
- Emptiness
- Stop and Go
- New Insights
- Clarity

New Beginning
- Future Self Image
- Excitement
- Determination
- Growth
- Re-evaluation

Each phase has its ups and downs. For example, before an ending, you'll probably experience some uneasiness and resistance. You might deny that anything has changed. Other times, you might suffer in silence, realizing that things have changed and there's nothing you can do about it. At times, you might still think of yourself in the same way as before and cling to your old identity. What's going to replace the identity you've had for the last thirty or forty years?

It might take a while to process how things have changed.

You'll have to reach a point of no return to grow and move forward. Something has ended, and the only way out is by moving forward. You can't effectively move forward if you haven't removed the shackles from your past.

As you go through an ending, the goal isn't to ignore the pain. Instead, it's to accept the change, find peace of mind, and commit to finding a better way forward. Note that sometimes we find great comfort in regressing toward the old, but in the end, healthy change requires looking ahead.

> "We ain't what we oughta be. We ain't what we want to be. We ain't what we gonna be. But, thank God, we ain't what we was."
>
> ~MARTIN LUTHER KING JR., CIVIL RIGHTS LEADER

Once you're ready to accept an ending, you'll move into the neutral zone, or as I prefer to call this phase, the messy middle. You've accepted that things will no longer revert to the old ways, but you're unsure how to move forward or in what direction to move. You might find yourself in the middle of the ocean with different ways of reaching a safe harbor, but all the choices seem equally difficult.

Many people find the messy middle the most challenging phase of a transition. When it comes to retirement, I've seen countless people struggle with bouts of regret, emptiness, and defiance, quickly followed by moments of clarity and hope for the future. You'll likely vacillate between optimism and pessimism. Some days you'll feel sure you're headed in the right direction, and other days will be filled with indecision and confusion.

You'll experience tremendous personal growth in the messy middle as you learn about yourself, how you want to live, and what it takes to become your Future Self.

Some people whizz through their messy middle with confidence and poise, but most encounter many detours and delays until they finally gain enough clarity and motivation to find their way out of this confusing and uncertain phase before moving into a new beginning.

The goal is to get to a new beginning with a clear sense of where you want your life to go and who you want to become.

A new beginning doesn't arrive without its challenges. In this phase, you'll have moments of indecision, but the hard work of executing your plan for your Future Self will slowly take shape. You'll genuinely accept that the past is behind you. You'll take full responsibility for your life.

Eventually, your new beginning will feel normal—no more new car smell. Your senses will dull. You'll reach homeostasis; what was once new will lose some of its shine.

But then what? Our brains love novelty and challenge. So, you might feel a certain emptiness once you've reached the summit. Maybe you start wondering if there's another peak you should scale. Or perhaps you decide that the summit you're on is no longer the best place for your current season of life.

At some point, where you're at in your life will no longer serve you, or at the very least, you'll feel the need for yet another change and another challenge. You'll start rethinking your life again.

Our lives aren't static. We don't set a course and stop once we reach our goals. Deep down, we all know that we're never a finished product. Our circumstances change, as do our minds, bodies, and spirit.

Your Future Self, to some extent, will always be in a state of evolving. We seek new challenges and strive to improve ourselves. Sometimes, we get bored with the status quo. Other times, we shed unnecessary baggage.

Priorities change. Beliefs change. Our wants change. Your Future Self is malleable, a moving target for renewal and regeneration, should you accept the responsibility and challenge of transforming yourself.

> "Things change. We need flexibility to ensure that we can change, too."
>
> ~SUSAN DAVID, HARVARD MEDICAL SCHOOL PSYCHOLOGIST

IT'S EASY TO GET STUCK IN THE MESSY MIDDLE

Survey research shows that most people experience a brief one-to-two-year honeymoon right after retirement and then enter a season of struggle in their post-career phase.

Many people drift with the wind or get stuck in the messy middle during their retirement years. Retirement brings about a natural ending, but they often wonder: What is the new beginning?

Few people intuitively realize that the adjustment process, while externally motivated (you left behind a job), is actually much more about an internal realignment of your identity, beliefs, and aspirations. The external changes, such as not having to commute to work anymore and no longer getting a paycheck, are predictable. What a lot of people don't anticipate, however, are the thoughts and feelings emanating from within.

These could be feelings of emptiness, as your identity forged during three or four decades of work no longer fits your current situation. You could have anxiety because you no longer have a place to go throughout the day and your time is now one hundred percent your responsibility. Or they might be feelings of disappointment that you no longer have big goals to reach. It could be a blah feeling that something is wrong, but you don't know what it is.

You don't have to be already retired to experience these feelings. For many people, the process starts as soon as the possibility of retiring becomes more of a reality. Once the finish line is within sight, your brain and emotions start churning in anticipation. You're already stuck in the messy middle, whether or not you want to be. For some people, these emotions become too much, and they decide to postpone their retirement, hoping they'll find greater clarity and their feelings will vanish. They fall into denial. They're stuck between what they once were and what's next. They still must figure out what they want in the next phase of their life and who they want to become. In most cases, they postpone the inevitable and prolong their stay in the messy middle.

These hidden or out-of-the-blue challenges that you never expected can weigh you down. You get stuck in an infinite loop of uncertainty and disappointment. You can drift and accept everything as it is or choose to design your Future Self proactively. Getting stuck in the messy middle isn't a long-term option if you seek happiness and fulfillment.

It's easy to get stuck in the messy middle when you retire. The real question is: How long will you remain in the land of indecision, anxiety, and fog?

What's your pain threshold before you seek new possibilities?

How wedded are you to your past?

As we age, the average person tends to get stuck in existing patterns and ways of being. They stop imagining a future different from their present. They stop believing that they can change. They stop learning. They spend more time thinking about the past and are less open to new experiences. They lack motivation. They stay busy, not doing much of anything significant.

Do you want to be average?

Or do you want to fight these tendencies? Do you want to aspire to a new beginning that energizes and fulfills you for the rest of your life?

"Every next level of your life will demand a different you."

~LEONARDO DICAPRIO, ACTOR

GETTING UNSTUCK: YOU NEED A VISION AND A SYSTEM

We all get stuck. We all fight change because we prefer comfort and certainty. We prefer instant gratification. On the flip side, we all know nothing good happens without a plan, commitment, and effort.

Spending your retirement years stuck in the messy middle isn't a recipe for finding happiness and fulfillment. There must be more!

I'm here to tell you unequivocally that there is more, but with one major caveat. You must accept full responsibility for your life.

There are no magic solutions. You must let go of past failures as well as successes. Your focus should only be on the type of life you want to lead and the person you want to become—in other words, you should be focused on your vision of your Future Self.

Your vision of your Future Self combines your values, beliefs, aspirations, and purpose for why this is your chosen destiny. Your Future Self is your ideal you. It acts as your guide when you make decisions. It answers your *what* and *why*. It motivates you to navigate the inevitable roadblocks and changes—external and internal—that you'll encounter.

Your vision of your Future Self on its own is not enough. You also need to commit to taking action, and you need a system for creating the change you want. You need a system for holistically optimizing all aspects of your life. A system that provides structure and focus for navigating your journey towards your final destination.

"You do not rise to the level of your goals. You fall to the level of your systems."

~JAMES CLEAR, AUTHOR OF *ATOMIC HABITS*

The **NET WEALTH** system that I use in my retirement coaching practice helps you do the following:

- Focus on the key areas of your life that make up your Future Self
- Understand areas of your life that need your attention
- Prioritize your goals
- Make more informed and intentional decisions
- Become accountable for your actions

The **NET WEALTH** system covers all major areas of your life. It starts with the traditional drivers of retirement planning—where you live (your **NEST**), your money situation (**EARNINGS**), and how you spend your **TIME**. It then focuses on the other areas of your life that can truly turbocharge your happiness and fulfillment: sharing your knowledge and experience (**WORK**), regulating your emotions (**EMOTIONAL ENERGY**), pursuing meaningful goals (**ACHIEVEMENTS**), growing spiritually, emotionally, and intellectually (**LEARNING**), remaining engaged deeply in the lives of family and friends (**TRIBE**), and staying physically and mentally fit (**HEALTH**).

Each important area of your life included in the **NET WEALTH** system will be covered in chapters three through eleven. But first, in chapter two, we'll explore your vision for your Future Self further.

Let me ask you: Are you ready for a new beginning?

Are you ready for a new beginning that:

- Transforms you from where you are today to where you want to go?
- Unlocks possibilities rather than constraints?
- Looks beyond money?
- Brings joy and fulfillment to your life?

Intentional change is emotionally demanding. It's much easier to remain stuck if the pain doesn't become too debilitating.

Many people choose to live with the pain and get stuck in the messy middle.

I don't want you to be one of them.

CHAPTER 2
DESIGNING YOUR FUTURE SELF

"If you have a clear vision of where you want to go, you are not as easily distracted by the many possibilities and agendas that otherwise divert you."

~TIMOTHY GALLWEY, AUTHOR OF *THE INNER GAME OF TENNIS*

HAVE YOU EVER STOPPED TO VISUALIZE WHAT YOUR LIFE WILL look like when you finally leave behind your primary career? Will your days be filled with nothing but fun activities and your nights surrounded by friends and family engaged in lively conversation? Will you cruise down the Danube River, soaking up the history and culture of the region?

It would be nice if that is the future today's retirees face, but we know that's unlikely. Many retirees struggle with uncertainty and fear of the future. Their identities are often tied to their previous occupations and family roles, and they're not quite sure who they are anymore. They think about the past and wonder about their future. What will retirement bring?

Most people have only a vague notion of what their life will be like in retirement. They might dream of moving to Florida to get away from shoveling snow. They might anticipate enjoying endless rounds of golf. Maybe they envision lots of exciting foreign travel interspersed with family reunions.

Often, these dreams are nothing more than warm, fuzzy thoughts because soon-to-be retirees lack a plan for making them a reality. Author Katherine Patterson once said in her book, *The Invisible Child*, "A dream without a plan is just a wish."

When I entered my fifties, I didn't have the faintest idea of what to do with my life. For the first time, I started thinking about my mortality and the end game. I only knew that things would be different, having divorced recently and watching my career as an investment manager go down the tubes. I had a vague sense of what I was interested in but no plan. Some days I just wanted to escape and never look back at my previous life. Actually, I did escape! I moved a thousand miles away for a job I thought would cure all my ills. I wasn't so lucky! Two years later, I was back in Boston and finally ready to admit that I was the only one responsible for my life. Nobody was coming to my rescue. Another job, or even winning the lottery, wouldn't help get me out of my funk.

Little by little, as my emotional life stabilized, I started thinking about my future again. That's when my journey of discovery began. I put shape and form into my dreams and sketched a rough plan. What did I want out of life? What type of person did I want to become? What dreams did I have? I hadn't thought of these questions in a long time, but they kept popping into my head.

Many people go to their deathbeds with regrets. I didn't want to have any more regrets than I already had. A good friend suggested therapy. I tried that, but what really helped was reading a book by Bronnie Ware, a palliative caregiver in the UK. The book, *The Top Five Regrets of the Dying: A Life Transformed by the Dearly Departing,* is a short read but not insignificant. In Ware's experience caring for the dying, she heard these five common regrets:

- I wish I had the courage to live a life true to myself.
- I wish I hadn't worked so hard.

- I wish I had had the courage to express my feelings more openly.
- I wish I had stayed in closer touch with friends.
- I wish I had let myself be happier.

Sobering, right?

I wasn't dying, but it made me think that if I didn't shape up and start taking responsibility for my life, I would have some of those same regrets.

Another thing I did was I read a ton of books and blogs on personal growth and self-improvement from the usual cast of characters in those fields, such as Tony Robbins to Brendon Burchard. Somehow, I came across the field of positive psychology. I had always believed that psychology was about digging up the bad stuff in your life and then analyzing it. Positive psychology is different because the focus is on things that might actually help you lead a happier and more fulfilling life. I took a couple of online positive psychology courses, which opened my eyes even further, forcing me to consider deep questions I'd not thought about before, questions such as:

- What does it mean to be happy?
- What does it mean to be fulfilled?
- What is a good life?

These are some of the oldest questions humans have grappled with over time.

I had been on this planet for over five decades and never thought about these questions before, but now I was deeply interested in finding the answers.

I concluded that I wanted to be happy *and* fulfilled in my life. I didn't want to live for short-lived spurts of dopamine and end up with long-term regrets and unfulfilled dreams. I felt I still had plenty of fuel in the tank to work on my dreams. I also felt that I had something to contribute for the first time in my life.

Too many people in or near retirement focus solely on comfort and pleasure —having a nice house, playing golf or tennis, traveling, and, for the most part, living day-to-day. They look at the past and live in the moment for themselves. They live a life where tomorrow is no different from today.

Their happiness is hostage to short-term pleasures that don't bring long-term fulfillment.

Some people are fine living only for comfort and pleasure, but I knew I needed something more meaningful to look forward to and feel like I mattered. I needed to tackle some of my dreams and aspirations. I needed to give something back to society. These thoughts weren't entirely selfless. Looking forward made me feel good about myself like I was in control and not just using up resources and time. Being of service to others also made me feel good.

I concluded I needed to live a life that satisfied the following for me to be *both* happy and fulfilled:

- Covering the basics of my lifestyle, such as having a place to call home and enough financial security to pay my bills.
- Having pleasurable and enjoyable experiences, such as playing tennis, gardening, and taking a couple of trips each year.
- Feeling content, grateful, and at peace with my life regardless of my circumstances.
- Contributing to the greater good of society and future generations by getting involved in sustainable causes and being available to mentor younger generations
- Working on my dreams and aspirations, such as growing a retirement coaching business that gives my life meaning and purpose

I label these various needs as **Comfort, Pleasure, Freedom, Legacy,** and **Meaning**. I think of them as directives on how to live in broad terms. I imagine these areas as concentric circles that overlap (as depicted below). For example, many goals I've been working on give me meaning and pleasure.

You'll have your own needs, which may look radically different from mine. What brings happiness and fulfillment is unique to each one of us.

A good, fulfilling life is about more than comfort and pleasure, as many think, especially as they anticipate retirement. It's also doing things that allow you to control your life, give back, and spend time on meaningful and purposeful activities and goals. The following graphic shows how all these pieces intersect:

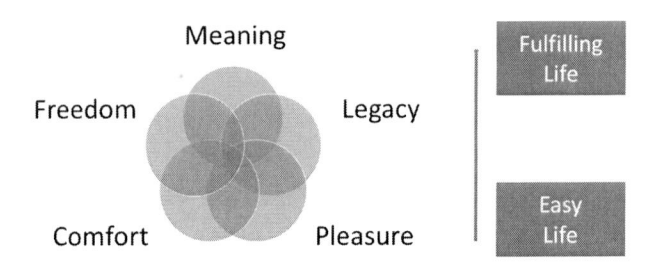

Meaning — Freedom — Legacy — Comfort — Pleasure

Fulfilling Life | Easy Life

DO YOU WANT AN EASY LIFE OR A FULFILLING ONE?

The traditional retirement industry orients toward comfort and pleasure—what I call the "Easy Life." For some people, that's enough. You only need to worry about yourself and the next dopamine hit.

But for many others, there's a nagging feeling that there must be more to life than a nice house, endless rounds of golf, and dining out. They want to keep growing and engaging with the world. They still have dreams they want to achieve. They feel they still have plenty of "juice" left and seek ways to share their elder wisdom. They want to look forward in life rather than backward. They know it would be easier to focus on comfort and pleasure, but they believe leading a life focused on happiness and fulfillment aligns more with their values, beliefs, and aspirations. They accept that pursuing fulfillment requires more work, persistence, and discomfort than the Easy Life, but that's a tradeoff they're willing to take.

Seeking fulfillment is more challenging than being happy now. Fulfillment is like a marathon, whereas happiness is like a short sprint. The two are intrinsically tied together, and most people would agree you need both, but there's a difference between seeking what scholars call "hedonic happiness," which involves pure pleasure-seeking, and "eudemonic happiness," which comes from meaningful pursuits often involving others. In that sense, I distinguish in this book between a life based on comfort and pleasure—what

I call the easy life—and a life incorporating meaningful pursuits and legacy, or as I call it, a life of fulfillment.

Often, seeking fulfillment means embracing delayed gratification, discomfort, challenges, and uncertainty on the path toward meaning and growth. Fulfillment takes work. You won't always be happy. You'll struggle at times. There will be obstacles, and, at times, you'll feel discouraged. Sometimes you may wish you had chosen the easy life, but you'd be missing out on the rewards—a life of meaning and contribution.

Fulfillment lasts longer than happiness. Fulfillment, hopefully, stays with you for the rest of your life. Fulfillment is earned long-term satisfaction because you have to work for it.

IT'S NEVER TOO LATE TO PURSUE FULFILLMENT

For many of us, life has led us in directions that, many years ago, we'd have never anticipated. Many good things have happened, but we've also had our share of disappointments and setbacks. We're here today, having followed our unique paths. At times, much of it would've seemed improbable, yet some of it has turned out how we envisioned it.

Many people believe that once you reach retirement age, your life is all set, but, in reality, retirement is merely the beginning of a new phase of life. People mistakenly assume their lives will follow a straight line until the near end. Psychologist Daniel Gilbert calls this the "End of History Illusion." When asked, people recognize that there's been a lot of change in their lives, but they still have the impression that in the future, their lives will be as much the same as today. They fail to anticipate how much change they will likely face in the future. They assume a linear life from this point forward.

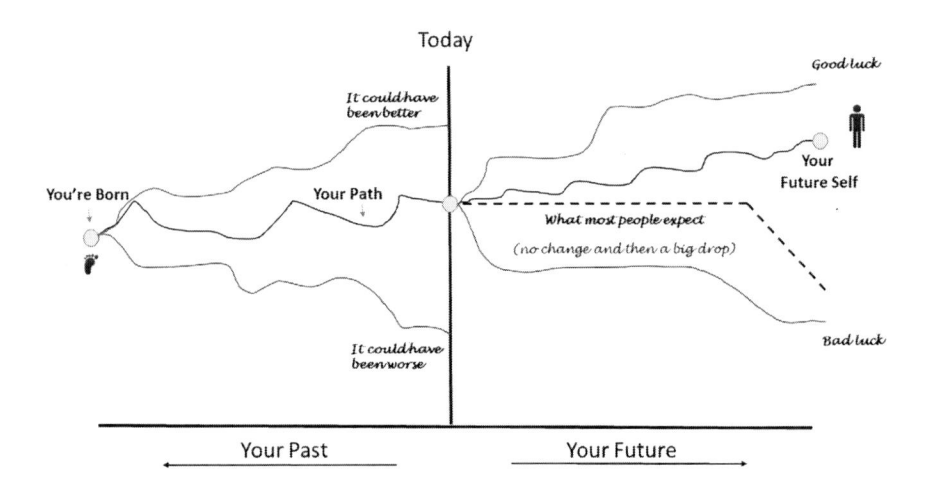

It's easier to remember the past rather than imagine the future. Research has shown that people have a narrower view of life as they age. They stop trying new things, and their social circles become stagnant. They assume who they are now is who they'll be for the rest of their lives. They assume the world around them won't change in any meaningful ways. They lack confidence in their ability to control their lives and can't imagine a future full of possibilities. They give up on the one superpower all humans have—our ability for creative imagination.

These are self-limiting beliefs that keep people stuck in the past. They needlessly expose people to the randomness of life and the inevitable change around us. They transfer control away from the individual when they need it the most—and time is becoming increasingly precious. They limit the upside of happiness and fulfillment.

"You are going to go through life either by design or by default."

~RICK WARREN, CHRISTIAN PASTOR AND AUTHOR

CONTROL YOUR DESTINY BY DESIGNING YOUR FUTURE SELF

Some people believe that once they retire, there's nothing they can do to change where they end up in life. They might get lucky and have a great life, or their lives might turn out terribly because of bad luck. They shape their actions by their present life's short-term rewards and challenges. They prefer getting a dopamine hit now rather than investing in their future. They fail to see that small actions compound into more considerable outcomes in the long term. They are disconnected from who they'll be in two or three decades. Where they end up in life will be a function of luck. They *hope* things will work out for them.

Hope, however, is not a good strategy. Relying on good luck is unreliable. Just because you've been lucky in the past doesn't mean that you'll be in the future. You'll end up somewhere, but it might not be somewhere you like. You'll be like a boat without a rudder, drifting at the whim of the current and the wind. It won't matter how big or fancy your boat is. Without a sense of direction and knowing where you want to end up, your final destination is out of your control.

To maintain control over your life, you need to imagine your future. Where do you want to end up? What kind of life do you want to lead? What kind of person do you want to become?

Your Future Self is all about these things. Your Future Self is you a year or even decades from now. You'll be older, but it's still you. Right now, there are two of you, your current self and your Future Self, but, over time, the two selves will (hopefully) converge.

As author Stephen Covey suggested, think ahead to your eightieth birthday party. Who do you want to be there with you? What is the mood? Where will the party be held? How will you look and feel? What will people say about you?

Imagining your Future Self is important to your well-being. It's the vision that moves you forward in life, despite the inevitable hurdles and challenges that will undoubtedly come your way.

A clear vision of your Future Self shows you the way forward when short-term distractions and quick dopamine hits tempt you. It keeps you on your chosen path, not the random path found by luck. It'll enable you to cut through the noise and complexity of daily living by narrowing down your choices to those aligned with your values, beliefs, and aspirations. I'll allow you to live a life of no regrets, focused instead on happiness and fulfillment.

You'll find that the closer you feel to your Future Self, the more you'll behave in a manner consistent with the values, beliefs, and aspirations you have chosen for yourself. Every day, you'll be investing and committing to your desired future.

Your path toward your Future Self will have plenty of potholes, but your vision will keep you moving in the right direction. You'll figure out how to overcome hurdles as you go along. It won't always be easy, but you'll move through life with intention and a sense of responsibility for your destiny.

> "We must all suffer one of two things: the pain of discipline or the pain of regret and disappointment."
>
> **~JIM ROHN, AUTHOR, ENTREPRENEUR, AND MOTIVATIONAL SPEAKER**

Designing your Future Self involves answering three key questions:

- WHO do you want to be?
- WHAT are your most important and deepest dreams and aspirations?
- WHY does your life matter?

The answers to these three questions are the pillars supporting the life you want to build. They're the foundation of your Future Self.

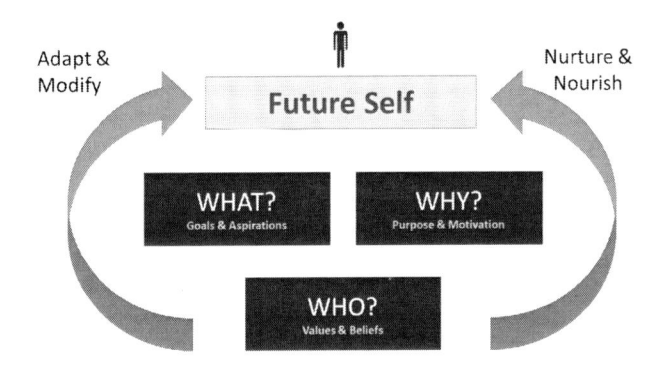

PILLAR 1: WHO DO YOU WANT TO BE? YOUR VALUES AND BELIEFS

Values. Your values are your guiding principles for your actions and decisions. They tell you what's right and wrong. They're black and white with only subtle shades of grey. They send signals to your head when you're not living according to your values. For example, if one of your values is directness, but you've chosen to sugarcoat the truth about a difficult relationship, ultimately, you will feel bad about your behavior.

Your values act as guideposts when making decisions. Awareness of your values gives you more focus and discipline in your life. By following your values, you'll behave more consistently with what you desire from life.

Living by your values helps you navigate the myriad choices we face daily. Some types of behavior fit our values, and others don't. Living by your values brings consistency to your life.

Values influence not only our actions but how we relate to other people. For example, if we value respect, we'll likely find it hard to work with someone who's frequently condescending and rude to waitstaff. The values we, as individuals, deem important often reflect how we want others to see us. For example, you may say, "I wish to be seen across as generous, honest, and wise."

Most people intuitively know the values a person of good character should possess. We know that lying is wrong and showing kindness is good. Since childhood, we've been conditioned to have a sense of right and wrong. But, as adults, we may not have thought deeply enough or have taken the time to reflect on what values are most meaningful to us and how they can create our vision of our future selves.

Examples of core values include honesty, respect, self-determination, courage, humor, and hard work. Instead of listing a litany of values, I prefer to use an online character assessment by the VIA Institute on Character. Over fifteen million people have taken this scientifically validated assessment. Dr. Martin Seligman, the father of positive psychology, is the organization's co-founder and active member. Dr. Seligman describes character traits as values in action.

According to the VIA Institute on Character, "Character Strengths are the positive parts of your personality that impact how you think, feel and behave." I've found this assessment to be of great value when working with clients. In general, I would say that most people already know their core values, but the assessment serves as a reminder of who they really are and helps them articulate those values.

I highly recommend that you take the assessment and reflect on the results. If you're uncomfortable taking the assessment, simply go through the list below and circle the values most important to you.

If you decide to take the Character Strengths assessment, here's some background. The assessment is structured around twenty-four character traits that define a person's value system. The twenty-four traits are arranged under six main categories described as the following "virtues:"

Wisdom: Creativity, Curiosity, Judgment, Love of Learning, Perspective
Courage: Bravery, Perseverance, Honesty, Zest
Humanity: Love, Kindness, Social Intelligence
Justice: Teamwork, Fairness, Leadership
Temperance: Forgiveness, Humility, Prudence, Self-Regulation
Transcendence: Appreciation, Gratitude, Hope, Humor, Spirituality

Each of these values can be manifested in myriad ways, and together, they make up your value system. Everyone possesses all twenty-four character traits in varying degrees. For example, my top three strengths are honesty, judgment, and love. My bottom three strengths are perseverance, prudence, and zest.

No pairings of strengths are better than another. All the character traits are good; some people simply emphasize more than others. The point is that we're all unique. We're not all-or-nothing creatures. We simply value some character traits more highly than others depending on our upbringing, personalities, and worldviews.

Do you know the core values you want to live by now and in the future?

Write down the five values you want to manifest in your life:

Value 1:

Value 2:

Value 3:

Value 4:

Value 5:

"Beliefs have the power to create and the power to destroy. Human beings have the awesome ability to take any experience of their lives and create a meaning that disempowers them or one that can literally save their lives."

~TONY ROBBINS, LIFE AND BUSINESS STRATEGIST

Beliefs. Now, let's turn our attention to your beliefs, the second component of how you envision your Future Self.

Beliefs are slightly different from values. First, they're usually hidden from public view. They're deeply personal, as opposed to values that tend to be driven by societal and cultural norms. They tend to be deep-seated and often subconscious.

Beliefs are assumptions a person holds as truth, whether they're factually correct. Many of the beliefs we hold in our hearts are nothing but figments of our imagination. Clients have told me they think they're bad with money, yet they've managed to amass impressive fortunes. I've also had clients tell me they're really good at making friends, yet their relationships are shallow and transactional.

You design your belief system. Your beliefs come from your life experiences and how you interpret events in your life. Two people may have identical value systems but radically different beliefs. For example, my two sisters and I share very similar value systems, but our beliefs can be completely different in some areas of life, such as personal growth. Even though we grew up in the same household, we had different experiences growing up, which likely led us to interpret things differently and end up with our own unique beliefs systems.

Our beliefs generally involve:

- **Ourselves:** our ability to adapt to new situations, easily make friends, or overcome difficult personal situations
- **Others:** whether other people can be trusted, whether they respect you, or look beyond your social status
- **The World:** the idea that the world is full of danger or that society treats all people the same

Beliefs don't only reside in our heads; they drive all our decisions. You act based on your beliefs. It's as simple as this: if you think you can do something, you'll try; if you believe you can't do something, chances are you won't even give it a shot. Henry Ford once said, "Whether you think you can, or you think you can't—you're right." I couldn't agree more. Your beliefs drive your choices.

As opposed to values or character traits that tend to be fairly static through life, beliefs are malleable. We typically positively describe values or character traits, but we often shy away from talking about beliefs because they're personal and, at times, don't portray us in a positive light.

Our beliefs can empower *and* limit us, depending on how appropriate they are in the context at hand.

Beliefs that allow us to take chances in the hopes of a bigger and better future are called "enabling beliefs." These beliefs portray optimism, hope, and confidence in our ability to overcome hurdles to reach our goals. They empower us to take action.

Some examples of enabling beliefs are:

- I can adapt to any situation.
- I will succeed because I work harder than anyone I know.
- I will emerge from my struggles as a better person.
- I know that my skills will lead to opportunities in the future.

Then there are "limiting" beliefs. These beliefs correspond to thoughts that prevent us from acting and seeking a better future. These beliefs may be true, such as I will never win an Olympic gold medal. But many times, they keep us from even trying. When a limiting belief is untrue, we're more likely to refrain from taking risks, even if taking that risk is beneficial. We stay stuck, our possibilities capped by the narrowness of our belief system.

Some examples of limiting beliefs are:

- I'd like to live abroad, but I'm not good at other languages.
- I don't have the social connections to succeed in business.
- I don't have enough money to enjoy my retirement.
- I've always been shy, and I'll never make new friends.

All these limiting beliefs, under most circumstances, are untrue. They may hold some water in the short term, but there's no reason why these objections can't be overcome. Everyone can learn a second language if they're committed enough. Everyone can make new friends if they're open and engaging. People can change if they're committed to the process but removing metal barriers is the first step.

Your beliefs influence the range of possibilities that lay before you. If you believe your life in retirement is already set and done, you probably set and reach new goals or develop a better future. Lewis and Virginia Eaton Professor of Psychology Carol Dweck, Stanford University, calls this way of thinking a fixed mindset. If you hold to limiting beliefs, you'll probably continue doing the same things you've always done. Your future is capped by your belief that your life is already determined.

On the other hand, if you view retirement as the freedom to try new things and reinvent yourself, you're likely to invest your time and effort into developing a brighter future. Professor Dweck calls this a growth mindset. People with growth mindsets seek brighter futures, even when facing challenges and detours.

Research by Professor Dweck and others has shown a link between having a growth mindset and achieving one's goals. Believing in one's ability to learn new ways and overcome challenges leads to a greater strength of will, resilience, and the "take action" set of behaviors necessary to achieve your goals.

With a growth mindset, you would take the prior set of limiting beliefs and reframe them as enabling beliefs:

- I would like to live abroad, so I should start taking classes in another language.
- To help my business, I can grow my social connections in the following ways.
- I have many options to increase my income during retirement.
- I can always get better at making friends.

Let me turn it back to you.

When you think about your future, what five enabling beliefs will allow you to lead a happy and fulfilling life in retirement?

Belief 1:

Belief 2:

Belief 3:

Belief 4:

Belief 5:

All this may all sound very abstract to you. Frankly, I never thought about beliefs until my fifties, and it took me several tries to come up with my go-to set of enabling beliefs to lead a happy and fulfilled life.

I will share my list with you, hoping you'll find something of value as you craft your list. Here it goes:

- **Good and bad things happen, but I am one hundred percent in charge of my life.** This belief keeps whiny why-me moments short-lived and empowers me to take action rather than fester in self-pity.
- **My actions today determine the quality of my life in the future.** I invest daily in my future by living a healthy lifestyle, taking care of my relationships, and working on my goals.
- **I already have enough material wealth.** More stuff won't make any difference to my happiness or sense of fulfillment.
- **I can always improve, even if the improvement is barely visible in the beginning.** Small actions compound over time.
- **The greatest legacy I can leave behind is the example of how to live, serve others, and love.** I want to be a retirement superhero like my uncle has been to me.

As I mentioned before, beliefs are personal. Your beliefs are assumptions you're making—not absolute truths. Your actions and behaviors are, in turn, driven by these assumptions.

By writing your beliefs down, you can identify your drivers of success. These empowering beliefs will drive your behavior, especially when times get tough.

You may also want to take the time to identify what beliefs are holding you back. Are there limiting beliefs you wish you didn't have?

Ask yourself this question: Are these beliefs true? Is there any way you can reframe these dis-empowering beliefs into a work-in-progress set of commitments to reach your Future Self?

PILLAR 2: WHAT DO YOU WANT TO ACCOMPLISH? YOUR DREAMS AND ASPIRATIONS

What do you want out of life? Are you living day by day and taking whatever comes your way?

Have you stopped wishing for a better future? Is lack of time your excuse, or is it the limiting belief that nothing will ever change?

Many people find it easier to ride the wave, but you don't have to. You're likely to spend two or three decades in retirement. That's a long time to surf life's waves.

Wouldn't you rather spend your time pursuing your dreams? What dreams keep coming up over and over? What do you aspire to do in the various areas of your life?

Many people think that retirement means your dreams and aspirations are buried forever, along with your paycheck. This sad, limiting belief isn't good for living a happy and fulfilled life.

Author and Doctor Gordon Livingston once said that humans need three things to be happy:

- Something to do
- Someone to love
- Something to look forward to

I think that these are the bare-bones requirements. Most people should aspire to happiness *and* fulfillment, not just getting through the day. A big part of living is waking up every day and looking forward to working on one's dreams and aspirations—something beyond daily survival. Waking up the next nine thousand days with nothing new to look forward to beyond the usual wash, rinse, and repeat cycle is depressing, at least that's what I think.

"What man actually needs is not a tensionless state, but rather the striving and struggling for a worthwhile goal, a freely chosen task. What he needs is not the discharge of tension at any cost, but the call of a potential meaning waiting to be fulfilled by him."

~VICTOR FRANKL, HOLOCAUST SURVIVOR

Some people choose easy lives focused on comfort and pleasure. They live their lives in the present with hardly a thought paid to their future selves. They're over-invested in the present. They're motivated primarily by how they feel in the moment, but, over the long term, they're likely to find life a bit empty and too predictable. Maybe they wish they'd spent more time thinking ahead because every day is the same. As my mother used to say, "Anything done in excess becomes boring." They choose a life focused on a series of short-term satisfaction rather than a life with a more fulfilling future.

At the other end of the spectrum are people who want to spend time pursuing things they've always wanted to do but didn't have the time to pursue. They want more out of life than comfort and pleasure. They feel they still have juice in their tanks to tackle their dreams and aspirations. They see futures bigger than their present situations. They're willing to invest in their future selves. Now retired, they have the time and freedom to pursue meaningful things. Maybe they want to spend their time and money on social causes? Maybe they want to work on a long-forgotten dream of theirs. Maybe they want to start a small business? Maybe they don't quite know what they want to do, but they feel something interesting pulling at them?

If you want a future greater than your present, you need to get clear on what combination of **comfort, pleasure, freedom, legacy,** and **meaning** is optimal for you. What will create happiness and fulfillment over the long term? Are there dreams and aspirations you harbor within each of these areas? What is going to make you look forward to doing something?

Let me walk you through an exercise that my retirement clients often find eye-opening.

What thoughts and desires keep tugging at your heart?

For creating comfort:

For creating pleasure:

For creating freedom:

For leaving a legacy:

For finding meaning:

What activities make you feel vital and alive?

Family & Friends:

Caregiving:

Fitness & Sports:

Personal Hobbies:

Community Involvement:

Professional Interaction:

Volunteer Work:

What unique skills, knowledge, and experiences do you have that would benefit others?

Skills:

Knowledge:

Experiences:

Can you identify three to five high-level aspirations of your Future Self?

Future Self Aspiration 1:

Future Self Aspiration 2:

Future Self Aspiration 3:

Future Self Aspiration 4:

Future Self Aspiration 5:

For example, for me my high-level aspirations are:

- To build a sustainable business focused on retirement advice and coaching
- To become healthier and fitter
- To remain engaged in the world
- To be an example of how to live according to one's values and beliefs
- To remain fully vested and engaged in the lives of my family and friends

PILLAR 3: WHY DOES YOUR LIFE MATTER? FINDING YOUR PURPOSE AND MOTIVATION

When I watch a movie, I usually try to figure out the main characters' key motivations. In well-made movies, you typically get a clue toward the beginning. Of course, you may not get the full story as motivations are often held deep within, and good films can surprise you. Eventually, you're led to what else is driving their behavior beneath the surface.

Like in the movies, we all have more profound reasons for our actions and how we lead our lives. What you see on the exterior isn't always consistent with the real motivation behind our actions. Sometimes, even we're not aware of what is driving our behavior.

What about you? Do you know what truly motivates you? Do you know why you do what you do?

These are deep thoughts that often drive your behavior subconsciously.

Your "why" is your purpose for doing things. It motivates your actions even when things get tough. It gives you clarity.

Determining your purpose is a deeply personal experience that requires dedicated thought and patience. You're not going to nail it the first time you try it. Keep asking yourself why certain things in life are important to you. Drill deep until your "why" is stripped of all external or societal "must-haves." After all, it's your "why."

Often, your "why" is about giving or contributing to someone or a cause, and it's not all that surprising. When people start to face their mortality, their purpose often shifts toward making a difference in the lives of others.

As an example, here are my "whys:"

- To be an example of re-invention for my kids
- To help fellow baby boomers find more enjoyment and fulfillment in retirement
- To bring a small measure of joy every day to at least one person

Your "why" is related directly to your dreams and aspirations.

If you decide to lead a happy and fulfilling life, you'll have to get crystal clear about why your dreams and aspirations are important to you; this is your "home cooking," not someone else's.

Ask yourself these questions:

- Is my motivation internally driven?
- Is what I'm trying to do worth the effort?
- Will pursuing these things make me feel good about myself?

Your "why" provides clarity. Your "why" should evoke positive emotions, such as joy, contentment, and pride. Do the things you aspire to do draw out positive emotions? The goal is to get really clear about why your main dreams and aspirations are important to you.

Research shows that the most fulfilled people derive their purpose from a higher calling. Research by University of Pennsylvania instructor Emily Esfahani Smith shows that a vital component of your life satisfaction is using your strengths to serve others. Giving is the reward.

Your purpose can take many forms and shapes. Your interests, skills, and special talents make you unique. You *can* find purpose in your life by sharing them with other people.

For example, your purpose could be:

- Sharing your professional expertise with the younger generation
- Helping abuse victims regain control of their lives
- Creating a beautiful piece of art or music to share with your community
- Volunteering at your local library to organize a series of lectures
- Planting a community garden that teaches people about our food supply and provides food for families in need
- Starting a business to provide a reasonable income to employees
- Traveling to a lesser developed country to rebuild communities devastated by a natural disaster
- Taking care of your grandchildren after they come home from school

> "The good news and the bad news of growing up and growing older are the same: you have no one else to blame if you do not live a life of your own imagining."
>
> ~RICHARD J. LEIDER AND ALAN M. WEBER, AUTHORS OF *LIFE REIMAGINED: DISCOVERING YOUR NEW LIFE POSSIBILITIES*

Spending time crafting the three pillars supporting your vision of your Future Self is important. Your values, beliefs, dreams, aspirations, motivation, and purpose in life make you unique. The beauty about retirement is that it allows you the freedom to become the best version of yourself in the form of your Future Self.

It might take a couple of iterations before you settle on the form and shape of your three pillars, but the clearer you are about where you want to go, the more proactive and focused you'll be making everyday choices.

The following nine chapters will help you plan and structure how to transition from where you are today to your Future Self in all the important areas of your life that make up your **NET WEALTH**.

Here's a quick rundown on what's coming.

YOUR NET WEALTH SYSTEM

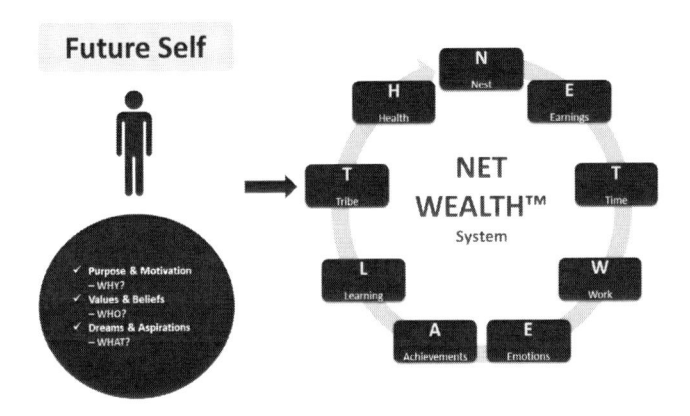

The **NET WEALTH** system incorporates all the major areas of your life—financial and non-financial. It's a system that helps you identify the areas in your life that need your attention and those where you excel. It helps you monitor your progress and establish priorities. When followed closely, this system lets you focus on what's important to you and how to ignore the environmental noise and societal pull toward a one-size-fits-all retirement.

The **NET WEALTH** framework isn't a magic solution. You still need to do the work, but it gives you structure and is designed to help you go from thinking and planning to take real action toward becoming your Future Self.

Let's take an inventory of all the **NET WEALTH** ingredients.

We'll start with the familiar territory—where you live (**NEST**), your money (**EARNINGS**), and your **TIME**. The first three ingredients of your **NET WEALTH** are the ones you're used to seeing in commercials.

Your **NEST** is where you live and the type of lifestyle you lead. The "E" in **NET** stands for **EARNINGS**. Whatever direction you want your life to go, and however you decide to get there, your Future Self requires fuel for the journey. A big challenge facing today's retirees is turning assets into a sustainable earnings stream to fund their lifestyle.

The next ingredient in your **NET WEALTH** framework is **TIME**. Specifically, how do you want to allocate your time? Time is our most precious resource, especially in retirement, but many people still treat it as a renewable resource.

The first part of the framework (**NET**) deals with the big picture, the planning and the design of retirement life—where you want to end up living, earning enough to fund the journey, and properly managing your time. Figuring out where you're going to live, having enough fuel in the tank, and properly managing your time is the beginning of optimizing your quest for fulfillment. These are all big, important steps, but like planning a road trip across the country, you still need to figure out lots of details, such as who is going on the trip with you, what sights you'd like to see, and how you're going to stay alert and awake at the wheel.

The second part of the **NET WEALTH** framework involves you as the driver and what it will take to put it all together. Unlike a self-driving car, you can't simply jot down a list of instructions into a computer. Road trips, as most of us know from experience, don't work that way.

The **WEALTH** part of the framework deals with all the things that make our lives worth it:

- The things you do every day
- The work you care about
- Your social connections
- The goals you're trying to achieve
- Your emotional and physical health

Think of the **WEALTH** framework as the "driving experience." It's all about the little things to make your journey as fulfilling and enjoyable as possible.

Let's start with W, which stands for **WORK**. Many people believe that once they retire, they will never work again. The reality is that most people will work again in some capacity, whether for pay, social connection, or commitment to a cause that matters to them. Some of the push to continue working will be economical. Besides the money, some people will continue working to feel connected and alive. Others spend their time working on a social cause that's important to them.

The next ingredient in your **NET WEALTH** system is the letter "E", which stands for **EMOTIONS**. We are emotional creatures. Research has shown that our emotions drive our behavior. Understanding our emotions and appropriately responding is a critical life skill. It's well-known that as people transition from full-time work, feelings of uncertainty, loss, and even fear become more common. Managing those feelings that arise naturally with aging is a primary component in maintaining a healthy emotional balance and resilience.

The "A" in the **NET WEALTH** framework deals with **ACHIEVEMENTS**. Research in positive psychology has found that happier and more fulfilled individuals seek new challenges. These individuals set goals and make necessary plans and action steps. Having something to look forward to gives our daily lives structure. Goals provide clarity and a sense of direction, keep people from focusing on the past, and motivate them to look ahead.

Next up is the "L" for **LEARNING**. Learning doesn't stop once you graduate from college or leave the corporate world. In today's world, we all need to become lifelong learners to keep up with all the changes around us. The benefits of learning go beyond simply attaining more skills and possibly earning more money. Learning also has many mental health benefits.

Social connections, or your **TRIBE,** are the next component of your **NET WEALTH.** Humans are social animals. We need for physical and emotional connection as well as love. Maslow's Hierarchy of Needs places belonging right after our need for food, water, and shelter. Social connections are the most important factor in determining global happiness.

The final component of your **NET WEALTH** consists of your **HEALTH.** Your physical health drives much of your daily satisfaction with life. As people live longer, the focus shifts to the quality of life. According to the 2010 online article in Scientific American, *Live Long and Proper: Genetic Factors Associated with Increased Longevity Identified*, research shows that our genes only account for about 30 percent of our overall aging. That means that 70 percent is due to the environment and the lifestyle choices we make.

YOU NEED A VISION AND A SYSTEM

An approach such as the **NET WEALTH** system is ineffective without a well-specified vision of where you want your life to go. Likewise, a great vision without a detailed plan and execution is insufficient for creating a life of joy and fulfillment. That's why you need a vision of your Future Self and a system.

In this chapter, we focused on creating the vision of your Future Self. We discussed the three pillars of WHO you want to become as a person regarding your values and beliefs, WHAT you want to achieve in your life, and WHY you want a life that brings you meaning and purpose.

The following nine chapters cover each of the components that make up your **NET WEALTH** system that, together with your vision of your Future Self, create the winning combination for a life of joy and fulfillment.

is a critical determinant of the types of routines and the lifestyle you adopt. In fact, research by Dr. Benjamin Hardy shows how your environment is a much more powerful influence on your behavior than willpower alone. Often, we're not even aware of how our environment affects us. In his book *Willpower Doesn't Work: Discover the Hidden Keys to Success*, he states, "Much of your behavior is unconsciously cued by your environment." After reading Dr. Hardy's book and being a member of his Accelerated Momentum Program (AMP), I firmly believe that where we live must sync with our vision of our future selves. Who we want to become, what type of life we want to lead, and what meaningful goals we aspire to achieve are all interlinked within our environment and where we live.

Your housing decisions are one aspect of your environment. Where you decide to live needs to be naturally in sync with all other areas of your life to sustain the vision of your life in retirement. The type of house you choose to live in, is intimately tied to your financial resources. Here's why:

- **The equity in your home is probably your most significant financial asset.** Look at your house not only in terms of shelter and emotional utility but in terms of financial value. Being house-rich and cash-flow poor won't do much for your happiness. At the end of the day, cash flow funds your lifestyle, so if your house prevents you from doing the types of things you find enjoyable or getting in the way of becoming your Future Self, it's time to re-evaluate.
- **Your house is probably your most considerable living expense**. You'll need to figure out what you're willing to spend for shelter, including all the costs of home ownership. If your financial means are stretched, you need to consider lowering costs by exploring options such as downsizing, moving to a cheaper location, or renting.

My goal for this chapter is to help you make the best housing decision possible by holistically considering the overall environment you wish to live in and your financial constraints. I wish for you to think strategically of your housing decision in the context of all areas of your life and your aspirations for the future. Too many people end up house-rich and lifestyle-poor

CHAPTER 3
YOUR NEST

"If you don't shape your environment, it will shape you."

~BENJAMIN HARDY, AUTHOR AND EXPERT ON FUTURE SELF SCIENCE

ONE OF THE FIRST QUESTIONS PEOPLE STRUGGLE WITH WHEN they begin thinking about retirement is: Where should I live? Should I move to a tax-friendly place with plenty of year-round sunshine like Florida or Arizona? Should I stay put, given the familiarity of my surroundings? Should I move closer to family? Should I downsize and move from the suburbs to the city? Or should I stay put and remodel?

NEST is more than the house where you live. I want you to think more strategically. Your house is an important part of your environment, but so are your physical surroundings, the people you interact with, the community you live in, what you do each day, and, in general, everything that surrounds you.

Where and how you decide to live should reflect the importance your environment plays in shaping your thoughts and behaviors. You may never have thought much about your surroundings before, but your environment because they fall prey to an emotional over-attachment to their current living situation without thinking about all aspects of their lives.

THE IDEAL ENVIRONMENT FOR YOUR FUTURE SELF

Remember the exercises in the last chapter that asked you to crystallize your vision of your Future Self? Did you come up with a vision for how you'd like to live in retirement? Do you have a clearer picture?

If you're still working on it, don't worry. Mine continues to evolve, but where I once drew a blank, I now have a blueprint I work from daily. My ideal living situation involves the following:

- Living with my wife in a low-maintenance, small-ish house or condo with an outdoor area to grow flowers and vegetables
- Spending spring and summer in New England, fall and winter somewhere warm (We're still working on this. Right now, it's a tie between Mexico and Costa Rica.).
- Surrounded by people we actively engage with daily, either through work, volunteering, or hobbies such as gardening and tennis.
- Enough activities and events to keep my wife and me busy and entertained. For me, that involves live music, interesting lectures on current events, and sporting events. For my wife, it involves dining, creative pursuits, and beaches.
- Near an airport to easily visit family and close friends, and a decent communications infrastructure to work remotely.
- Affordable so that all-in expenses on housing are less than 25 percent of my retirement income.

Does this help?

You probably already have a good sense of what lifestyle you would like in retirement, but you may still be fuzzy on the details. I urge you to think strategically. Narrow down your choices by considering the following factors:

- **Life stage fit**: By this, I mean the type of housing most suitable for your desired lifestyle. For example, if you want to travel a lot, you're probably better off living in a condo where you can simply turn the key and leave without much thought. Or, if you're having mobility issues, you should probably live in a place with easy in and out access. Think about some of these questions. At this stage of your life, do you want to live in a low-maintenance condo, or do you want a lot of space? Do you want to remain mobile, moving every couple of months to a different location? Do you prefer city living at this stage? Or do you prefer the quiet of the suburbs or the country? You probably don't want to lock yourself into any arrangements that are hard to get out of, should you change your mind.
- **Climate and weather**: The choice isn't only about sun versus rain or hot versus cold. It's also about what type of climate you prefer. I love warm temperatures, but humidity zaps my energy. I love trees and mountains, but I also like being close to a body of water to cool down in the summer. As you know, there are always tradeoffs, but what is a deal-breaker for you? Can you live with the average winter temperatures of your desired location? Is the summer too hot? Again, you would rather be safe than sorry. Several years ago, I went to Panama to research whether I would like to live there in retirement. I absolutely loved it—especially the people—but the weather was too hot and humid for my taste. That was a deal-breaker.
- **Social network and family**: Humans are social creatures. You may not feel that you need anybody around, but what about when you're feeling down or need some help? Having family around is important, especially as one ages. And it's not just family that's important, but also a lively circle of friends and acquaintances. Loneliness is a serious problem among retirees. You need good social connections for your emotional and physical health. Can you picture yourself surrounded by friends and family in your chosen retirement location?
- **Affordable and quality health care**: Health care might not be as important to you when you first retire but you'll appreciate being

close to quality health care as you get older. Quality health care comes at a cost, but the it varies significantly depending on where you reside. In the US, health care is expensive. It's much cheaper abroad, and the quality may be perfectly acceptable to you. If you need specialized care, you'll need to carefully research the available medical facilities and capabilities in the area. Health care is one area where you don't want to make any assumptions.

- **Cultural and entertainment options**: These areas can also be important, especially if you love socializing. Getting out and about can be beneficial to your mental health. Having easily accessible cultural and entertainment options can enrich your life. In many areas, these options are free. If you're looking for world-class options, you'll probably be restricted to a big city. If you're easily entertained, as I am, then most locations should offer adequate options.
- **Outdoor activities**: Like the previous category, you may find great satisfaction in spending time in nature hiking, bike riding, or simply admiring nature. If you're fond of the outdoors, being in a climate where you can be outside most of the year will play a crucial part in deciding where to live. I have a friend who moved from Connecticut to Idaho. I never saw him as a big, outdoorsy person, but he has always been into running and photography. One of the reasons he moved to Idaho was the state's natural beauty and wide availability of running trails. Idaho is a good fit for him.
- **Work opportunities**: More people than you might imagine "un-retire" after a brief honeymoon period. They either go back to work full time, or they choose to work part-time (the more likely scenario). If you intend to work in retirement, you need to live close to where the opportunities are. In today's mobile world, remote working is possible, but those opportunities depend on the type of work you're interested in and industry norms. Not all industries have embraced the remote working culture, so do your research ahead of time.
- **Quality of infrastructure**: We often take our roads, utilities, and government services for granted, but all it takes is for our internet

or electrical service to go out, and our entire world stops. In many lesser developed countries, these interruptions are expected. People work around them, but if your lifestyle depends on 24/7 access to quality infrastructure, you want to confine your search to cities with recent investments in modern infrastructure. I know this is an area of great stress for many Americans living abroad. They are often surprised that the things that we take for granted in the US are deemed not as important in other countries.

You'll also need to consider your housing choice's financial ramifications. Three areas come to mind in this respect:

- **Cost of housing**: Do you live in an expensive area like California, or like me, in New England? Think in relative terms given other housing areas you'd consider moving to. In my case, I am interested in evaluating the Playa del Carmen region of Mexico, not only for a cheaper cost of living but for the weather. Boston, where I live now, is very expensive.
- **Living costs**: Cost of living includes everything beyond owning or renting your house. Taxes are a big consideration for retirees, as are everyday living costs, such as food, clothing, transportation, and entertainment. Consider these expenses in relation in your typical consumption basket.
- **Medical:** The cost of your health care can vary considerably depending on where you live. You consume these services locally, so your location determines the type of care available to you and how much it costs. Even within the US, the cost of services like assisted living can vary widely. According to Senior Living in 2022, the average annual cost of assisted living will be lowest in Alabama ($37,800) and highest in Delaware ($80,280). That's an impressive big gap! According to the American Health Care Association, the average length of care is twenty-eight months, so where you live matters a lot regarding your retirement health care expenses. The differences are even starker when considering health care costs outside of the US. Many retirees motivated primarily by lower health care costs move to countries such as Mexico.

Thinking through all these pieces of the retirement puzzle can get overwhelming, so I created a tool to help you identify gaps. The worksheet may lend some structure to your decision-making. It incorporates the key factors to consider when evaluating where to live and the type of lifestyle you want. Look at it as a starting point and refine your criteria over time.

NET WEALTH COMPONENT	Current Rating (A)	Target Rating (B)	Desired Change (B-A)	Immediate Priority	90-Day Goals
NEST	10=Best, 1=Worst	10=Best, 1=Worst		10=Most, 1=Least	Be as specific as possible.
Cost of Housing					
Non-Housing Living Costs					
Life Stage Fit					
Climate/Weather					
Social Network, Including Family					
Cost & Quality of Health Care					
Outdoor Activities					
Work Opportunities					
Quality of Infrastructure					

Here's how the tool works.

First, on a scale of 1-10 (with ten being the best), how do you evaluate your current living situation? Fill in column A with your answers.

Second, complete the ratings in column A to match what you envision life to look like as your Future Self? Write down your desired ratings for each category in column B.

Third, are there areas where there's a big gap between your current and desired ratings? Simply take the rating in column B and subtract the rating from A.

Fourth, independent of your ratings, rank your most immediate focus areas in column D. What factor is most important to you?

Finally, pick the two or three areas that matter the most to you and write down what you plan on doing in these areas over the next ninety days. Be as specific as possible.

Can you identify the areas that require your attention?

Taking the time to think strategically pays off in the long term. A serious drag on the financial health of retirees is moving around too much in retirement. My parents lived in three different countries during their retirement, which seriously depleted their savings. Moving isn't only expensive; it's also stressful.

Research by Ken Dychtwald at Age Wave, an organization that addresses issues relating to aging, shows that, on average, retirees move twice during their post-career days. The first move is to a place that meets lifestyle requirements for cost, climate, proximity to family, and activities. The second move occurs much later in life and is motivated by the availability of health care and proximity to immediate family. By planning for your needs now, you can save money and quickly fulfill your vision for your Future Self.

THE BIG DILEMMA—SHOULD WE STAY OR GO?

To a financial advisor, your house represents a financial asset. In many cases, it's your biggest asset. To you, your house means a lot more. It's where you sleep and eat most of your meals, but it's also the place containing many of your memories.

As you contemplate retirement, you inevitably start thinking of your home differently. With the recent boom in real estate values, you've probably peaked at Zillow or Redfin to get an idea of what you could get for your house. I do it, and so do all my friends and clients.

My wife and I constantly ask ourselves whether it's time to sell our condo in Boston. We've been lucky. Who would've thought a pandemic would increase real estate values? But then we think about our neighborhood and friends around us and we pause.

Should we stay, or should we go? As they say, it's complicated. Yes, it's a financial decision but also an emotional one. It's a decision about our current lives, but what we want our lives to look like in retirement.

Deciding whether to stay or move can be a difficult, especially when so many other things are changing around you. Not only are you leaving your primary career behind, but you're also trying to figure out who you are and what you want out of this new phase in life we call retirement.

It's not the easiest decision. Right? You probably have mixed emotions. You're facing an uncertain future that requires lots of decisions. From an emotional and financial standpoint, this is one of the toughest decisions.

Here are some options to consider.

Stay put. Do nothing. Contrary to conventional wisdom, most retirees elect to continue living in their current homes, but that may not be the wisest choice for everybody. Is it for you? I know it wouldn't be a good decision for my wife and me. We live in a second-floor walk-up. It's already not fun having to carry bags of groceries up the steps, and I can't imagine we will feel any more energetic two decades from now.

Staying put is the default option for most people. If you have plenty of financial resources and like where you live, don't sweat it. You might live in an expensive home, but if you have no problem covering your monthly mortgage, stay put. That's assuming that your current house supports the vision of your Future Self and the lifestyle you anticipate having in retirement.

What if money is an issue? You may not want to admit that you're living beyond your means, and staying in your current home limits your ability to do things you may want to do in retirement. If that's the case, it's time to consider other options. In the long run, you'll be better off. I've had clients who refused to tap into their home equity, which wasn't a pretty picture. Eventually, they acknowledged the reality, but they had wasted valuable time.

Downsize. Sell your current home and buy a smaller house. Do you need to continue living in a four-bedroom house with a three-car garage? Do you use fewer areas of your current home, but it requires a lot of effort and money to maintain?

Finding a suitable alternative might involve trading from a house to a condo or townhouse. It might also involve a change of scenery, such as moving from the suburbs to an urban area. From a financial standpoint, freeing up some of the equity in your home may be a smart decision that gives you the financial freedom to do things that you otherwise might not be affordable.

Move to a cheaper area. Many people fantasize about this option, especially if they live in an expensive area, such as New England or the West Coast. You might wonder: What could we get in [city] for the price of our house? The all-in costs of home ownership can be substantial, and in the early years of retirement, housing costs represent, by far, the largest expense you'll incur. Saving money in the early retirement years can yield considerable dividends down the road.

You can gauge living costs by researching housing prices, taxes, and overall basic living expenses, such as utilities and food. However, when seeking out lower cost-of-living options, there are tradeoffs that you shouldn't minimize. You might be farther away from family, and moving will require you to spend more money on trips.

I believe that people are often reluctant to move because they're afraid of change. They're looking at things from the perspective of loss rather than an opportunity to reset and thrive during this next chapter of life.

Rent. Renting is becoming more common worldwide. Baby boomers have been brought up thinking that renting is throwing money down the drain. Other generations have more favorable opinions about renting. The reality is that whether you own or rent, having a place to live will cost money. You can shell out money to a mortgage company or write a check to a landlord.

Renting offers two advantages: You free up capital, and you have mobility. The two primary disadvantages are that you may have to move if the landlord sells the property, and you can't make the place your own in terms of décor and design.

You must decide which tradeoffs make sense for your financial situation and life goals. Holding onto an expensive home that sucks up your hard-earned money may cost you happiness and fulfillment. That's probably a poor tradeoff.

Staying put, downsizing, moving to a cheaper area, and renting are your basic options, but I want to throw out two other options which have recently become part of the retirement conversation.

Become a landlord. Don't worry. I'm not telling you to pitch a tent in your backyard and rent your home permanently. It's a bit more nuanced. If you're not using all your space, or you spend part of the time away from the house, consider renting your home, at least temporarily. With the emergence of the sharing economy and services such as VRBO and Airbnb, renting your home has become more feasible and quite lucrative option.

If you live in an area tourists frequent, why not jump on this opportunity? The rent you can fetch during a premium week—for example, when a special event is happening nearby—is mind-boggling. Imagine what you could do with that extra cash. You could use the money to fund your dream vacation.

Another option, if you prefer to stay close to home, is to take in a renter. This option especially appeals to solo retirees who could use the cash to fund their lifestyle but would benefit from the company. Clearly, this option isn't for everyone, but if you can find the right person, you might create your version of *Golden Girls*.

Get a reverse mortgage. Reverse mortgages aren't wildly popular in the US, but as more baby boomers approach retirement with inadequate liquid assets and houses with substantial, this mortgage option will rise in popularity. Many retirees have the bulk of their net worth tied to their homes and lack sufficient cash flow to fund their living expenses. A reverse mortgage is one solution to this problem.

A reverse mortgage is a loan that allows you to continue living in your own home without a monthly payment because you're borrowing against your home's equity. You get to take money out of your house, continue living there, and postpone repayment until you die, move out, or sell your home. When either of those three situations occurs, you, or in many cases, your estate, pay back the loan balance, including accrued interest.

Many consumers have difficulty understanding reverse mortgages, but don't let that discourage you from seeking help if your ultimate goal is to stay in your home and use your home to fund your continuing living expenses. Speak with your financial adviser or someone you trust to learn more about this option and if it's the right choice for your situation.

There is nothing wrong with taking some equity out of your house but know that if you take out a reverse mortgage, it's not free money. You're legally bound by the terms of the contract you sign. Also, keep in mind that interest rates on reverse mortgages are typically higher than traditional mortgage interest rates.

"It's easy to underestimate the real cost of home ownership."

~SUZE ORMAN, AUTHOR AND PERSONAL FINANCE GURU

MAKE SURE YOU UNDERSTAND THE TRUE COST OF YOUR HOME OWNERSHIP DECISIONS

For most people, their home is much more than a financial asset; it's a highly emotional asset. But the emotional attachment to one's home may come at a high cost.

Even if you love your current home, do you know how much it really costs you?

As any homeowner knows, there are many expenses besides paying the mortgage. Property taxes need to be paid. You need to pay the insurance bill. The roof needs to be replaced periodically, as do the air conditioning and heating systems, not to mention the normal maintenance costs like lawn care, snow removal, and HVAC and water heater servicing.

When you add up all the bills, home ownership is expensive.

But all these out-of-pocket expenses pale compared to the one item that nobody talks about: imputed rent. Imputed rent is a concept that refers to how much it would cost to rent your current home if you didn't own it.

Why should you care? It's not affecting your cash flow, right? Yes, but what if you want to do more in retirement and being house-rich prevents you from truly enjoying life? In a perfect world, would you purchase your house again?

In the investment world, there's a popular saying: You buy and sell your portfolio every day. It means you should never get too attached to any of your investments. You shouldn't let sunk costs determine your actions today. Every day you should re-evaluate if the investment still makes sense.

Now, I understand that your home is more than the average investment. I get that, but the point is that, as with stock investments, you shouldn't get overly attached to your home, especially if owning it prevents you from pursuing the type of life you aspire to live in retirement.

I don't want you to think you must sell your home. Instead, I'm asking you to look at home ownership differently. Sometimes it takes a different way of looking at things to understand whether they're helping you or holding you back.

Let's imagine that, instead of living in your house, you decide to rent it out. How much rent would you charge?

You'd probably base the rental amount on the rent for comparable properties in your area. Or you might use Zillow to determine what they deem to be the estimated rent, which is actually your home's imputed rent value.

Let's do a couple of simple calculations. Let's assume a house price of five hundred thousand dollars. Let's also assume that the house is paid off (for simplicity's sake). Zillow estimates a likely rent of two thousand dollars per month or twenty-four thousand dollars per year.

Your imputed rent is twenty-four thousand dollars a year. Now ask yourself: Would I pay that much to live in my home? Only you can answer that question.

What if the Zillow rent estimate for your home was ten thousand a month? Would you be willing to write a monthly rent for that amount?

There are no right or wrong answers. What you're willing to spend on your home's imputed rent is up to you. Only you can make the tradeoff between the economics of living in your home versus the emotional benefit.

If your imputed rent is too high given your financial resources, you should consider moving to a place where the cost is more aligned with what you're willing to pay.

Being house-rich but not able to enjoy life isn't a reasonable tradeoff. Many of my retirement clients reframe how they view their homes after analyzing the actual cost of ownership.

People won't ever see their home as purely a financial asset, but they shouldn't ignore its monetary value, especially when being house-rich impacts their desired lifestyle.

THINKING BEYOND THE OBVIOUS: HAVE YOU CONSIDERED LIVING ABROAD?

Most people explore a narrow range of possibilities. They either stay put, or they flock to where other retirees live.

However, a small but growing portion of retirees is looking beyond the usual choices. They're looking at countries like Mexico, Ecuador, and Costa Rica—three well-trodden destinations for ex-pats. In recent years, many other countries have joined the list of possible retirement places, such as Belize, Colombia, Thailand, Portugal, and Spain.

The world is more homogenous today than several years ago. Living abroad doesn't seem so remote anymore, given the availability of communication services such as Facetime and Zoom.

People are considering living abroad for a variety of reasons. Lower cost of living is still the main reason, but regaining a sense of adventure and having access to affordable health care are important reasons to consider living abroad.

The cost-of-living advantage of living abroad can be substantial. Numbeo, the world's largest cost of living database, maintains a Cost-of-Living Index comprising the top six hundred cities worldwide. The index is constructed to have a value of one hundred for New York City. Boston has an index value of eighty-nine, or about 11 percent cheaper than NYC. Charleston,

South Carolina, a popular place for retirees, has an index value of eighty. Charlotte, NC, comes in at seventy-three, or 26 percent cheaper than NYC.

If you look abroad, the comparisons relative to NYC get even better. Panama City comes in 41 percent cheaper. San Jose, Costa Rica is 48 percent cheaper, and Cuenca, Ecuador is projected to be 65 percent cheaper.

You might not have thought about living abroad, but many baby boomers and members of the F.I.R.E. movement have been giving it a try. It's an option worth exploring. Living abroad may not be for you, but if you need to reduce your living expenses drastically, it's an option to keep open. Beyond the obvious pull of a lower cost of living, moving abroad may be what you need to pursue your goals and lead the lifestyle of your dreams. For example, I know of a couple who moved to Guatemala simply to learn Spanish and assimilate into a foreign culture. I also know a former university professor who moved to Panama to pursue his love of marine life and snorkeling. Money wasn't the driving force for moving for either of these people.

CONSIDERATIONS FOR YOUR FUTURE SELF

Your living situation must align with your overall life goals and the lifestyle you wish to have during your next phase in life. It's shortsighted to view any aspect of your life in isolation. The key is maintaining a balance between all aspects of your **NET WEALTH** and thriving.

My uncle recently taught me this lesson. He's ninety-three years old, and he shuttled between the US and Costa Rica for thirty years. Three years ago, he sold his large farmhouse in Costa Rica and rented a beautiful condo nearby. Last summer, he sold his house of fifty years in the Washington DC area. I never thought that he could do it. I felt that it would be too painful for him. I recently talked to him about this, and he told me that he spent several years thinking about this decision, and, finally, when he sold his beloved home, he was ready. He hasn't had any regrets. He knew that it was the right decision for him. Selling your home is never an easy decision, but sometimes it's the right one, given your stage in life and your goals and aspirations.

Your environment, your physical surroundings, the people you interact with, the community you live in, what you do daily, and, in general, everything that comprises your surroundings greatly influences your thoughts and behavior. You might not even be conscious of the pull exerted by your environment.

Your housing choices are an integral part of your well-being, as they heavily influence the environment in which you live. You want to bloom where you're planted and avoid the constant search for greener pastures. Your happiness is influenced more by your experiences than by the things you own. Your house is more than a financial asset, but don't make the mistake of becoming over-attached to it and becoming house-rich and lifestyle-poor.

In the next chapter, we'll look at your entire financial picture and assess ways to create a sustainable earnings stream from all your financial assets.

CHAPTER 4
EARNING A SUSTAINABLE LIVING

"Planning is bringing the future into the present so that you can do something about it now."

~ALAN LAKEIN, AUTHOR OF *HOW TO GET CONTROL OF YOUR TIME AND YOUR LIFE*

As people approach retirement, the thing they usually focus on is money. Survey after survey shows that not having enough money is the number one worry people have when considering retirement. Up to that point, they have always felt they could fall back on the comfort of a paycheck, but in retirement, they lose that security.

When you retire, things, understandably, change. The sense that the margin for error—extra cash to go out to lunch or dinner with friends, a new tennis outfit, or a couple of tickets to a concert—is no longer there.

Now what? The whole mindset of going to work and getting a paycheck is thrown out the door. You can freak out and ignore reality for a bit, but the pile of bills on your desk will always be there, and eventually, you must deal with it.

Your mindset will need to shift from working for a paycheck to creating a sustainable income stream from your investments and possibly post-retirement work. This chapter will go over the basics of creating a sustainable earnings plan geared toward your unique circumstances, goals, and risk profile.

GETTING PROACTIVE WITH YOUR FINANCIAL HEALTH

Most people don't think about retirement until their fifties. Many other things compete for their time and money—climbing the corporate ladder, kids, aging parents, etc. But as the kids leave home and careers start winding down, most people start thinking about retirement, and finances become the main topic of discussions. Some typical questions that I've heard over the years are:

- Are we on track with our savings?
- What's our net worth?
- Could we retire in five years, or do we need to keep working?
- Is it too late?
- How much could/should we spend in retirement?
- Do we need to buckle down and save more?
- Can we afford a second home and a boat?
- Do we have to pay taxes once we retire?
- Should we play it safe with our investments?

These are typical questions with complicated answers.

Dealing with money issues can be emotionally draining. There's always that nagging feeling that it would be nice to have more. We all want to feel safe and live a comfortable life in retirement.

Who wants to deal with money issues when there's already a feeling of apprehension or perhaps even fear about life in retirement?

My goal is to keep things simple. I give you a light financial planning approach to figuring out your financial picture through the **PROACTIVE** system, which I use with my coaching clients. The system consists of nine steps divided into three main categories:

- Steps 1-3: Your unique circumstances, personal preferences, and financial goals
- Steps 4-5: Your financial assets and cash flow
- Steps 6-9: Your available options and strategy for implementing your financial plan

Working with the **PROACTIVE** system, you'll identify a sustainable spending rate, develop a suitable investment plan, and create a comprehensive outlook for thriving financially in retirement.

Even if you already have a financial advisor or plan on getting one soon, going through the methodology will strengthen your financial education and empower you to make financial decisions. At the end of the day, remember that even if you have an advisor, the ultimate responsibility for your financial health lies with you.

The **PROACTIVE** system isn't a fancy algorithm that will magically solve all your issues, but it will embolden you to take control of your finances. The methodology helps you organize your thoughts and develop strategies for satisfying your long-term financial goals.

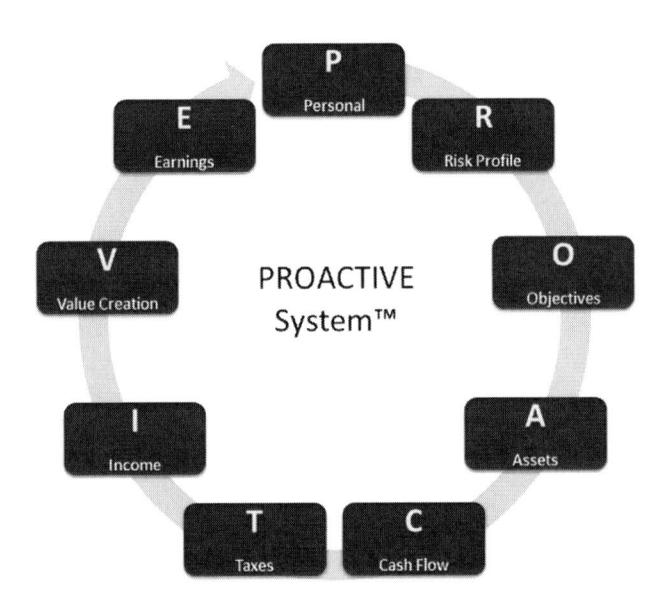

PROACTIVE System™

- P — Personal
- R — Risk Profile
- O — Objectives
- A — Assets
- C — Cash Flow
- T — Taxes
- I — Income
- V — Value Creation
- E — Earnings

STEP #1: PERSONAL SITUATION

A good plan is customized to your needs and requirements. It starts with an overview of your age, career stage, marital status, children, and overall family structure. If you're working with a financial advisor, this is step one before you have an in-depth financial discussion.

Your financial plan needs to be in sync with your vision of your Future Self. Your finances are only one aspect of your **NET WEALTH**. Look at your finances as the necessary fuel for funding your desired lifestyle.

In the last two chapters, we covered how to determine the lifestyle you want in retirement. Congratulations! You're on your way. Being clear on your needs and wants is the first step in developing a plan suitable for you and your circumstances. Let's move on to the next step.

STEP #2: RISK PROFILE: HOW YOU FEEL ABOUT UNCERTAINTY

Planning is easy on paper, but things often get messy when you get into the real world. Unfortunately, it is often the case that what we expect does not exactly happen as we imagined. Your financial life is no different. Good and bad things happen without apparent reason; expecting a linear path only happens in textbooks.

For example, take stock market returns. The average return in the US is about 11 percent, but can you recall when the actual return was exactly in line with the average? Hardly ever. Some years, the return will be north of 30 percent, and other years the return will be south of 30 percent. That's what professional investors call volatility, and the layman calls uncertainty.

In other words, stock returns fluctuate from year to year and are unpredictable—at the least, they fluctuate within a wide range. It's likely that, at some point, your expenses and income had a similar range of variation. Think about it. Can you predict accurately when your home heating system will die or what your income will be in ten years? The world is uncertain, knowing how to best manage our financial affairs in situations beyond our control is important.

The world is full of unknowns. It's a basic human trait to want to control life, but much of what happens is unpredictable. Rather than driving yourself crazy, your best bet is to anticipate how you would feel and react to events beyond your control.

When it comes to your financial health in retirement, the key uncertainties involve:

Investment returns:

On average, your 401(K) and other investments go up yearly, but occasionally, you experience large investment losses. Who can forget 2008? Losses can jeopardize your financial health, especially if they happen near or early into retirement. Here are some questions to ponder that will shed light on how much uncertainty you can deal with:

- How do you feel about losing money in any given year?
- How do you feel about losing money several years in a row?
- Do you have the emotional perseverance to wait for your investments to recover, or do you panic at the first sign of trouble?
- Do you have enough of a financial cushion to absorb losses?
- Do you have a solid understanding of historical capital market returns?

How long you live:

Your money needs to last for however long you and your spouse/partner live. Do you have a reasonable expectation, given your health, of how long that will be? If you die early, you'll probably have money left over. On the other hand, if you live longer than expected, you might run out of money. Given today's longer lifespans, it's prudent to assume that you and your spouse/partner will live into your nineties. It's better to be safe than sorry. Ask yourself these questions:

- How long does your money need to last?
- Could you ramp down your lifestyle spending needs if you're forced to do so?

- Will your sources of safe money, such as pensions and social security, if you're in the US, be enough to live on for the rest of your life?

Large, unexpected expenses:

Life is full of surprises, some of which we should reasonably expect and others that come out of nowhere. When they plan for retirement, most people don't account for large, unexpected expenses and get taken by surprise. These surprise expenses include long-term health care and home maintenance issues. Here are some other things to consider:

- Have you factored in large increases in health care expenses in your later years, say from age eighty-five onward?
- Do you have an annual home maintenance budget that allows for large, one-time repairs?
- Are there any other expense categories where you could realistically see a big jump in cost in the future?

Inflation (the loss of purchasing power):

Remember when a movie ticket was $3.50? Now, it's more like ten or fifteen dollars. If your income hasn't kept up with inflation, you'll afford less and less every year. Instead of going to the movies once a week, you may only go four times a year. That's what inflation does to your purchasing power. Like adding an inch every year to your waistline, the loss of purchasing power isn't that noticeable at first, but over two or three decades in retirement, your ability to sustain your desired lifestyle becomes seriously imperiled. My father frequently complained about inflation after being retired for a couple of decades. He watched his lifestyle erode even in the face of historically low inflation levels. In today's post-COVID-19 world, retirees face tough challenges given the jump in inflation. Dealing with inflation might be one area where a financial advisor can really help you figure out questions such as:

- Does your lifestyle have enough wiggle room to tolerate a significant jump in inflation?

- Can your investments reasonably keep up with inflation?
- Are your expenses going up faster than the rate of inflation?

Nobody likes uncertainty, but it's a fact of life. When it comes to your financial health, it's important to take a long look in the mirror and honestly determine how much uncertainty and financial risk you want in your life.

One key consideration is that in retirement, you no longer have the safety cushion of a paycheck. The good news is that your financial resources are probably the highest they've ever been. The bad news is that you also have more at stake should your finances come under stress.

Few people in retirement risk as much as they did in their youths, but how risk resilient are you in the face of adversity? Can you take your lumps as they're handed to you, or do you panic at the first sign of trouble?

Everyone in retirement, whether a baby boomer or a member of the F.I.R.E. movement, faces similar financial risks, but how one reacts to financial stress is highly personal. Some view risk as an unavoidable part of life and aren't much affected. They exhibit moderate amounts of risk aversion. Others catastrophize every adverse event, leading to high levels of risk aversion.

What's your risk-aversion level? Ask yourself these questions:

- How much risk can you afford to take, given your financial resources and lifestyle requirements?
- Do you have a financial cushion should your expectations turn out to be too rosy for the actual situation?
- Are you comfortable taking risks to make more money, or are you content where you are financially and don't want to push your luck?
- If a shortfall were to occur, do you believe you'd have the mental fortitude and time for your portfolio to recover?

After answering these questions, do you think you're a risk-taker like Evel Knievel—willing to bet the farm at every turn? Or are you more of a middle-of-the-road risk-taker like Warren Buffet, willing to wait out any market distress? Or, maybe you're incredibly risk-averse, as many of the people growing up during the Great Depression were who couldn't stand the thought of losing any money at all. Do you know what sort of risk-taker you are?

There are important questions that most people struggle with answering because answering them requires introspection and intellectual honesty. It also requires an understanding of your emotional makeup. The questions are meant to get you thinking but don't search for too much precision in your answers. Close enough is good enough.

If you're overwhelmed, I strongly suggest hiring a financial advisor to help guide you assess your risk profile. You can, alternatively, go to my website https://www.retirewithpossibilities.com and take a standardized risk questionnaire.

Assessing your risk profile is a science and an art. No questionnaire can fully capture everything about you and your unique circumstances. I highly recommend discussing your financial situation with an advisor, or at the very least with someone financially literate.

STEP #3: OBJECTIVES

When it comes to your financial aspirations, there is usually a hierarchy of needs and wants. At the bottom of the hierarchy is your need to maintain a comfortable lifestyle. Making sure you don't run out of money for your necessities is quite important. Having adequate shelter, food, and health care represent your bare minimum needs. These are your minimum financial requirements.

If your financial resources are ample, what would you like to do with your money? Maybe go on some trips, eat at a nice restaurant, buy a fancy new camera, or remodel your kitchen? How about buying a second home or paying for your grandchildren's educational expenses? These represent your wants. They're not necessary for your survival, but make your life more enjoyable. These are your highly desirable goals.

Some people also have stretch goals. These are goals way beyond your current means. Achieving these goals would transform your life. The goal might be to grow wealth from one million to ten million over the next decade. It might be to own a string of apartment buildings generating over one hundred thousand dollars a month in rental income and paying off all your debt. These are the types of goals that, when you tell them to your friends, they snicker behind your back. Let them snicker. Stay focused on meeting goals that are meaningful to you.

Finally, there are legacy goals. You may want to leave money for your relatives when you pass. This money will make their financial lives more comfortable. Legacy goals could also involve leaving money to a social cause. Many people wish to leave their homes to their children.

Your financial goals must align with your vision of your Future Self.

- What are your minimum financial requirement goals? For most people, it's to cover basic living expenses (shelter, health care, food, utilities, and basic entertainment) for the rest of their lives.
- What niceties in life would you like to enjoy? These would involve spending on vacations, hobbies, nice clothes, fine dining, or a new car once in a while.
- If you stretched financially, what would that entail? For you, maybe it's a second home, a sailboat, a large hobby farm, or a trip around the world.
- What do you hope happens to your remaining assets once you pass? Is this of importance to you? Do you want your descendants to inherit anything left or leave some money to a social/environmental organization?

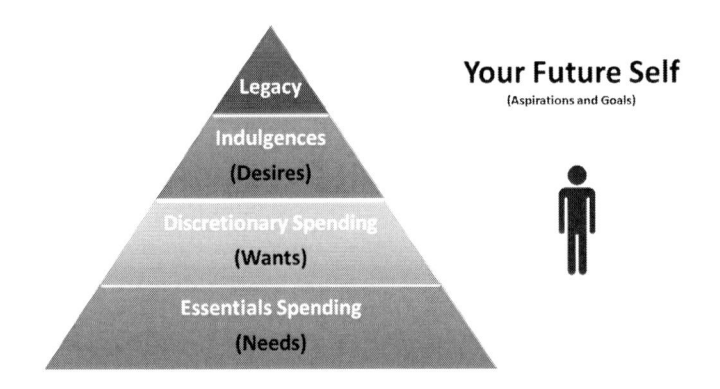

STEP #4: ASSETS

A big part of any financial plan is taking an inventory of your assets and debts. In this step of the PROACTIVE process, the goal is to create your Household balance sheet. Think of this step as an overview of your financial health. You'll have a positive net financial cushion if you own more than what you owe. Knowing the size of your financial cushion is and determined by the size of your cash flow, which we'll calculate in the next step. For now, be patient. Financial planning can be like watching a cricket match where, to the naked eye, nothing seems to be happening, and then, bang, everything happens at once.

Bear with me, please. Many of my clients find the exercise of tallying all their assets eye-opening. It's not something they would do for fun, but in hindsight, they realize that it's a critical part of assessing your financial health. Otherwise, how would you know how much you could safely spend in retirement without running out of money?

The first step is understanding what you own and how much each item is worth. You should include the value of assets you don't plan to sell, such as your primary home. Some advisors don't include the value of your home at this stage, but as discussed in the previous chapter, you need a sense of whether you're house-rich or lifestyle-poor. Moreover, your home is typically your largest and most significant asset. The goal is to get a realistic assessment of the value of what you own.

Let's drill down the list of your assets. The main ones are:

- **Cars and other big-people toys**
- **Club memberships**
- **Collectibles**
- **Financial accounts**—401(k), the cash value of your pension if you have one, savings accounts, any deferred compensation coming to you, trusts, variable annuities, other forms of cash value insurance
- **Real estate**—your home and other property you own
- **Private equity assets**—your business if you own some of the equity, other silent partner investments

You may also want to include the expected value of any inheritances you might receive. Skip this step if the value is highly uncertain or receiving an inheritance is a low probability event.

Here's a worksheet I use with my clients.

ASSETS	CURRENT VALUE	IN RETIREMENT	COMMENT
Taxable Assets			
Cash			
Bank Accounts			
Money Market Funds			
Investment Accounts			
Stock Option Grants			
Business Interests			
Partnership Interests			
Precious Metals			
Collectibles			
Personal Property			
Automobiles			
RVs & Boats			
Home			
Other Real Estate			
Tax-Deferred Assets			
401(K) Plans			
403(B) Plans			
457 Plans			
IRA			
Fixed Annuities			
Variable Annuities			
Deferred Comp Plans			
Life Insurance			
Series I-Savings Bonds			
Tax-Free Assets			
Roth 401(K) Plans			
Roth IRA			
Coverdell IRA			
Health Savings Acct			
529 College Savings Plan			
Other 1			
Other 2			
Inheritance			
TOTAL ASSETS			

Some of your assets are what I refer to as "use" assets. These are lifestyle assets that you use for consumption and pleasure, such as your house, cars, boats, and country club memberships. These assets have a value but, in general, require you to spend money every year to use them. They have what economists call a positive cost of carry. In layman's terms, you must write a check every year to keep using these assets.

Other assets, such as your 401(k) or brokerage account investments, are designed to yield a return. I call these "return" assets. There is no intrinsic use for many stock certificates or brokerage statements were it not for the fact that you expect a monetary return on those assets. You don't expect the same level of satisfaction from looking at your bank statements as, for example, taking a boat ride or driving a convertible.

Feel free to use the worksheet to tally up all your assets. I suggest using a "net of all fees" value for your assets. For example, the net value of your primary residence should involve a deduction for selling costs (taxes, fees, legal, and agent fees). I typically use an 8-10 percent range as a discount from the net value of your primary home. Another example involves the value of your 401(k) or IRA investments. These investments are taxed when you withdraw the money at your ordinary income tax rate. I use a 30 percent tax rate to arrive at a reasonable value on assets where taxes are due for simplicity purposes. Feel free to use an appropriate tax rate for your circumstances. The main point is the IRS keeps a keen eye on many of your assets.

Another modification I use with clients is to create an inventory of assets as if they were already retired. An inventory of assets is much more of a forecasting exercise and thus subject to greater imprecision. I recommend being conservative in your projections. For example, the housing market may have been going gangbusters lately, but historically real estate has yielded a 2-3 percent annual return rate. Have fun projecting future values but be conservative. This is where you can see the real difference between a "return" and a "use" asset. The value of the money in your 401(k) will very likely keep growing over the next decade (barring a market meltdown), but the value of "use" assets such as a boat will invariably decrease due to wear and tear.

Add up your debts. Of equal importance is tallying up how much you owe —mortgages, car loans, credit cards, etc. Include any long-term financial commitments that you've made if not legally bound.

Hopefully, your debt will be minimal to your assets by the time you retire. The difference between your assets and your financial commitments or debt is your net worth, and your net worth allows you to use your resources to generate an income in retirement.

Figuring out what you owe isn't a guesstimate. It's easier than figuring out approximate asset values.

Typical items that would fall under this category are:

- The outstanding balance on a home mortgage and home equity lines of credit
- Balance on other loans, such as on your car
- Any consumer debt you're carrying, such as credit card balances
- Student loans, not just yours, but for any loans co-signed by you
- Business loans if you own a business and have outstanding debts
- The value of lifetime alimony payments (if applicable)

Here's a worksheet to help you tally your debts and obligations.

LIABILITIES	CURRENT OBLIGATION	IN RETIREMENT	COMMENT
DEBT			
Primary Mortgage			
Secondary Mortgages			
Auto Loans			
Credit Cards			
Student Loans			
Business Loans			
Personal Loans			
Other Borrowing			
FUTURE COMMITMENTS			
Health Care			
Long-Term Care			
Legacy Bequeaths			
Vacation Property			
RV & Boats			
TOTAL LIABILITIES			

I usually add a column for what your debt is likely to be once you retire. For example, you might have one hundred thousand left on your mortgage, but in ten years, when you retire, the debt balance might be significantly lower. Same with other forms of debt such as business and student loans.

Before you declare mission accomplished, think again. Have you left anything out? Have you forgotten about some obscure asset or financial obligation?

Determine your financial cushion. So, now that you have tallied everything you own and owe, take the difference, and voila! That is what I call your financial cushion.

Your Household Balance Sheet

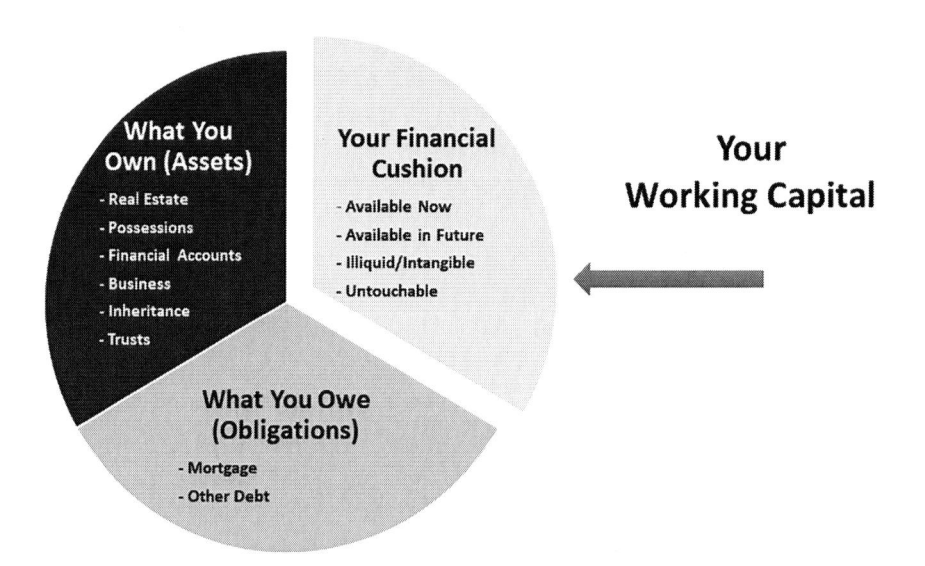

What You Own (Assets)
- Real Estate
- Possessions
- Financial Accounts
- Business
- Inheritance
- Trusts

Your Financial Cushion
- Available Now
- Available in Future
- Illiquid/Intangible
- Untouchable

Your Working Capital

What You Owe (Obligations)
- Mortgage
- Other Debt

Your financial cushion is your working capital for funding your lifestyle. In the next step of the PROACTIVE process, we will go over your household cash flow. The size of your financial cushion becomes relevant in the context of your cash flow. For example, if your financial cushion is large, but your expenses are more, you'll eventually be in financial hot water.

If you're having trouble conceptualizing all this financial "stuff," think of your assets as a water reservoir. In this step, you just calculated the size of the reservoir. Knowing how large of a reservoir you have is not that useful if you don't know how many people and businesses it serves and the intensity of use. The next step is calculating your cash flow. You'll figure out how much water comes into the reservoir (income) and how much gets consumed (expenses). Only after this step can you assess the reservoir's health. If more water gets consumed than replenished, the reservoir's health becomes compromised, and, eventually, it will dry out. The same applies to the relation of your financial cushion to your net cash flows.

STEP #5: CASH FLOW

In contrast to your household balance sheet, your household cash flow is dynamic. It changes all the time as you earn and spend money.

The two need to work together. You can't spend prodigious amounts of money forever without resorting to draining your financial cushion by selling assets.

Your cash flow is the sum of all your sources of recurring income minus your expected expenditures. Sources of income could include pension payments, social security, and wages if you still work. In terms of expenditures, it's helpful to separate them into essential and discretionary. It's also beneficial to anticipate expenditures that may not happen repeatedly but that you anticipate making in the near term.

As with managing a water reservoir upon which people and businesses rely, managing your household cash flow is probably the most important and challenging task to maintain your financial health in retirement.

Add up all your sources of income. Let's tally up the most frequent sources of income in retirement:

- Pensions from a previous employer
- Government support—in the US, that would mean a monthly check from the Social Security Administration
- Interest from investments
- Dividends
- Annuity payments
- Earnings from a job, wages or contract work, such as consulting
- Profits from an ongoing business

- Other forms of earnings from assets you own, such as rental income or royalty payments
- Investment account principal that you're drawing down

The first two sources of income – pensions and government support – are usually the safest and most reliable sources of earnings.

Here's a worksheet that I use with my clients. If you're already retired, fill out the information in the first column. If you're not yet retired, please also fill out the third column with your income estimates once retired.

INCOME	CURRENT	IN RETIREMENT	COMMENT
Fixed Income (Monthly)			
Net Paycheck			
Personal Support Payments			
Pension			
Social Security			
Annuity Payments			
Rental Income			
Other 1			
Other 2			
Variable Income (Monthly)			
Bonus			
Commissions			
Royalties			
Passive Business Profits			
Side Gig			
Other 3			
Other 4			
TOTAL INCOME (MONTHLY)			

Add up your expenses. How are you spending your money? Are you spending it on the monthly mortgage, car payments, groceries, cable, internet, entertainment, or other expenses? Now that you think about it, the list is probably longer than you initially thought. In this step, you're asked to provide your monthly expenses instead of how much you owe. For example, you may have a minimum payment of fifty dollars a month on your credit account but owe two thousand dollars on the card. You're not double counting if you include your credit card's outstanding balance among your debts on your household balance sheet. Remember, your outstanding debt is like a water reservoir. The monthly payments are analogous to how much water gets consumed.

Here's a sample worksheet to help you tally all your expenses.

EXPENSES	CURRENT	CATEGORY	IN RETIREMENT	COMMENT
Fixed Expenses (Monthly)				
Primary Mortgage		Essentials	$	
Other Mortgages		Essentials	$	
Consumer Debt Payments		Essentials	$	
Student Loan Payments		Essentials	$	
Auto Loan		Essentials	$	
Real Estate Taxes		Essentials	$	
HOA/Community Fees		Essentials	$	
Home Insurance		Essentials	$	
Auto Insurance		Essentials	$	
Life Insurance		Essentials	$	
Health Insurance		Essentials	$	
Club Dues		Discretionary	$	
Allowance/Support		Essentials	$	
Charity		Indulgences	$	
School Tuition		Discretionary	$	
Cable/Internet/Phone		Essentials	$	
Variable Expenses (Monthly)				
Utilities		Essentials	$	
Auto Gas & Maintenance		Essentials	$	
Groceries		Essentials	$	
Clothes		Discretionary	$	
Prescriptions		Essentials	$	
Personal Care		Essentials	$	
Home Maintenance		Discretionary	$	
Dining Out		Indulgences	$	
Entertainment		Indulgences	$	
Pet Food & Care		Essentials	$	
Transportation		Discretionary	$	
Travel		Indulgences	$	
Other 1		Unexpected	$	
Other 2		Unexpected	$	
Other 3		Unexpected	$	
TOTAL EXPENSES (MONTHLY)			$	

If you tally all your expenses, you might be surprised to see how much you spend on everyday items such as dry cleaning, Starbucks, take out, etc. You might discover that all those dinners and drinks with friends are almost as expensive as your mortgage or rent. All of these "hidden" recurring expenses can really add up.

What about the "one-timers" that suddenly show up in your inbox, such as insurance premiums and automatic annual renewals. These add up, too. What about unexpected expenses that keep on happening? For example, cars break down, teeth get chipped, and roofs need replacing.

Creating four buckets is an excellent way to think of your lifestyle expenses. Each bucket serves a different purpose and generally aligns with the objectives in step three.

Fill your essentials bucket with your basic living expenses – money for food and shelter (rent or mortgage plus property taxes and upkeep), utilities, health care, phone, basic transportation, and clothing. These are your basic needs. It's what you need to survive in your current situation.

The **discretionary** bucket includes items or services that make your life better but aren't required for bare minimum survival. These are items such as entertainment, gym memberships, and hobbies. These are your wants. Discretionary expenses allow you to enjoy your daily living. Which of these expenses would you have a hard time giving up?

The third bucket is filled with **indulgences**. Indulgences correspond to our stretch goals or desires. These are items we don't need for daily living and are a bit extravagant, even in our own eyes. If any of these indulgences disappeared, we would miss them, but our overall well-being would not be permanently affected.

What constitutes an indulgence? You'll have to decide this for yourself. I'm a pretty simple person. My biggest indulgences are nice shoes, a trip to the US Open with my son, and a winter vacation to a warm fun-filled destination.

If these indulgences were to go away, would I be sad? Sure, but I would get over it in time. My life wouldn't be affected in a meaningful way.

The final bucket is filled with **unexpected** expenses. These expenses are hardly ever discussed, even in financial planning sessions. They include fixing the roof, buying a new dishwasher, and replacing old tires. Spending money on these unexpected events gives us no pleasure. We would rather ignore these expenses.

Creating these expense buckets helps us get a sense of our priorities. Clearly, our highest priority is to satisfy our basic needs. The second-most priority is our wants or short-term discretionary spending, followed by our indulgences in stretch goals. Finally, we arrive at legacy spending. This item doesn't typically involve a monthly recurring expense but a lump sum contribution directly from our household assets. For that reason, I don't usually include a large legacy bequest in the household cash flow statement. Instead, it's a future obligation on your household balance sheet.

Your Household Cash Flow

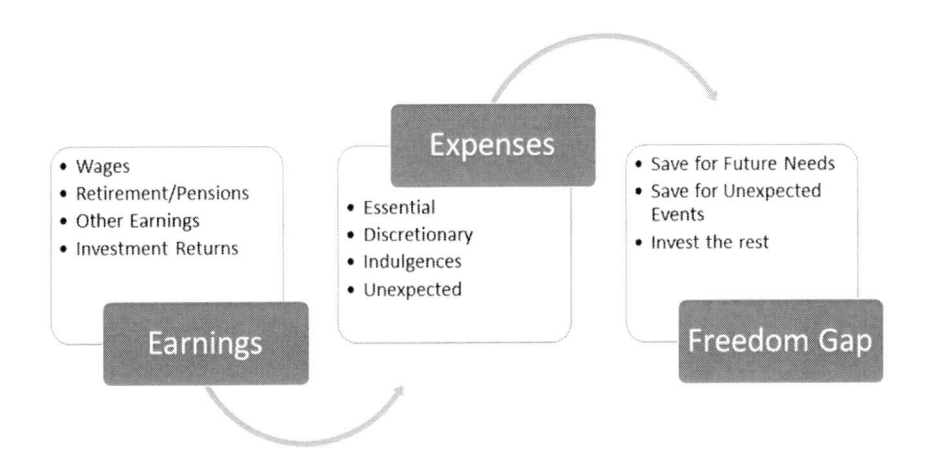

Earnings
- Wages
- Retirement/Pensions
- Other Earnings
- Investment Returns

Expenses
- Essential
- Discretionary
- Indulgences
- Unexpected

Freedom Gap
- Save for Future Needs
- Save for Unexpected Events
- Invest the rest

Why should you care so much about your cash flow?

Very simple. Your earnings/income need to at least match your expenses. That's your goal. If your expenses exceed your income, your financial reservoir slowly drains away. You'll sooner or later risk running out of money and depleting your financial cushion. On the other hand, if your earnings/income exceed your expenses, you will have excess money to set aside and invest

Your freedom gap is the difference between your earnings/income and your recurring expenses. If your freedom gap is consistently positive, you'll enjoy the ability to fund some or all your indulgences and further strengthen your financial health by increasing the balance of assets on your household balance sheet.

It's easy to get confused with all these financial terms. If you refer back to the reservoir analogy, you'll be able to distinguish between the concept of a balance sheet (the reservoir) and your cash flow (the flow of water coming versus leaving the reservoir). If positive, your freedom gap replenishes your financial reservoir's water table. I hope that this analogy clarifies the concept for you. These are vital concepts to understand for your financial wellbeing.

The most crucial financial requirement in retirement is that expenses not exceed sustainable sources of income. Your **household cash flow** is the tool designed to keep earnings and expenses in balance. You'll have to draw down the balances from your financial cushion if you're running a deficit. If you draw down the balances judiciously and invest appropriately, your money should last for your lifetime. If you overspend and invest poorly, your financial resources will deplete sooner than anticipated.

This whole topic leads me to the million-dollar question that keeps people and financial advisors up at night: How much can I safely spend in retirement?

The answer requires a comprehensive financial plan beyond the scope of this book, but there are rules of thumb that you can follow.

For example, advisor William Bengen came up with the 4% rule, which has become the most often used shortcut to a complete financial plan.

The 4% rule allows individuals to withdraw an inflation-adjusted 4 percent a year from their financial assets over thirty years with a reasonable expectation that they will not run out of money.

The 4% rule makes many assumptions, but it's a decent first pass.

It works as follows. Let's assume you have five hundred dollars of savings. If you use the 4% rule, you'd be able to withdraw twenty thousand dollars a year. If you had a one-million-dollar portfolio, you would be able to withdraw forty thousand dollars.

Let's say that the 4% rule states that you can spend a maximum of twenty thousand dollars a year, but you really need thirty thousand dollars to fund your lifestyle. What can you do?

If you face a persistent deficit, there are only three courses of action:

- Increase your earnings/income (maybe go back to work, rent out an unoccupied property, or get a higher rate of return on your financial savings)
- Spend less (cut out your indulgences and maybe even some of your discretionary spending)
- Do a little of both, increasing earnings/income and cutting back your expenses

Once you've identified your household financial cushion in step four and your cash flow freedom gap in step five, you'll know where you stand. Only then will you understand whether your lifestyle is sustainable.

Now let's turn our attention toward implementing your financial plan. The next step involves looking at ways to manage your taxes.

STEP #6: TAXES

Are you looking forward to not paying taxes anymore? Think again. Just because you're retired doesn't mean that the tax authorities have forgotten about you. You may no longer have to pay payroll taxes, but you still need to pay almost every other tax. Step six will help you determine how best to structure your financial assets and decide where to live to minimize your lifetime tax bill.

Regarding your investments, the general principle is to hold assets with the greatest tax burden in tax-exempt and tax-deferred account types. On the flip side, investment vehicles with small or non-existing tax burdens should be held in taxable accounts. In this way, overall portfolio taxes will be minimized.

There are usually tradeoffs between paying taxes now versus later when it comes to retirement planning. You will still have to pay taxes at some point, but the timing and amount can be optimized to lower lifetime outlays. Financial professionals refer to this as tax arbitrage.

Many people believe that your tax bill goes down massively in retirement. The truth, however, may be quite different depending on what type of investment accounts you own, how you allocate your assets, and where you live.

Taxable, tax-deferred, and tax-exempt accounts. Examples of the three types of accounts include a brokerage account, a 401(k), and a Roth IRA. The key difference between these types of accounts pertains to how taxes are calculated.

You pay yearly taxes on interest payments, dividends, and realized gains on investments sold in a taxable account. In a tax-deferred account, such as a 401(k), you pay taxes on withdrawals at your marginal tax rate for ordinary income. Finally, in a Roth type of account, you have already pre-paid your taxes when you set up your account, so any withdrawals are tax-free.

Asset location—where different investments are held. The US tax code distinguishes between interest income and dividends from qualified and non-qualified entities.

Interest income is derived from the coupons paid by bond investments. Banks also pay interest income on CDs and savings accounts. Interest income is typically taxed as ordinary income tax, which is usually a higher rate than capital gain taxes. That's why fixed-income investments are taxed at the highest rate.

As of 2022, dividends are taxed at a 20 percent tax rate if IRS rules qualify the company. Most publicly traded companies and companies domiciled in tax jurisdictions with reciprocal tax agreements with the US meet the criteria of a qualified company. The most notable exceptions are Real Estate Investment Trusts (REITs). REIT dividends are taxed as ordinary income, making these investment vehicles fairly tax-inefficient.

Without going into all the tax code intricacies, here's a ranking of popular investment vehicles by tax burden.

Greatest Tax Burden Real Estate Investment Trusts (REIT's)
Commodities
Corporate Bonds
Government Bonds
Actively Managed Stocks
Cash/Money Market/CD's
Index Funds
Smallest Tax Burden Tax-Exempt Bonds/Municipal Bonds

Choice of legal residence. Where you live will make a difference in terms of your tax burden. Your federal taxes will be identical, but there is a big difference at the state level. For example, at the moment, nine states don't have a state income tax: Alaska, Florida, Nevada, New Hampshire, South Dakota, Tennessee, Texas, Washington, and Wyoming.

Twelve states don't tax Social Security income, and fourteen states don't tax other pension income. Three states (Illinois, Mississippi, and Pennsylvania) don't tax 401(k), IRA, or pension distributions.

According to Smart Asset, an online financial advice firm, the seven "very tax friendly" states are Alaska, Florida, Georgia, Mississippi, Nevada, South Dakota, and Wyoming. They also classify seven states—California, Connecticut, Maine, Minnesota, Nebraska, Rhode Island, and Vermont—as "Not Tax Friendly."

If you're considering retiring abroad, things get even more complicated. You'll still be subject to U.S. Federal taxes but not state taxes. You will, however, be taxed by the country where you're residing. Every country has a different tax code. Countries generally deemed tax-friendly to US citizens include Panama, Ecuador, Belize, Portugal, and Greece.

The takeaway from this section is that you'll still have to pay taxes in retirement, but how much you pay is highly dependent on the types of investment accounts you own, what types of investments you own in each account, and where you live.

Nobody likes paying taxes, but sometimes people can go too far with tax avoidance tactics. Living in a tax-friendly locale simply because you strongly dislike paying taxes gives way too much power to the tax authorities. Your decision where to live should account for taxes, but not as the sole criteria. Similarly, with your investments, don't refrain from selling an investment that has appreciated significantly simply because you don't want to pay capital gain taxes. You always want to consider the tax implications, but don't let it cloud your judgment.

In steps seven to nine, it's time to create an investment plan that will generate the necessary income to fund your lifestyle, build a risk-adjusted portfolio that outpaces inflation, and construct a growth-oriented portfolio with the remaining assets. Let's talk investments now.

STEP #7: INCOME GENERATION PORTFOLIO

This step discusses creating a very low-risk portfolio of investments to fund your lifestyle expenses over the next three years. The choice of how many years of expenses to set aside in this bucket is arbitrary. Some advisors use five years, but I prefer to use three as capital market conditions typically move in three-year cycles.

In your overall PROACTIVE portfolio, there will be three distinct buckets of assets, each with its own investment strategy.

- An Income Portfolio (Step #7) is designed to fund your lifestyle expenses over the next three years
- A Value Creation Portfolio (Step #8) structured to protect you against the loss of purchasing power over the next decade
- A Growth Portfolio (Step #9) built to make your money last over your whole life

PROACTIVE Portfolio Structure

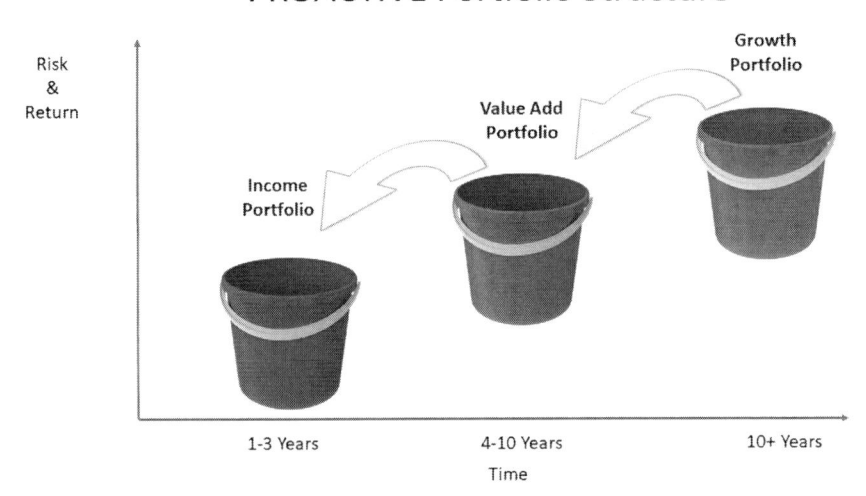

This section will explore the first bucket, the Income Portfolio, designed to fund your necessary living costs for the next three years.

Based on your cash flow analysis in step five, let's assume you need $125,000 a year to fund your lifestyle. This amount would include your necessities and discretionary spending, but not indulgences or legacy expenses. Let's further assume that social security for you and your spouse will be fifty-five thousand a year. A rental property you own nets two thousand dollars a month (after maintenance expenses), or twenty-four thousand dollars a year. Your spouse also has a pension paying one thousand dollars a month. You expect to bring in ninety thousand a year, resulting in a thirty-four thousand dollar a year shortfall between all these sources. This shortfall needs to be funded from savings. Based on your cash flow analysis in step five, you have enough financial assets to sustain this annual spending rate comfortably.

I suggest you set aside three years of lifestyle expenses as a starting point. The strategy would work as follows:

First, you would set aside 3 X $34,000 or $102,000 in the Income Generation Portfolio. The money would come from your savings, be it in withdrawals from a 401(k), Roth accounts, or another form of savings.

Second, you would pick suitable investments from the following list:

- Bank savings accounts and short-term Certificates of Deposit
- Money Market mutual funds
- Short-term (one to five years maturity) government, high-quality corporate, and municipal bonds. These could be mutual funds or exchange-traded funds (ETFs)

All these investments are very low risk. The yields on these investments will be low due to their low risk.

Third, you'd withdraw thirty-four thousand dollars from this portfolio every year to fund your living expenses.

Because these investments are very low risk, you don't need to obsess over any stress in the stock market. Even if something happens in the market, your chances of losing money are tiny. The whole purpose of the Income Portfolio is to allow you to sleep well at night without worrying about how to fund your lifestyle over the next few years.

The next component of your PROACTIVE portfolio is geared at generating a rate of return above inflation. Because there is no free lunch in financial markets, you'll need to accept some additional investment risk in this bucket. Let's take a look at step eight.

STEP #8: VALUE CREATION PORTFOLIO

It's essential to keep your money working for you. The strategies used in the Income Generation portion of your portfolio in step seven don't provide any form of protection against inflation. The **Value Creation Portfolio** aims to generate returns *above* inflation consistent with your risk profile. Your Value Creation Portfolio is designed to outpace inflation by investing in a suitable mix of stocks, bonds, and alternative assets fitting your risk profile.

How do you beat inflation?

Certainly not by playing it safe. To beat inflation, you'll need to take investment risk.

But how much risk will you need to take?

The short answer is that you will need to include high-return but high-risk assets in your **Value Add Portfolio**. Assets fitting this bill include:

- Intermediate to long-maturity (three to twenty years maturity) corporate bonds (Bonds)
- Inflation-protected (TIPS) government bonds (Bonds)
- Domestic and International stocks (Stocks)
- Real Estate Investments Trusts (Alternatives)
- Commodities (Alternatives)

The goal of the **Value-add Portfolio** of your PROACTIVE portfolio is to outpace inflation by taking a reasonable amount of risk.

By how much should you attempt to beat inflation? That will depend on your Risk Profile, which we covered in step two. Are you comfortable living with portfolio volatility and financially and emotionally able to take the risk?

- Yes, it doesn't bother me much.**Low-risk Aversion**
- It depends, but I get nervous.**Moderate-risk Aversion**
- Not really. I tend to panic.**High-risk Aversio**n

Where do you fall?

If you have low risk-aversion, your **Value-add Portfolio** can contain a higher stock allocation. If you're very risk-averse, your portfolio will allocate a smaller amount to equities.

Here are some guidelines. The allocations to stocks may appear high, but remember that a portion of your assets has already been allocated to very safe investments in your **Income Generation Portfolio**.

RISK AVERSION	STOCKS	BONDS	ALTS	CASH
Low	75%	15%	10%	0%
Moderate	60%	30%	10%	0%
High	40%	45%	10%	5%

These are suggested allocations, but only you know how much risk is appropriate for you.

Deciding on your target allocation is probably the most important investment. Your investment portfolio will be much more influenced by the mix of stocks, bonds, cash, and alternatives than by what mutual funds you hold. Focus on the big picture first. Fill in your target allocation in the chart below.

Your Target Asset Allocation

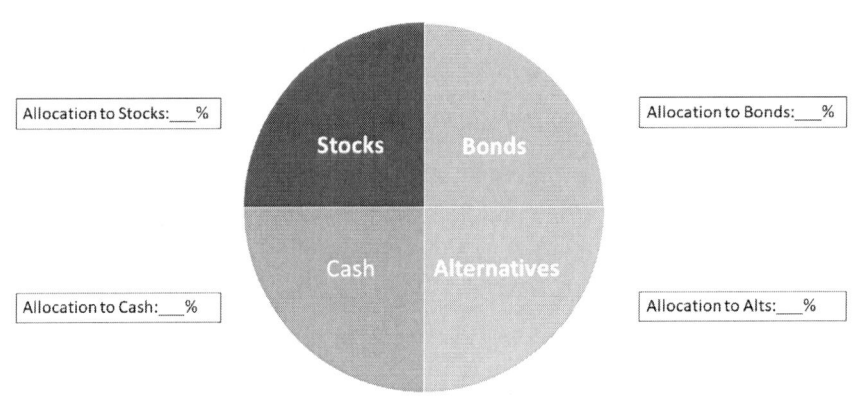

Allocation to Stocks:___%

Allocation to Bonds:___%

Allocation to Cash:___%

Allocation to Alts:___%

Total Portfolio: 100%

Let's now move to the growth portion of your PROACTIVE portfolio.

STEP #9: GROWTH PORTFOLIO

Many people become more risk averse as they age. That is understandable, but avoiding all risks has significant implications when it comes to financial matters. Financial markets work on the premise of risk and return. The two are tied together, as more risk provides more potential return. If you play it too safe, your return is likely to be low and probably won't surpass what you're losing in the form of inflation.

There are two main reasons for holding part of your PROACTIVE assets in a growth portfolio. Your **Growth Portfolio** is designed to take advantage of the outperformance of stocks over the long term. On average, stocks in the

US have returned close to 11 percent per year. Nothing in the public markets comes even close to that rate of appreciation, but there is a cost in terms of a higher level of volatility and occasional corrections, such as during the financial crisis of 2008.

The reason why I think you should always allocate some portion of your portfolio to the Growth bucket is twofold:

- The first reason is to provide a way to deal with the longevity of today's retirees. The chances are that if you retire in your sixties, you'll live for twenty to thirty years more. Some portion of your assets should be geared at funding your lifestyle way out in the future. Historically, stocks have been able to outpace inflation over the long term. If your portfolio isn't designed to last upwards of thirty years, you'll need to cut your living standard drastically.
- The second reason is to provide for a legacy if that is important to you. You don't intend to use these assets for your consumption but want to hold on to them until you die. Investing in a way to maximize appreciation while outpacing inflation is likely to be in the best interests of your beneficiaries.

Given the long-term nature of this bucket of assets, the type of investments held in your Growth Portfolio typically includes:

- Stocks of companies with high growth and profitability potential
- Private Equity
- Venture Capital

These investments are inappropriate for funding your lifestyle expenses in the short and intermediate run. They are high risk, high return, and require a patient long-term time horizon to succeed.

YOUR PROACTIVE PORTFOLIO

Your overall portfolio consists of three buckets designed to fund your lifestyle expenses over the short-term (one to three years), grow your assets at a rate exceeding inflation over the intermediate-term (four to ten years), and provide a financial cushion in the long-term (ten or more years).

The Income and Value Add Portfolios are the most important in terms of priorities. If your assets are plentiful, you're in a position to consider setting aside an allocation to the Growth Portfolio. Whether you intend to protect your lifestyle should you live longer than expected or leave a legacy behind, this portion of your portfolio should only represent a small portion.

Your most important goal regarding your financial wealth is to fund your lifestyle. The pecking order is, therefore:

- Pay for your current lifestyle over the next three years
- Protect yourself against a loss of purchasing power
- Have enough resources leftover in the case you live longer than expected or wish to leave a financial legacy behind

Here's a quick recap of your PROACTIVE portfolio.

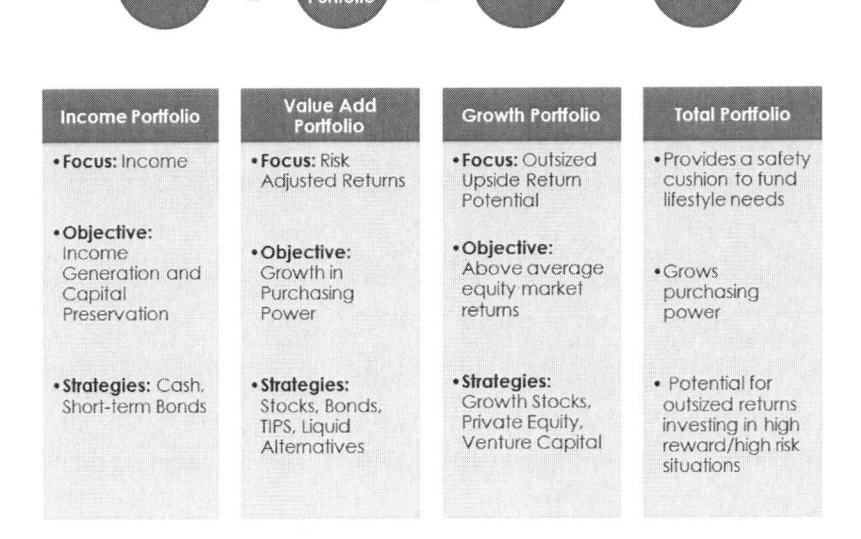

Income Portfolio + Value Add Portfolio + Growth Portfolio = Total Portfolio

Income Portfolio	Value Add Portfolio	Growth Portfolio	Total Portfolio
Focus: Income	**Focus:** Risk Adjusted Returns	**Focus:** Outsized Upside Return Potential	Provides a safety cushion to fund lifestyle needs
Objective: Income Generation and Capital Preservation	**Objective:** Growth in Purchasing Power	**Objective:** Above average equity market returns	Grows purchasing power
Strategies: Cash, Short-term Bonds	**Strategies:** Stocks, Bonds, TIPS, Liquid Alternatives	**Strategies:** Growth Stocks, Private Equity, Venture Capital	Potential for outsized returns investing in high reward/high risk situations

"The best time to plant a tree was 20 years ago. The next best time is today."

~CHINESE PROVERB

CONSIDERATIONS FOR YOUR FUTURE SELF

Your financial health is an integral part of your **NET WEALTH**. It provides the fuel necessary for your journey. In this chapter on earnings, you learned about high-level financial planning. Making your savings work for you is critical to making your money last and protecting your lifestyle from a steady erosion of purchasing power over time.

KEY TAKEAWAYS:

- Get to know yourself—your goals, preferences, and attitude toward risk.
- Take an inventory of all your assets and cash flows.
- Use your assets to generate income at a sustainable rate.
- Play it safe with your short-term funding lifestyle needs.
- Protect yourself against the erosion in purchasing power by investing in a risk-managed portfolio of stocks, bonds, and alternative assets.
- If excess assets are relative to your lifestyle needs, manage those using a long-term strategy incorporating growth stocks, private equity, and venture capital.
- Strive for balance amongst all components of your PROACTIVE system.

The trick for your long-term sustainability is to keep your expenses aligned with your overall income. A rule of thumb frequently used by retirement professionals is to spend between 3 and 4 percent of your portfolio assets in any given year.

If you're overspending and lack the resources to make more money, you'll likely run out of money. All steps in your PROACTIVE system need to be aligned.

There was a lot of information in this chapter. If you're feeling overwhelmed, I suggest talking to a financial advisor or retirement planning coach.

In the next chapter, we'll look at the next component of your **NET WEALTH**: time. Like managing your finances, how you allocate and use your time in retirement involves tradeoffs and a strong vision for your Future Self.

CHAPTER 5
GETTING A RETURN ON YOUR TIME

"We have a finite amount of time. Whether short or long, it doesn't matter. Life is to be lived."

~RANDY PAUSCH, FORMER COMPUTER SCIENCE PROFESSOR

TIME IS LIKE A RIVER RUNNING DOWN FROM THE MOUNTAINS. It always moves in one direction, and the second the flow of water touches you, it's past you. You can't stop the flow, and, unlike a river, time doesn't get replenished.

When the flow of time is plentiful, you take it for granted, but as it diminishes, you notice it more and value it more. Over time, the flow of time starts drying out. and the flow becomes a trickle and eventually stops. Time becomes more valuable as we have less of it.

Computer science professor Randy Pausch faced this reality when he was diagnosed with terminal pancreatic cancer in August 2007 at forty-six years old. Doctors gave him three to six months to live. He eventually passed away in July 2008, but not before delivering one of the most-watched YouTube videos of all time.

A self-described efficiency freak, Randy preferred to answer his phone while riding his bike (not sure I would try this). He joked once in a lecture that he had yet to find a way to make more time, but he was trying.

While Randy never did find a way to make more time, he became an instant expert on what to do with his limited time on earth the minute he received his terminal diagnosis. As is customary for retiring faculty at Carnegie Mellon, he was asked to deliver a final lecture.

After his terminal diagnosis, his wife Jai didn't think that giving a lecture was a good use of his limited time, but there was something inside of Randy that kept pushing him, and he committed to a September eighteenth date.

It took Randy a while to figure out precisely what he wanted to say, but it finally dawned on him that all the things he valued in life were rooted in the dreams and goals he had as a child, so he aptly named his last lecture "Really Achieving Your Childhood Dreams."

The lecture has been viewed over twenty million times on YouTube, but its popularity has less to do with achieving your childhood dreams and more with how to lead your life the right way. "If you lead your life the right way, the karma will take care of itself. The dreams will come to you," Randy said.

Nothing makes you realize the value of time more than knowing that your time is finite. As Randy said, "Time is all you have. And you may find one day that you have less than you think."

How you spend your time directly impacts your quality of life. Invest your time wisely, and your life will blossom. You'll feel energized and enjoy a sense of fulfillment. Waste it, and every day will feel the same as the last. You'll drift with the wind.

THE PROBLEM WITH TIME

Most people don't think much about how they'll spend their time once they retire. Sure, people have dreams and ideas of what they would like to do, but not a concrete vision.

One of the significant changes that retirement brings is that you go from time-constrained to time-affluent. As you retire, your problem goes from trying to fit too many commitments into your day to finding enough activities to fill the time once dedicated to commuting and working.

In surveys by the US Bureau of Labor Statistics, the average daily hours of leisure per person increased from 4.5 hours for 45–54-year-olds to 7.4 hours for people over the age of 65. On the surface, that is a good thing—people generally retire to increase the amount of time they can spend on leisure activities. There's a problem, however, when you dig a bit deeper. Most of that leisure time gets spent on passive activities such as watching TV.

In a larger survey, this one done by the University of Michigan, they found that while most retirees would like to spend their leisure time on active activities, such as socializing, walking, and exercising, the reality is that they spent most of their time on passive activities. Even more telling is that these passive activities increase with age, despite survey respondents increasingly indicating a preference for more active pursuits.

The hard reality for many people in retirement is that they're spending a lot of their time on passive activities that don't bring them much satisfaction. They're spinning their wheels on low-return activities while their time is becoming scarcer.

Have you ever had days when you're really busy, but feel like you accomplished nothing at the end of the day? The following nine thousand days (yes, that's the average number of days spent in retirement in the US) could feel like that if you treat time as a disposable commodity with little value. Those words may read harsh, but it's the reality of daily living for many retirees today; busy doing lots of things but not necessarily the things that provide purpose and meaning to our lives.

We know that time on earth is a blessing, but somehow, we don't treat time with the same respect and attention as other scarce resources, such as money. We often believe that we'll always have more time to do what we want in life. There's always tomorrow, but as author Sam Horn points out, "Tomorrow is not a day of the week."

In this chapter, I'll help you get the most out of your time in retirement by focusing your attention on activities that provide a meaningful and high return on your time. First, I'll teach you the value of your time by dispelling some of the most widely held misconceptions about your time in retirement. Then, I'll introduce you to a structured way of thinking about allocating your available time best and follow up with tactics for re-optimizing your valuable time.

Let's get started.

SOME PRECONCEIVED NOTIONS ABOUT TIME THAT COULD BE TRIPPING YOU UP

Most people don't think much about the meaning of time, and, as a result, they squander it. One day, they realize that the river of time has passed them by, and they don't have enough time left to do everything they want to. They consistently fall prey to several misconceptions, what I call "time traps," that prevent us from living our best lives while we still have time.

Time is money. Most people value their money more than their time, obsessing over their account balances and reaching their retirement number. People do this often because quantifying the value of time is nearly impossible. You can't read the *Wall Street Journal* and find the price of time like you could for a mutual fund. Your time's value is determined by what matters to you. For example, taking time to travel can be highly desirable to somebody who values new cultural experiences and the thrill of new learning. Yet, it's of little value to somebody who isn't interested in learning about other cultures.

I'll have time to do all the things I want some time in the future. As Randy Pausch sadly found out, you may not have a tomorrow. Many things can happen in the future, not in your control. Don't tempt fate by postponing action.

I'm so busy now, but someday I'll have more time to work on my dreams. Like the previous belief, you may never get a chance down the road to realize your dreams. Remember that your river of time is always fuller now than it will be in the future.

I'm waiting for the right time or situation. Many people wait for something to happen before they feel given the green light to pursue their goals. They're waiting for permission. For example, many people would love to start a business but wait to have millions in the bank before pursuing their entrepreneurial dreams. The self-imposed hurdle becomes the excuse for never acting.

A busy life is a successful life. Busyness is a lack of priorities and a lack of understanding of your time's value. Saying no is often the first step to increasing the return on time on those activities that truly matter to you. You want your time to be spent wisely and not on everything that comes across your desk.

I don't have the time left to change my life. Retirees often use this excuse for not changing. Change happens when you commit. Change happens when what you're trying to achieve is meaningful to you. Change can happen on a dime. The challenging part is starting and persevering when the inevitable discomfort sets in. Calendar time is not the limiting resource mindset.

"Make every day your masterpiece."

~JOHN WOODEN, UCLA BRUINS HEAD BASKETBALL COACH

What do you think? Have you ever used any of these excuses? I have, but I know now that these limiting beliefs hurt me. I think it was once I turned sixty that I realized time was shortening. If I wanted to accomplish my goals, I needed to speed up and not place so many imaginary roadblocks in the way. I've always been very time-conscious, but, in all honesty, I never realized how much time I wasted hoping for the perfect situation to arise before committing to my goals. I realize now that it's the other way around. First, you commit, and then you invest the time. Today will vanish anyway, so you might as well spend your time on something you find meaningful and valuable. In the next section, we'll explore these thoughts further.

THE VALUE OF YOUR TIME

We all have twenty-four hours in a day, and whether we are doing things we enjoy or not, the time gets spent anyway. Some of our time we spend sleeping and the essential chores of living. We also spend time working and on leisure and idle activities. Your time machine deposits 86,400 seconds every night at midnight, and—*poof*—they're gone twenty-four hours later!

Unlike money, you can't hoard time, but what would happen if we started to treat time more like we treat money?

In the seventies, grocery stores held promotional contests to see how much you could fit in a shopping cart. Contestants had a limited amount of time (usually five minutes) to fill up their carts with anything they wanted in the store. The whole strategy consisted of maximizing the dollar value of what you managed to put in your cart. Once your time was up, you got to keep everything in your cart.

If you filled up your cart with low-value goods such as sugar, flour, or sweets, you would be leaving a lot of money on the table compared to those people who rushed in with a plan to only focus on pricey goods, such as exotic spices, specialty foods, and home goods. Once time was up, they would tally up the value of all the goods in the contestant's cart and calculate the financial return on the contestant's time. If they picked lots of high-priced goods, their return on time was high. If they didn't, their return on time was low, and they were laughed at for their poor strategy.

Life isn't a game, but indulge me for a moment. Think of your life like this supermarket contest. Imagine that your daily activities are like items in a grocery aisle. Say you start your day at 7 a.m. and get until 10 p.m. to do whatever you want. How will you spend your time? Which activities would you pick? Which activities would you avoid? Which activities would you do first? You might not be all that unfamiliar with this game because when you choose where and how to spend your time, you're doing the same thing the game show contestants did. Many of your decisions may be unconscious, but you're still making a choice. Even if you spend all day on the couch surfing Netflix because you're tired, that's a choice. But is it a choice that improves your life, or one that only feels comfortable at the moment? Time passes regardless of your choices, but the return on your time varies drastically depending on whether your choices align with your Future Self or they keep you stuck in the mud.

When I started looking at time this way, I immediately realized how much time I spent on low-return activities that only soothed me in the short term. I became more conscious and intentional about how I used my time. I learned to prioritize and schedule my high-return activities while minimizing time spent on passive activities, such as watching TV or scrolling through Facebook. I learned to say no to things that weren't of any genuine concern to me. I re-discovered a simple tool from my MBA days designed to bring structure to any decisions regarding time.

THE TIME ALLOCATION MATRIX

I believe this tool originated with General Eisenhower, and executive coach Stephen Covey popularized it in the 1980s. I adapted the framework to reflect how to optimize our allocation of time. The diagram below has four segments partitioned by the importance of an activity and its urgency.

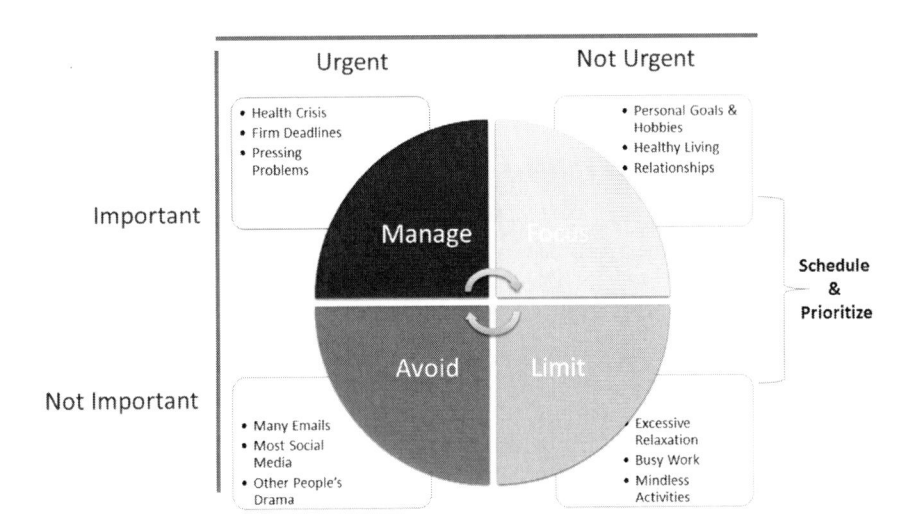

	Urgent	Not Urgent
Important	• Health Crisis • Firm Deadlines • Pressing Problems **Manage**	• Personal Goals & Hobbies • Healthy Living • Relationships **Focus** — Schedule & Prioritize
Not Important	• Many Emails • Most Social Media • Other People's Drama **Avoid**	• Excessive Relaxation • Busy Work • Mindless Activities **Limit**

My available time is any hours that haven't already been allocated to something in the day. For example, sleep and basic self-care are allocated.

Let's assume those two things account for ten hours a day. If you're still working full time, you'll need to cut another nine to ten hours a day from your available time. Let's look at two scenarios and do the math.

Scenario 1: You're still working full time. Let's assume you're spending twenty hours a day between self-care and work during the workweek. That leaves you four hours a day to allocate any way you see fit. Assuming you're not working on the weekends, you also get an additional twenty-eight hours of available time.

Under this scenario, you have forty-eight hours a week to allocate to whatever activities you want. When I first did this math, I was surprised by the number of "free" hours per week. It's like having a second job. Isn't it? You can do a lot with forty-eight hours a week, but you'll need to pick wisely. Otherwise, those forty-eight hours will pass unnoticed.

Scenario 2: You're retired, and you've got oodles of time. Under this scenario, you get the benefit of being retired. Retirement means time freedom. You can allocate your time any way you want, and you have lots of it. Here's the breakdown: You have fourteen hours a day, seven days a week. Every day is Sunday! The total number of available hours is ninety-eight a week. Wow, that's like having two jobs!

When it comes to time, you either use it or lose it. Instead of working for a paycheck, you work for yourself. You've become an entrepreneur in charge of *all* your time. As with any entrepreneur, your job is to allocate scarce resources (your time) in such a way as to get the highest return. Your return comes in the form of happiness and fulfillment.

Now that we've done the basic math, let's figure out how to use the time allocation matrix to allocate time to the most meaningful and value-enhancing activities.

Let me briefly describe the four segments of the matrix.

SEGMENT #1: IMPORTANT AND URGENT ACTIVITIES (MANAGE)

Fires that need to be put out immediately comprise the first quadrant. You need to drop everything and deal with the crisis at hand. It could be a personal issue, such as a health crisis or a miscommunication with a loved one. It could mean a flood in the basement or a deadline to file for social security benefits.

You can't predict the time you might spend on these urgent but essential activities, but they require your immediate attention. You must manage under the circumstances as best as possible. Otherwise, you risk severe repercussions. By immediately dealing with a crisis, your return on time is super high, but, hopefully, you don't have too many of these moments.

SEGMENT #2: UNIMPORTANT AND URGENT ACTIVITIES (AVOID)

These activities are drama-filled. They appear urgent, but, upon reflection, they're not. For example, you don't need to respond to every posting on your Facebook feed. You don't need to respond immediately to your friend's latest conflict with their partner. Sometimes the best course of action is to wait it out. As with most drama, things tend to work themselves out.

These urgent, but unimportant issues, won't affect your life once you put them out of your mind. The best way forward is to avoid spending any time on activities that appear urgent but aren't necessary because the return on your time is harmful. You're using precious energy on stuff that doesn't matter. It would be best if you minimized the time spent in this segment. Even better, say no!

SEGMENT #3: IMPORTANT AND NOT URGENT (FOCUS)

This segment is where your time has the most value. This is the time you spend on your goals and aspirations that you sketched as the vision of your Future Self in chapter two. This is the time you invest in healthy living habits such as nutrition, exercise, learning, and other forms of self-care. It's time you spend with family and friends, deepening your bonds.

You need to schedule this time because you want to protect it at all costs. This is the time allocated to daily actions that lead to a life of happiness and fulfillment. This is the time segment where you work toward becoming your Future Self. It should be the focus of your day. This is the first group of activities written in pen when scheduling your time. These are the non-negotiables in your life. These are the non-negotiables in your life.

SEGMENT #4: UNIMPORTANT AND NOT URGENT (LIMIT)

Activities that fit this segment involve a passive consumption of your time. They are activities like watching TV and busywork around the house such as paying bills. For the most part, none of these activities require much brainpower. They're mindless and, if unchecked, can lull you into a sense of complacency.

Take watching television. You might intend to catch up on the news at six o'clock but get sucked into watching the latest episode of *Entertainment Tonight* after the news ends. Pretty soon, you're eating dinner in front of the TV, watching whatever show is on, and by ten o'clock, you're asleep on the couch. Four hours have passed in the blink of an eye. You didn't intend to spend so much time in front of the TV, but you're right at the national average of four hours a night. That's twenty-eight hours a week of passive consumption that hasn't done one iota for your happiness or sense of fulfillment.

You've traded your valuable time for very little return. If you care about your well-being, you must limit your time on these mindless activities. Beware of the power of "easy" and "comfortable." They take over your time without you even noticing it. Many retirees have fallen prey to a lifestyle spent on the "not important and not urgent" without realizing the great disfavor they're doing to themselves over the long term.

"The best way to maximize your time is by not wasting time. This requires planning and having an awareness of how you spend your time throughout the day."

~TASHA HOGGATT, AUTHOR

USING THE MATRIX TO PRIORITIZE YOUR TIME

The matrix gives you four different boxes to allocate your available time. The two boxes on the top are where your investment of time bears the greatest reward. These boxes address the real crises in your life and where you work on becoming your Future Self.

We would spend all our time in these two boxes in an ideal world, but let's be realistic. We're not robots; we'll always waste time on activities that might feel okay momentarily but don't contribute to our happiness and sense of fulfillment. We're often content to allow time to pass without giving the passing a second thought.

I value my time, and you value your time, too. When I worked through the time allocation matrix, it was the first time I noticed that I was seriously underinvesting in my future. I simply didn't spend enough time working on my goals and the areas of my life that made me happy and gave me a sense of fulfillment. Busyness deferred my dreams. I let my day job suck all my energy and reenergized by idly watching too much TV at night. I would joke that I was working at 30 percent capacity without getting a return on the other 70 percent of my time. At the end of the day, I was the fool for not prioritizing my time the right way.

At this point in my life, my time allocation was split roughly into the following segments:

- 10 percent on "Important and Urgent"
- 30 percent on "Unimportant and Urgent"
- 20 percent on "Important and Not Urgent"
- 40 percent on "Unimportant and Not Urgent"

I was shocked. I always thought of myself as someone who actively planned for my future life. But in a sense, that was in itself part of the problem. I was good at planning and terrible at execution. I also realized that I was simply not spending enough time on what mattered to me.

My priorities, even allowing for some waste, should have been more along the lines of:

- 10 percent on the "Important and Urgent"
- 5 percent on the "Unimportant and Urgent"
- 75 percent on the "Important and Not Urgent"
- 10 percent on the "Unimportant and Not Urgent"

When you do this exercise, you'll probably have the same realization. You're underinvesting in your future and overinvesting in your present. I don't know too many people who genuinely maximize all their time. Our human tendency is toward comfort and the familiar, which guarantees us the status quo for the most part.

What is your current time allocation? Are you happy with where it is? Will your time allocation lead to happiness and fulfillment? What changes in your priorities do you need to make to close the gap with your Future Self?

Let's start by writing down your optimal allocation of time?

- On the "Important and Urgent" _____%
- On the "Unimportant and Urgent"_____%
- On the "Important and Not Urgent"_____%
- On the "Unimportant and Not Urgent" _____%

Are you committed to the goals and aspirations for your future that you sketched out in chapter two? Is your time allocation aligned with these objectives?

Wisely investing your time requires thought about what matters to you (covered in Chapter two), a plan (what are you going to do with your time covered in this section), and action (creating practices and habits designed to maximize the return on your time). Taking action is the subject of the next section.

> *"Until you value yourself, you will not value your time. Until you value your time, you will not do anything with it."*
>
> ~M. SCOTT PECK, AUTHOR OF THE *THE ROAD LESS TRAVELED*

GET A HIGH RETURN ON YOUR TIME

It's one thing to allocate your time towards your high-value activities and another to use the time effectively. The first step toward maximizing the return to your time is to allocate the necessary time to the activity. That's what we did in the previous section. We shifted our time allocation away from low-return to high-return activities.

But what if all you do with your time is waste it? What if, despite your commitment to becoming your Future Self, you don't seem to be making much progress?

I don't want you to think that you should allocate every waking minute of the day. One of the great benefits of being retired is picking activities and living in a way that inspires you. I'm saying that if you have goals and aspirations, you allocate the necessary time to make progress. My goal for you is to get the most happiness and satisfaction from your time and that you don't waste it on mindless activities that keep you busy but don't do much good over the long term.

To maximize your return on time, you'll also need to be effective, not just have good intentions. You'll need to overcome inertia and distraction. You'll need to be able to execute your intentions, but let me warn you that there are no magic bullets. Sometimes it's as simple as putting your head down and getting the work done. At other times you'll need tactics to get the ball rolling.

Here are some suggestions that have worked well for me.

SCHEDULING

Managing your schedule is an absolute must, especially if you're retired. If you don't schedule your time, I guarantee you'll lack consistency. One day you'll do great; the next, you won't spend a second on your most important goals. Please do not buy the conventional wisdom that you should throw out your alarm clock and do whatever you feel like once you retire. I guarantee that what you'll feel like doing is taking it easy, and time will drift away.

The whole point of scheduling is to remind you to work on activities that, in your words, are meaningful and important, such as those you came up with in chapter two. A schedule is a daily reminder of the lifestyle and vision you have of your Future Self. Decide how many hours you spend on these structures and activities, and then schedule them.

You don't need a fancy scheduler to remind you what you need to do. I do my weekly schedule in Excel, but paper and pen work, too. I break up my available time into thirty-minute increments. I feel like I need at least half an hour to get anything done, but you may be okay with smaller chunks of time.

I don't specify the nitty-gritty of everything I want to accomplish. I use broad categories such as client meetings, research, exercise, quiet time/meditation, and lunch (guys can't go without it). My weekly calendar blocks my time, but I also have a specific daily to-do list, which I write out by hand the night before. For example, it'll say go to the gym and do cardio work.

At first, when you get into the habit of scheduling your week, you'll probably overcommit yourself. You won't leave enough time between tasks. I always give myself at least five to ten minutes to transition. I need that time to declutter my brain and gain focus on the next item on my list.

It's important to be realistic with what you can accomplish in the selected time slot. The key is to focus on the activity at hand single-handily. You'll make a lot of progress some days. Other days, you'll tread water with little progress. Stay consistent and focused on seeing results.

> *"The best advice I ever came across on the subject of concentration is: Wherever you are, be there."*
>
> ~JIM ROHN, AUTHOR, ENTREPRENEUR, AND MOTIVATIONAL SPEAKER

CREATE AN EMPOWERING ENVIRONMENT WITH RULES THAT PROTECT YOUR TIME

You must set up your environment conducive to whatever you're attempting to do. For example, if you want to write the next great novel, you need an environment that allows you to focus on writing. If you're going to get fit, you need an environment where fitness is a core value.

You may think that you're good at removing distractions from your brain, but the research is clear about our inability to be effective when attempting to multi-task. Distractions rob our focus.

I also highly recommend setting some ground rules when you need to focus. For example, I never take phone calls when writing and refrain from answering emails. When my children were little, I had a home office in the basement. When the door was shut, Dad was working, and no interruptions were allowed. When the door was open, they were welcome to come in and keep me company.

Your environment exerts a powerful influence over your behavior. If you rely on willpower alone, you'll likely lose. Design your environment to support your goals, and you're much more likely to make the progress you want to make.

PERIODICALLY RE-EXAMINE YOUR TIME-WASTERS AND EXCUSES

Do you ever find yourself bargaining with yourself to get out of doing what really needs to get done? You might say: I'll skip today's spin class so I can go out with friends for drinks, but tomorrow I'll take an extra intense spin class and lift some weights. You know where I'm going with this. Tomorrow you'll feel too tired to work out and make another deal with yourself. And so it goes on.

We tend to think that we can make up for today's shortfalls by overcompensating for tomorrow. Everybody does it, but you need to look inside and figure out what's really going on to break the cycle.

Why are you making these deals with yourself, knowing you're sabotaging your goals? Are the goals you set for yourself not that important anymore? What is triggering you?

You'll keep repeating the same pattern if you don't understand what's happening. That's why it's a good idea to write in a journal. Write down your go-to excuses. Then, next to your excuses, write down why these excuses are total BS and what you'll do the next time you feel these disempowering emotions creeping in. Also, remind yourself why the goal is important in the first place. Be specific. Don't just write down: I want to be fit. Instead, write down: I want to be strong enough to play tennis twice a week in a competitive league this summer. Come up with a plan for dealing with your excuses.

ACCOUNTABILITY

We are incredibly creative about coming up with excuses. They often sound rational to us and give us a way out. We can justify almost anything to ourselves, but the same doesn't hold true with others. Others can sniff out when your excuses do not hold water.

If you can't be intellectually honest with yourself, it's time to get a no-BS accountability partner. An accountability partner is somebody to who you report your progress. You may text them daily or hold a weekly review session. The deal is that they keep you accountable for your actions, and you do the same for them. Your accountability partner can give you a different perspective and ask the tough questions you're afraid to ask yourself. They're not feeling the same disempowering emotions as you when you come up with excuses. Maybe they'll give you a pass initially, but after hearing the same set of excuses for a while, they'll likely feel disappointed in you or, even worse, upset that you're wasting their time.

I have been on both ends of the accountability bargain. I've administered tough love and been on the receiving end of it. There have been periods when I went without an accountability partner and found myself drifting. Nothing beats the discipline of openly stating your commitments and having somebody else hold you accountable. It forces you to do what you said you would, lest you risk embarrassment and disappointment. And, who wants to do that, right?

CLUSTER UNPLEASANT TASKS

We all have to do grunt work, whether writing bills, cleaning the basement, or folding clothes. Many of these things fall under the "Unimportant, Not Urgent" category but still need to get done.

My best suggestion is to batch this work. In other words, schedule time on your calendar to do nothing but this type of work. Don't try to fit it in whenever you have a moment to spare. Schedule it. Admit to yourself that it's not going to be fun. That way, you'll see it right on your calendar, and all you have to do is show up and get started. No excuses.

There are many things in life that people have to do on a routine basis that they don't enjoy. In fact, in many instances, the very thought of having to do something makes people sick to their stomachs. Take sales calls, for example. If you're running any business, especially a startup, you understand the importance of sales. You have to put yourself out there and face possible rejection and maybe even embarrassment. Most people hate sales calls for this reason, but there is no easy way out if you want to have a successful business. Unless you outsource the task to somebody else, you must force yourself to make the sales calls. Darren Hardy, the author of *The Compound Effect,* offers a great example of how to do this without endlessly ruminating. He simply schedules his sales calls for the same time every week. For instance, he might reserve Wednesday afternoon from 3:00 p.m.-5:00 p.m. for making calls every week. He doesn't make sales calls any other time unless they're scheduled ahead of time. This way, he doesn't allow himself to come up with excuses. He's totally focused on one thing only—sales.

You may not need to make sales calls in your life, but I'm sure there's some activity you need to do on a routine basis that you dread. I recommend creating a big bucket category in your schedule for such tasks and getting them over within the prescribed time block.

I hope that you understand the importance of focusing on activities in your life that give you a high return on your available time. We all get the same twenty-four hours a day, but how we use that time is life's great differentiator between those who are squandering it unconsciously and those that intentionally set out to maximize its value.

"How you spend your time defines who you are."

~OPRAH WINFREY, MEDIA MOGUL

CONSIDERATIONS FOR YOUR FUTURE SELF

How you manage your time will determine the quality of your days. It's easy when you retire to consider all your free time as leisure time. For a while, it might be nice to relax and regroup after leaving a long career behind. At some point, however, you'll need to look at your day and decide for yourself if you will make your time count.

Your time in retirement is precious. The value of your time has increased (because you have less of it left), yet many people squander their lives on passive activities that bring little long-term joy and fulfillment to their lives. Passive translates to easy and comfortable today but hard and uncomfortable in the long run.

I want to conclude this chapter with some reminders of the value of time by Steven Griffith in his book *The Time Cleanse:*

- To realize the value of ONE YEAR, ask a student who failed a class.
- To realize the value of ONE MONTH, ask a mother who gives birth to a premature baby.
- To realize the value of ONE WEEK, ask the editor of a weekly paper.

- To realize the value of ONE HOUR, ask the lovers waiting to meet.
- To realize the value of ONE MINUTE, ask a person who missed a train.
- To realize the value of ONE SECOND, ask a person who just avoided an accident.

Thought-provoking, isn't it?

Let's be honest. It's easy to waste time, but it's not wise. Investing your time in high-return activities requires discipline, focus, and follow-through. It requires knowing where your time is going in the first place and then, based on that knowledge, deciding where it could go instead to create more meaningful experiences.

Your time is worth what you decide to do with it. You determine its value by doing the things that bring joy and fulfillment to you. You can't just mimic what everybody else is doing and expect that to work for you. You get to decide, and then you spend the day on activities that matter to you. Your allocation of time reflects your priorities.

The person you are in retirement is no different from the person who worked for three or four decades, but you have a choice to make. What will you do with the time you previously spent at work? Do you invest it in passive leisure, or do you seek more balance in your life by investing it in activities and pursuits that compound over time to long-term happiness and fulfillment?

In the next chapter, we'll focus on the next component of your **NET WEALTH**—work. In a sense, work seems the polar opposite of time. Research has shown that many retirees "un-retire" after a brief honeymoon. When people first retire, they expect to have lots of free time, but many soon find they miss work. They often decide to forego some free time to go back to work. The next chapter will explore why work may be highly beneficial to retirees.

CHAPTER 6
WORK

"We work to become, not to acquire."

~ELBERT HUBBARD, AMERICAN AUTHOR AND PHILOSOPHER

WORK IS INCREASINGLY BECOMING A FIXTURE IN THE retirement landscape. Ironic, wouldn't you agree? Isn't retirement about not working anymore? Your parents' and grandparents' retirements certainly were, but nowadays, with people living much longer s, working in some capacity makes sense, both from a financial and a non-financial perspective.

And it's not, as you might think, about the money. According to the 2014 Merrill Lynch report *Work in Retirement Myths and Motivations*, only 31 percent of retirees who go back to work do it for the money. Sixty-two percent said it was to stay mentally active. In comparison, 46 percent said it was to remain physically active, and 42 percent cited social interaction as their reason for going back to work.

In fact, did you know that about two-thirds of retirees go back to work a couple of years after they retire?

Many retirees approach retirement with the idea of never working again, only to discover that they miss it after a couple of years. Often, they decide that working is not that bad if you're spending your time on meaningful and enjoyable activities. They refocus their work lives around activities that bring greater meaning, joy, and flexibility.

It's estimated that people will have three primary careers in their lifetime and change jobs six to ten times. I wouldn't be surprised if these estimates prove way too low, given how fast technology and work practices have changed.

In this chapter, you'll learn why many retirees choose to keep working not for the paycheck but the social interaction, mental stimulation, and engagement with the world. Retirement has given them the freedom to choose meaningful work and share their wisdom and life experiences as engaged contributors.

WHY WORK IF YOU DON'T HAVE TO?

After spending a couple of years in retirement, many people are surprised when they start missing workdays. Working fulfills an internal need they didn't realize they needed during their primary careers.

Working in retirement is rapidly becoming the norm. People live longer and stay healthier today and want more out of life than simply leisure and comfort. They want to keep participating in life and hate feeling their age makes their opinions irrelevant. I can't think of one friend who, after a successful career, has at least not dabbled in working during retirement.

Working is one way to stay engaged in life. In fact, working has several proven benefits that can make your life in retirement more rewarding.

"It's hard to finance a 30-year retirement on a 40-year career."

~JOHN SHOVEN, CHARLES R. SCHWAB PROFESSOR OF ECONOMICS AT STANFORD

WORKING CAN HELP YOU CREATE A SUSTAINABLE LIFESTYLE

As discussed in chapter four, many retirees find that their savings and investments don't provide the cushion they were hoping for after retirement; for most people, there's a gap between what they want to spend and how much they have. Working after your primary career days will be necessary for many people as they seek to supplement their savings to last over a longer lifespan.

Most retirees don't own a business or have other passive income streams that keep generating profits—although, hopefully, after reading chapter four, you've thought of a few! Instead, they rely primarily on savings accumulated over their careers, supplemented by what they're entitled to from government assistance programs. In the US, for example, social security is expected to only account for about 30 percent of the average person's retirement needs. Savings, interest, or dividends need to make up the shortfall, but what if you're constantly dipping into your principal investments? Eventually, you'll run out of money.

Famous rappers might argue that more money brings more problems, but the more significant issue for many retirees is not having enough money, which brings substantial problems.

It's a tall task to accumulate enough assets during your career and live two or three decades living in retirement comfortably. Something needs to fill the gap, and increasingly that something is working.

But that's not necessarily bad news! Working has many emotional and social benefits.

WORKING INCREASES SOCIAL INTERACTION

Many retired people miss the daily interaction with co-workers, clients, and customers. They miss being engaged with society.

Loneliness is a serious problem in many countries where the social fiber of family connections has broken down. A recent University of California San Francisco (UCSF) study found that 43 percent of people over sixty-five years old feel lonely. Many retirees cite social interaction as the reason for going back to work. While work friends will likely never replace family intimacy, the workplace has become a social hub for many people.

The daily work routine of getting up in the morning, having a coffee with a co-worker, chatting around the water cooler, going to a planning meeting, and being on a committee becomes part of the fabric of our lives. Something we don't tend to value until it's no longer there. Many things we complain about while working full time become important later in life and help us stay connected to people.

Finding work in retirement can be a great way to establish new routines and ensure you encounter meaningful social interactions.

WORKING PROVIDES INTELLECTUAL STIMULATION

Another aspect of work that retirees miss is intellectual stimulation. You can get mental stimulation at home, but it's not the same. Usually, a certain sense of purpose and camaraderie in the workplace creates much-needed social bonds.

The workplace is also where a lot of knowledge takes place, not abstract learning from an online course or book, but real-world applicability. For example, going through the recent COVID-19 scare forced workers to learn the power of online video calls quickly. It didn't take long for people to realize they could easily use video technology platforms such as Zoom to maintain social links with friends and family. Having that first experience in the work environment made it much easier to apply these skills outside of work.

WORKING OFFERS MEANING AND PURPOSE

Whether or not you get paid, finding meaningful work is important. At this stage in your life, it's not about merely showing up and hoping the job fills the void you feel.

A paycheck isn't necessary to find satisfaction in one's work. Working in a meaningful role is often enough of a reward. Just ask a stay-at-home parent or a youth soccer coach! People are finding out that the benefits of work extend beyond a paycheck.

"Strive not be a success but rather to be of value."

~ALBERT EINSTEIN, PHYSICIST

FINDING YOUR ENCORE CAREER

We are all different. What one person finds interesting another finds boring. Some people like to feel challenged and constantly seek new learning opportunities; they enjoy testing new scenarios. Other people prefer to take a slower, more methodical approach. They don't mind doing the same thing for a long time; they may enjoy the repetitive nature of some activities.

We've all had jobs throughout our careers that weren't a fit. Maybe we didn't like the people we worked with, but more likely, we didn't enjoy the type of work.

Some of your motivations may have followed you from your career days; others may be a byproduct of your new phase in life. You may be more interested in mentoring the younger generation or working for a cause that resonates with you. You may be more interested in taking a U-turn and doing something totally different from before.

At first, when people retire, they tend to be a bit about what they want to do as an encore career. They might have a sense of what they generally would like to do but lack clarity.

Here are some questions to get you going:

- Would you consider doing something like you did during your primary career days?
- Does the thought of sitting in front of a computer all day make you yawn? Maybe you need a job with a good deal of social interaction.

- Do you want a role that requires decision-making, or do you prefer a non-leadership role?
- Do you love interacting with people? Do you derive energy from talking to people? If so, a customer-facing role may be an excellent choice.
- Are there specific industries in which you would love to work? Maybe these industries attract you because of their philanthropic missions, such as social causes, or perhaps you're drawn to the industry simply because of your interests and hobbies.

For many people, their ideal work scenario simultaneously fulfills several of their needs. For example, my friend Greg found a way to combine his love of the seas, problem-solving, and interacting with people by working as a charter boat captain.

What are you looking for in a job?

Here's a worksheet designed to help refine your thinking. By ranking the attributes you find important in a job, you'll have an easier time assessing the job type that suits you. If you're already employed, these rankings may serve as a check-in; to whether the job is the right one for you. I also include in the last column my rankings to give you a sense of my priorities regarding work. My most important attribute in a job is that it's for a worthwhile cause, followed by using and enhancing my skills.

NET WEALTH	Most Important Criteria	My Most Important Criteria
WORK	10=Most, 1=Least	10=Most, 1=Least
Financial Compensation		4
Growth Potential		7
Worthwhile Cause		10
Status		1
Social Connection		2
Time Away From Home		3
Mental Challenge		6
Preserving Knowledge		8
Developing New Work Skills		9
Schedule Flexibility		5

There are no right or wrong answers.

If your household budget is currently in deficit, you'll probably place much greater importance on compensation. Your priority is bringing enough money in to close the gap.

On the other hand, some people are more motivated by professional challenges; others are driven by what they can contribute to a social cause. Everybody is different, but knowing yourself will save you headaches as you explore a new direction in your work life.

The work world is becoming more fluid and subject to change every day. The pressures faced today were hardly imaginable a decade ago. The pace of change is accelerating, and our skills and mindset must adapt to the times. As the world moves faster, we need to anticipate better what skills and experiences will be valued in the future and understand where and when we can contribute while also working in a role that provides more than just a paycheck. At the same time, you need to seriously think about what you want from a job in terms of life satisfaction.

RETHINKING THE FORTY-HOUR WORKWEEK

Jobs take different forms and shapes today. As a retiree, you may decide to work for a paycheck, start a new business, or volunteer.

Instead of working eight to ten hours a day, you may decide that three or four hours is optimal. Enough to get you out of the house, socialize a bit, and be back home in time for lunch.

You could also choose to work only part of the year. For example, if you work in a coastal community or vacation town, you might work full time from May through September, then spend the remainder of the year relaxing, traveling, or learning a new skill.

ADJUSTING TO A NEW SWEET SPOT

The transition from full-time to part-time work can be challenging for people. Primarily, there needs to be an internal re-alignment of expectations. Retirement marks an end to your primary career. People often find themselves at a loss during this in-between period (Remember the messy middle we talked about?) before expectations form and new goals crystallize.

It's common to experience bumps as you seek new work opportunities, whether for pay or pro-bono work. I observe that it usually takes a couple of tries before retirees settle on the right work situation. Like anyone learning to live life in a new way, retirees must clear several hurdles.

Hurdle #1: Over-attachment to an old identity. The biggest challenges retirees face is that their old identity, forged over decades of work, may not be relevant anymore. It's very easy to pretend to be just taking a break from our old working lives. We convince ourselves that we are still the same person, but the world has continued changing.

The struggle to stay latched on to our old identity is real. We all crave the familiar, but we need to ask ourselves: Is our old identity serving or hurting us in our new phase of life?

Let's say you managed a large sales team before retirement. Now you work part-time for a small company and report to somebody half your age. Your role, as in most jobs, is initially undefined. How will you behave? Will your old work identity emerge? Will you feel like the boss again? Under your new circumstances, that might be a recipe for disaster. Your boss will likely resent you and question your fit with the company.

Is that what you want? Probably not.

Instead, you might want to model your behavior after Robert De Niro in the movie, *The Intern*. De Niro's character is an intern to a much younger, less experienced CEO played by Anne Hathaway. Rather than imposing his old identity on the role, De Niro elects to become an elder mentor to his boss. What many would have predicted to turn into a disaster and waste of time becomes a win-win situation for the older mentor/intern and the boss.

It's worthwhile remembering that every beginning requires an ending. You can't move forward if you're still hanging onto lots of baggage from your previous life. Who you were during your career is likely no longer a helpful identity. For some people, shedding their previous identity takes considerable time, but understanding the new context in which they wish to work in retirement becomes critically important.

Hurdle #2: Ignoring context. It's common for people to struggle with finding the right job in the early days of retirement. For example, if you used to manage a design team, you may feel a bit out of place as part of a smaller team where you're expected to focus on technical matters exclusively.

Another example might be a former corporate executive who wants to work for a non-profit organization. They're eager to contribute and share their experiences from their time in the corporate sector. They often assume that their corporate background gives them an edge, but are frustrated with the lack of receptivity to new ideas.

The key to work transitions is bringing value to the current organization, not the organization of your past. Spend some quiet time figuring out where you fit in and where you can make the most significant contributions. Take a page out of entrepreneur Chip Conley's book. At fifty-two, he was hired as a mentor by the much-younger founders of Airbnb. They wanted Conley to help them understand the hospitality business. He might have been tempted to sit back as a wise elder and impart his wisdom from his corporate perch. However, Chip soon recognized that he could learn a lot from the youngsters and that his greatest contributions had to fit the context of his new work role. He had to shed his old identity to move the business forward at Airbnb.

Your internal transition must sync with the external world when working. You must spend time thinking about how to fit in the best and provide value to your new organization. Otherwise, tension will build, and work will become the exact opposite of what you were looking for—all stress and no upside.

Hurdle #3: Underestimating your experience and skills. As people forge their way into their retirement years and explore various work options, being open to new ways of applying one's skills and experiences becomes critical.

You've accumulated so much experience and skills during your working career. You may think that all you know how to do is your old job, but many of your skills are transferrable. For example, as an investment manager, I often prepared detailed financial projections using Excel spreadsheets. I apply my Excel skills in my current work as a retirement coach—same skills, different applications, and context.

Managing people is another skill. Let's say that during your primary career, you managed your fair share of people. You probably developed a management style and understood what made each individual tick. Could you use those skills in a different context? My guess is that you could find a way to adapt your experiences and skills to the new situation.

Just because you're no longer working in your primary profession doesn't mean that your human capital has vanished overnight. The challenge we all face as we seek to reinvent ourselves in the workplace is how to apply our elder wisdom in a changing world. After three or four decades of working, we have the fundamentals down, but the game has evolved.

Do you have the mentality to keep growing and adapting to the new environment?

A central idea in Charles Darwin's work, *On the Origin of Species*, as paraphrased by Louisiana State University professor, Leon C. Megginson, is that "it's not the strongest of species that survives, not the most intelligent that survives. It is the one that is most adaptable." As a modern elder, you need to adapt to the practices and environment of today's workplace rather than expecting people to accommodate your way of doing things. If it means using Zoom to make calls, you figure out how to schedule them and use the software. If it means using Excel macros, you spend your spare time taking courses until you can do the work as well as anybody else.

"Indecision is the thief of opportunity."

~JIM ROHN, AUTHOR, ENTREPRENEUR,
AND MOTIVATIONAL SPEAKER

Hurdle #4: Looking for the perfect opportunity. Nothing in life happens without action, and nothing is ever perfect.

You could hold out for the perfect opportunity, but wouldn't you rather just get going?

Planning is great, but you'll never remove all the uncertainty. You'll likely go through a trial-and-error period before settling on work that suits your needs and wants in retirement. You won't know unless you try.

There are endless ways to use your experience and skills in today's world. Don't wait for all the stars to line up. Don't wait for everybody's approval. Take the initiative. If you don't ask, nothing will happen. Don't wait for the perfect opportunity. Maybe creating the perfect opportunity is what is meant to happen. If people see your value, they'll give you the latitude to create your perfect situation.

USING AGE TO YOUR ADVANTAGE

Some people feel they're not quite up to snuff keeping up with their younger peers in intellectual horsepower. They don't retain as much information; it takes longer to assimilate concepts, and focusing on subject matter doesn't last as long.

All these things are true. As you get older, your short-term memory doesn't function as well, your ability to focus for sustained periods decreases, and complicated tasks that require processing speed suffers.

You have to remember that no human—young or old—can compete with Google's data bank, but your experience and skills allow you to turn information into context-appropriate knowledge. Research has shown that with age and life experiences, you gain wisdom and an ability to connect the dots that the younger generation may not have.

Age and life experience also translate into greater emotional balance. You learned you don't always have to be correct. There are other viewpoints that matter. You see the big picture better; life has taught you to react slower and listen more. Your understanding of your environment has improved with age. You're probably much more empathetic than when you were younger.

There's no doubt that ageism exists in the workforce, but you can use your ability to connect the dots and get along with people to counteract the societal impulse to ignore your elder wisdom.

CONSIDERATIONS FOR YOUR FUTURE SELF

- Working in retirement is becoming the norm. For many people, it's about supplementing their savings and pensions with meaningful work to fund their lifestyle in retirement.
- Beyond the paycheck, the benefits of working in retirement include mental stimulation, social connection, and giving back. Many retirees elect to work for psychic income only.
- Let go of your past identity. Don't feel entitled to be the boss.
- Be creative in applying your skills and experiences to new work situations. You got the fundamentals, but you'll need to find the right fit to deliver value to an organization.
- Your greatest advantage might be your ability to connect the dots and bring a level of emotional intelligence to the workplace. Your wisdom garnered over three or four decades of work may be your greatest asset.
- Don't expect immediate success in finding meaningful work in retirement. It will probably take several tries until you find the right situation.
- Get started. Network, learn from others, and take that first step even if the ideal opportunity doesn't present itself.

CHAPTER 7
EMOTIONAL ENERGY

"My message for everyone is the same: that if we can learn to identify, express, and harness our feelings, even the most challenging ones, we can use those emotions to help us create positive, satisfying lives."

~MARC BRACKETT, DIRECTOR OF THE YALE CENTER FOR EMOTIONAL INTELLIGENCE

People have described me as an emotional person. My emotions are, at times, like a volcano, erupting and quickly receding into a long slumber until the next flare-up. These flare-ups sometimes resemble hot lava spewing harmless flares into the night sky, making for a beautiful photo op. Other times, the eruptions look like a grey mass rolling down the hill, burning everything in sight. For a long time, I assumed that was how I was built.

It never occurred to me I could manage my emotions. I knew that my flare-ups often left other people perplexed, and the consequences of my actions often took a toll on my relationships; they certainly did for my ex-wife and kids. Until I spoke to a therapist after my divorce, I didn't realize I could behave differently. I could make room between my visceral, raw emotion and my response to the situation. Utilizing time and space were the tactics I lacked. Realizing that I could choose my response instead of it choosing me felt like a lightning bolt had hit me.

I finally understood how to manage my emotions to make them work for me instead of against me. I became more aware of my emotional makeup and slowly gained the ability to respond to situations more amicably. I came to understand the effect emotions have on our quality of life.

Our emotions have power, and humans are emotional creatures. Our emotions influence how we feel about ourselves, our decision-making abilities, and our relationships.

Managing our emotions is as important as managing our physical health or finances. Emotional management is necessary at any age, but it becomes vital as you face the increasing daily challenges of aging. The inevitable physical and mental decline that happens to everyone over time may be the furthest thought from your mind now. I don't like to think about it, but I also know that just as I've had to change my tennis game to compete with younger players, I need to adjust my mindset to reflect on the inevitable shortcomings of aging.

This chapter aims to teach you how to offset the physical and mental limitations that come naturally with age through managing your emotional makeup to emphasize those feelings that empower and energize you to enjoy a happy and fulfilled life in retirement. Your emotional energy comprises a vital part of your overall **NET WEALTH**.

"Emotion is more powerful than reason. Emotion is the driving force behind thinking and reasoning. Emotional intelligence increases the mind's ability to make positive, brilliant decisions."

~DR. T.P. CHIA, ACTIVIST AND FORMER POLITICAL PRISONER

OUR EMOTIONS SHAPE OUR DECISIONS

We would all like to think that we make rational, well-thought-out decisions. Yet, psychologists have found that our emotions and how we interpret them subconsciously drive our behavior. We're not always the rational creatures that we think we are.

Psychologists use the emotional cycle to illustrate how emotions influence our behavior. The concept, while theoretical, has been widely used in the self-improvement industry. Understanding how we make decisions and react was very helpful when I realized that my emotions didn't always serve me in the best way. Becoming more aware of the effect our emotions have on us is an important life skill. The concept, depicted in the shape of a wheel, works as follows.

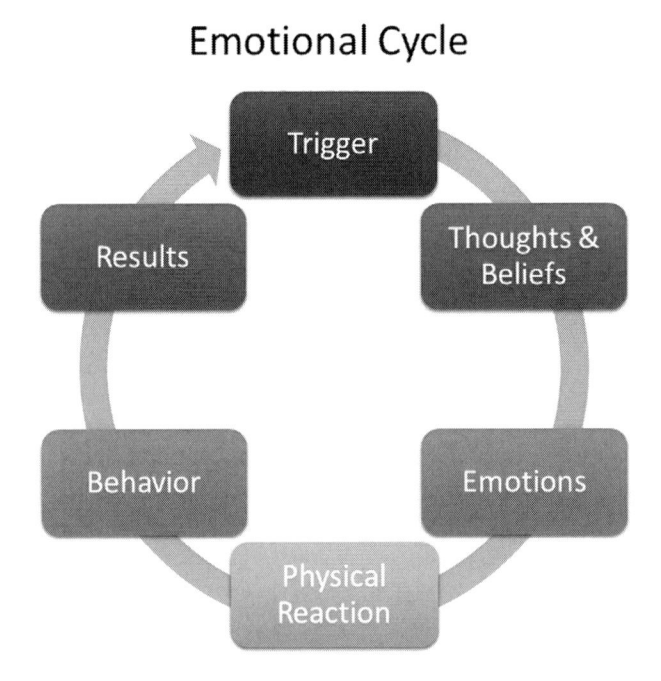

Emotional Cycle

Trigger → Thoughts & Beliefs → Emotions → Physical Reaction → Behavior → Results → (Trigger)

First, you experience a trigger. Your brain continuously processes input from your senses: sight, hearing, taste, touch, and smell. A trigger is anything coming from your senses that affects your emotional state. It could be a conversation with a friend, an article you're reading, a picture of your mother, a bolt of lightning, the fresh smell of lavender, etc.

That burst to your senses, in turn, activates your thinking brain. The raw information gets interpreted through the filter of your belief system, which is driven by your past life experiences, as we showed in chapter two. Depending on their beliefs, people can have radically different interpretations of the same trigger. Let's say you hear your neighbors whispering. You might believe that they're talking about you, and you get flustered, while another person may think they're talking about a death in their family and feel awful for them. The point is that we all have our own beliefs, which may or may not be entirely consistent with the truth of the situation.

Then comes a flood of emotions. Your emotions surface based on your interpretation of an event, such as a conversation with your friend or the smell of fresh lavender, your emotions surface. For example, you might feel anxious if you're having a difficult conversation with a friend. If you're looking at a picture of your deceased mother, you might feel love and sadness.

Emotions are often associated with physical responses in the body. If you're having a difficult conversation with your friend, you may feel anxious, and your shoulders and neck become tense. Afterward, you're likely to feel drained. Conversely, when looking at a picture of your favorite deceased grandmother, memories may come flooding in, and you may even feel a slight pressure in your chest.

These emotions and physical reactions influence our responses. If we feel tense and under attack, we may lash out in anger and storm out of the room. If the smell of fresh lavender bought back great memories of a trip to Provence, you might surprise your partner with a candlelit dinner that night.

Finally, the last step is assessing the results of our actions. As my mother used to say, "There are always consequences to our actions." We can't undo our actions. We only have the fallout. Was our behavior appropriate for the situation? Did we burn any bridges by taking our frustrations out on a friend? Did we grow closer as a couple by reminiscing on a great trip over a home-cooked meal? Could we have dialed down our response, given what the other person was going through?

Thinking of your emotions in this way isn't a theoretical exercise. Learning how to respond appropriately to life situations is essential to your well-being. Even if you think that you're always rational, contemplate the possibility that your emotions sometimes get the better of you. Can you think of a couple of instances when you made an emotional decision? How was your response? Did it serve you or hurt you?

Here are my takeaways from how emotions affected my life:

- I'll always wear my emotions on my sleeve. You'll feel my energy, good or bad. In any case, repressed emotions have a way of eventually escaping into the open.
- How I feel is based on my beliefs, which may or may not be accurate for the situation. Be honest with yourself. Nobody has a batting average of 1.00. We all bring baggage to our daily lives. Your baggage may have nothing to do with the situation at hand.
- I'm not afraid of my emotions, but I'm concerned about how I respond to them. I often need to put some space and time between my feelings and how I react, especially when the stakes are high; slowing down my Latino impulse to respond immediately to everything has proven invaluable. I believe that everybody can benefit from this practice, even the cast of *The Real Housewives of New Jersey* television show. We all control how we respond.
- I can't control the fallout from my actions, but I can re-evaluate if my response was appropriate given the situation. If my actions were poor, I feel bad and try to rectify the situation. Not everybody feels this way, but everybody should attempt to learn from their mistakes so that their responses are more appropriate in the future. Your happiness depends on it.

EMOTIONAL ENERGY

"Between stimulus and response there is a space. In that space is our power to choose our response. In our response lies our growth and our freedom."

~VIKTOR E. FRANKL, PSYCHIATRIST AND HOLOCAUST SURVIVOR

I hope you understand how important it is to your well-being to respond to your emotions appropriately. Too often, when stressed, we let our negative emotions control our behavior and regret our decisions. Our lives in retirement won't be all chocolates and roses. We'll face stressful situations as we have throughout our lives. We need to gain control over our emotions to make the best decisions, even when enduring the inevitable physical and mental challenges that the future brings.

Our emotions shape the quality of our decisions, but they also affect our overall sense of well-being. In the next section, I introduce you to the idea of viewing your emotions as energy in motion. It's safe to say that we all want more energy in our lives. Heck, we need more energy as we age to live a happy and fulfilled life.

People often mistakenly believe that their only source of energy is physical. They focus on getting fit or eating nutritional foods, assuming those things will give them the vitality they need. But you also need mental energy channeled from your positive emotions into additional fuel for your journey. According to psychotherapist Mira Kirshenbaum, author of *The Emotional Energy Factor: The Secrets High-Energy People Use to Beat Emotional Fatigue*, 30 percent of one's total energy comes from the body. The remaining 70 percent comes from their emotions. Naturopath and functional medicine practitioner Dr. Stephen Cabral said something similar during Episode 2201 of his podcast, *Cabral Concept*. He attributed the superior energy of many overachievers to their motivation and mindset, not to their physical conditioning.

THE POWER OF OUR EMOTIONS

Our emotions carry energy. The word "emotion" is derived from the concept of movement. The Latin derivative, "emotere," literally means energy in motion. When I'm experiencing negativity in my life or I have responded poorly to a situation, my energy levels drop drastically. I tend to feel tired and achy. My back starts hurting, and my legs feel heavy. I can't get myself to concentrate on anything, and my mind often creates entirely implausible catastrophes that feel very real to me. It zaps my energy to the point that I need a nap. On the flip side, when I feel good about myself and the world, I don't notice the time that often. Life feels fluid. Suddenly, my backache has vanished, and I have a spring in my step. I forget living through the New England winter. I'm ready to rock and roll with the best (yes, even at my age).

There is actual science behind my casual observations. In path-breaking research by Dr. David R. Hawkins, he classified common emotions along an energy scale, depicting the intensity of the feeling. Positive emotions give you energy, while negative emotions deplete it.

Different emotions have different degrees of energy. For example, contentment is a low-intensity positive emotion, while joy has a much higher degree of energy. Similarly, shame resides in a low-intensity state, while frustration quickly drains your energy. According to the research by Dr. Hawkins, negative emotions suck the energy out of you. It'll be hard to find the required energy to change the dynamic if your life becomes dominated by negativity.

I think of negative emotions as a leak on a boat. A leak won't initially sink the boat, but it will weigh it down and slow its trajectory. The leak will overwhelm your thoughts. Eventually, the boat will sink unless the hole gets plugged. In any case, the boat ride won't be as enjoyable or smooth as it could have been.

Upward Spiral

- Enlightenment
- Joy
- Love
- Enthusiasm
- Optimism
- Hope
- Contentment

Boost Your Energy

Emotional Energy Level

Downward Spiral

- Frustration
- Anger
- Disappointment
- Anxiety
- Fear
- Despair
- Shame

Drain Your Energy

Positive emotions, on the other hand, lift you. They make the boat ride feel lighter and faster. Positive emotions allow you to think about all the good things in your life and give you a sense of possibility. They give you more energy to pursue your goals.

Research by Dr. Barbara Fredrickson, who developed the broaden-and-build theory of positive emotions, shows people's thinking becomes more creative, flexible, and open to new facts and information when they feel good. The effects aren't short-term, as most people would expect. The real power of positive emotions makes people feel more resilient, socially connected, and optimistic about the future. Having positive emotions also counteracts the negative emotions we all feel at times. The research by Dr. Fredrickson also shows a direct link between feeling good and your health.

The byproducts of positivity are of great value to retirees, primarily as aging takes its toll on your physical and mental capabilities. A positive mindset can counteract the natural decline that we all experience. Think of physicist Stephen Hawking, who, at twenty-two years old, was diagnosed with **amyotrophic lateral sclerosis** (ALS). He chose to remain positive, despite his obvious physical challenges. In an interview with the *New York Times*, he said, "I'm happier now than before I developed the condition. I am lucky to be working in theoretical physics, one of the few areas in which disability is not a serious handicap." Dr. Hawking chose a positive mindset over physical constraints to lead an incredibly productive and inspirational life.

HARNESS YOUR EMOTIONS TO THRIVE

Having positive emotions makes you feel good in the moment, but as shown by Dr. Barbara Fredrickson, the effects last longer. I believe every time you experience something positive, you're adding gas to your fuel tank. By filling up your fuel tank, you'll gain a valuable reservoir of energy you can tap into when you need it.

Reflect on the unexpected challenges you've faced in the past. If positivity has played a role in your life, you're probably much at coping with adversity. Chances are, you find ways to overcome problems and move forward. When faced with a high-stakes decision, you're likely more flexible in your thinking if you've been blessed with an abundance of positive emotional experiences.

Wouldn't it be wonderful if we could force ourselves to have only positive emotions? That's not going to happen. Am I right? I wish we could, but we're human. What we can do is develop routines and habits to help us have more positive experiences.

I use the **Emotional Energy Grid** concept with my clients to assess whether their lives have an emotional energy deficit or surplus. This tool gives us thirty thousand views of their emotional health and helps them plan their lives.

To thrive, they need to experience a preponderance of positive emotions. But what will it take to create better emotional health if they're barely surviving?

The **Emotional Energy Grid** depicts four quadrants, depending on the negative-to-positive emotions ratio and the intensity of those feelings. More intense feelings, good or bad, require higher energy. Let me elaborate.

Emotional Energy Quadrants

	Survive	Thrive	
Energy Depletion	Fearful, Angry, Worried, Anxious	Engaged, Optimistic, Enthusiastic, Confident	**Energy Boost**
Energy Drain	**Burnout**: Exhausted, Depressed, Sad, Hopeless	**Sustain**: Content, Peaceful, Relaxed, Accepting	**Energy Recycling**

Negative Emotions | Positive Emotions

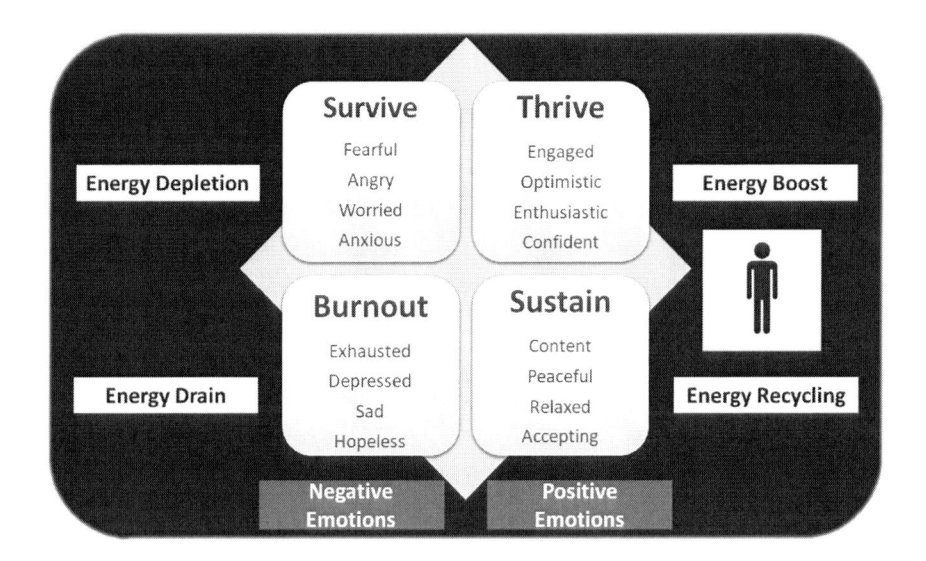

The four quadrants reflect four distinct states of emotional energy, each with a profile of emotions.

The burnout quadrant. A person feeling dispirited and overwhelmed with negative emotions, such as depression and sadness, would be in the burnout quadrant. They're always tired. Things feel hopeless. They feel like life is draining from them day by day.

The survive quadrant. A fearful or angry person faces a constant energy shortage, leaving them exhausted. This situation corresponds to the survive quadrant. People in this quadrant feel stressed most of the time. They just want to survive another day. They have little hope for change. Their negative emotions stay with them day in and day out. It's impossible to live in this state without blowing a gasket.

The sustain quadrant. Compare that with someone content and relaxed with their place in life—nothing much changes. They're happy with the status quo. This situation corresponds to the sustain quadrant. People living in this quadrant are operating at an above-average emotional energy level. Life is comfortable and emotionally predictable. Their emotions are generally positive, and their emotional energy is in a steady state—not too high, not too low. They always seem to be okay.

The thrive quadrant. This quadrant corresponds to a person living their best life. Their emotional energy is constantly boosted by the activities they participate in and their outlook on life. They're fully engaged in the world and remain optimistic and enthusiastic about their ability to lead a life of joy and fulfillment.

Given the benefits of experiencing positive emotions, as shown in the previous section, the two quadrants on the right—Thrive and Sustain—are where you want to be. Nobody wants to feel burnout continuously, or even worse, headed toward a life of endless stress and barely surviving.

Where in the **Emotional Energy Grid** do you find yourself most days?

Do you tend to be energized by your lifestyle, or are you constantly searching for that energy boost you get from positive experiences?

Some of my clients are perfectly content with their lives in retirement. Typically, there's a progression people go through. They may start retirement all gangbusters, going after their goals and living life to its fullest. After a decade or two of thriving, they may eventually settle down to enjoy the fruits of their labor and really appreciate life. They may still have aspirations and work on maximizing their positive experiences, but they want to tamp down the intensity of daily living. They're at peace with their lives. Their future and current Selves have become intertwined.

I see myself going through this progression. I intend to work hard on my aspirations and goals as long as they are meaningful and motivating. I hope to be in the Thrive quadrant for the next couple of decades. When I no longer have stretch goals, I'll hopefully reflect on my life with gratitude and focus more on enjoying the small things in life with my immediate family and friends. I think there's a time and place for everything, as long as you feel your life is on track.

I hope you understand why I think your emotional energy is such a huge part of your **NET WEALTH**. With the right amount of emotional energy, you can climb mountains and lead the type of life consistent with your vision of your Future Self. Without emotional energy, you're likely to always run on fumes and never have quite enough energy to reach your goals. Physical energy won't be enough. You also need emotional energy.

In the next section, I will show you how to put all this knowledge into practice.

INCREASE YOUR EMOTIONAL ENERGY BY BECOMING EMOTIONALLY INTELLIGENT

Best-selling author and researcher Daniel Goleman popularized the term emotional intelligence in 1995. He postulated that having emotional intelligence is sometimes even more important to our well-being than cognitive intelligence or IQ.

Emotional intelligence refers to a person's ability to recognize their own emotions and those of others and use that information to guide their thinking and behavior in ways that contribute positively to their well-being. There are four general ways to become more emotionally intelligent: perceiving, understanding, using, and managing emotions.

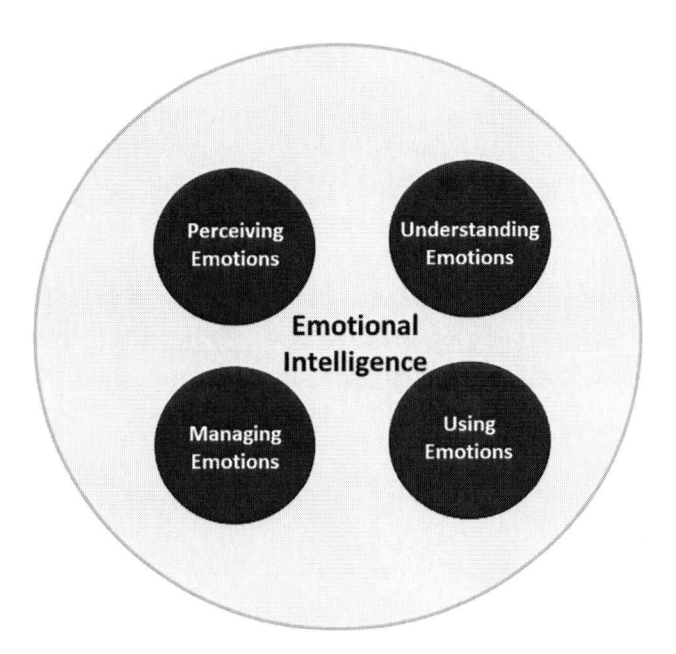

Let's go through each of these areas to see how they help.

Perceiving your emotions. Self-awareness is the first step. Instead of flying off the handle, you must take the time to sense what's happening inside of you and others. Naming your emotions is essential so you can distinguish what you're feeling. It's equally important to figure out what others are feeling.

Understanding your emotions. Why are you feeling a particular emotion? What are you reminded of by the situation? What similar instances from your past are influencing your feelings? Do you see how your emotions affected certain decisions you made in the past? Put yourself in somebody else's shoes. Do you understand what they might be feeling and why?

Appropriately use your emotions. Choose to respond in a manner that serves you and recognizes the likely feelings of others. It's how you communicate better with others. It's also how you delay immediate gratification in pursuing your goals.

Managing your emotions. Your ability to self-regulate by either responding or detaching from the situation is an incredibly beneficial skill to possess. It also involves your ability to redirect old patterns into healthier directions.

Your goal is to boost all components of your emotional intelligence to gain mastery over your emotions so, you don't get caught in a downward emotional spiral. Instead, you can use your emotions to further your progress toward your Future Self. You want to thrive rather than settle, or even worse, merely survive in retirement. A big part of your **NET WEALTH** is managing your emotional energy.

"Emotional intelligence is your ability to recognize and understand emotions in yourself and others, and your ability to use this awareness to manage your behavior and relationships."

~TRAVIS BRADBERRY, AUTHOR OF
EMOTIONAL INTELLIGENCE 2.0

Here are some tactics that may come in handy.

TACTIC #1: DEVELOP EMOTIONAL AGILITY

As we experience internal or external change, our capacity to deal with these changes positively is tested. Many times, we'll think that life is unfair or that we're just going through a patch of terrible luck.

You might have experienced the loss of a loved one, and your grief is off the charts. You might regret losing a ton of money on a speculative investment. You might have fought with your best friend and feel actual loss because you haven't spoken in months. You might be ashamed that your consulting proposal has been rejected by everybody so far.

Regardless of the reason for our challenges, we have three choices:

- Ignore the situation: bottle everything up and suffer the consequences later.
- Complain about the situation and slowly become more miserable, reinforcing a downward spiral that requires more and more effort to overcome and keeps you stuck.
- Seek to understand the negative emotions and take the necessary steps to move forward.

Rather than ignore negative emotions, Dr. Susan David from Harvard University's medical school and an expert on emotional agility, suggests four specific approaches to take when experiencing negative emotions.

Face your emotions and choose not to run away. Emotions often contain a message that may be difficult and uncomfortable to hear. You will need the courage to accept the truth, whatever it is. Choosing to ignore recurring negative emotions only postpones the day of reckoning.

Put some space between your emotions and actions. You'll need to detach for a moment from your immediate feelings. This action will create the necessary space to give you time to decipher the true meaning of your emotion. Take the impulsivity out of your actions.

Focus on your core values and most important life goals as reminders of what lies beyond your immediate hurdles. This approach uses selective ignorance by focusing on your inner motivation and purpose. For some people, religion plays a huge role in giving them the strength to overcome difficulties. For others, it is about a cause or deeply held belief that provides the necessary fuel for overcoming whatever challenges they face.

Tweak your mindset, motivation, and habits. Change and uncertainty are all around us. We cannot run away from risk, but we can manage it. Sometimes, it'll take a slight reframing of a situation to get past the negativity. Sometimes, we'll need to look inside and re-commit to our vision for ourselves. Sometimes, we will need to re-examine our tactics and approach. Life requires constant adjustments.

"Emotions are data. They are not directives."

~SUSAN DAVID, HARVARD MEDICAL SCHOOL PSYCHOLOGIST

TACTIC #2: INCREASE POSITIVE EMOTIONS

We all experience negative thoughts, but what if we could counteract this negativity by consciously increasing the occurrence of positive emotions? That is the tactic suggested by Psychology Professor Barbara Frederickson.

Her research shows that positivity is associated with higher levels of well-being and a whole host of positive residual effects, such as increased health and resilience. Positive emotions make us feel better in the moment and allow us to open up to new possibilities.

By experiencing positive emotions such as joy, gratitude, hope, pride, and love, we can offset the negative impact of feeling low. Unfortunately, our brains have evolved to feel more negative emotions than positive ones. For example, Dr. Robert Plutchik, an authority on the taxonomy of emotions, determined that out of the top eight emotions felt by humans, only two (Joy and Trust) were unambiguously positive. The other six emotions were either neutral or decidedly negative. Our brains are predisposed to danger, which is why we tend to have many more negative emotions throughout the day than positive ones.

Dr. Barbara Frederickson suggests developing tactics to cultivate more positive thinking to counteract the negative tendencies.

Besides taking a "happy" pill, here are some ideas for finding more positivity in our daily lives.

Socialize with people who have an upbeat outlook on life. Research has shown that emotions are contagious, so when you're feeling down, seek the company of naturally optimistic people. Socializing, in general, is a wonderful way to forget your problems and put them in the proper perspective.

Take the time to participate in activities that naturally divert your attention away from your problems. For some people, it might be taking a walk in nature or riding a bike. The best activities are those requiring movement and some concentration.

Re-interpret the situation that's creating negative feelings. Is this something that you caused or something that happens to everybody? You only control so much in your life. At times, everybody has bad luck; why should you be immune, right? Looking at life this way can relieve you from blaming yourself for things beyond your control.

Slow down, close your eyes and breathe. Take the time just to be. Some people advocate meditation as a way to let go of stress. Others swear to the act of controlling your breathing.

Figure out your response to negative emotions by planning. Nothing ever goes smoothly, right? Mentally prepare ahead of time so that when you face hurdles that are likely to derail you, you have a game plan to respond positively.

Focus your thinking on what you have, not on what you might have lost. Develop the habit of expressing gratitude for your life, however, challenged it might be. Focus on your progress rather than how far you have yet to go.

Use negative emotions to fuel positive actions. Channel the anger or disappointment you feel to push you forward. Athletes, for example, are often driven to succeed by perceived injustices in the past. Tom Brady and Michael Jordan come to mind.

Visualize how your Future Self would behave. Your Future Self represents your ideal. Model your behavior as if you're already the person you aspire to be. How would your Future Self respond to the negativity you're currently feeling?

TACTIC #3: CONFRONT YOUR FEARS DIRECTLY

Fear is the mother of all negative emotions. Call it plain-old fear or fear of the unknown; it doesn't matter. Nobody likes to be afraid. Fear stops us in our tracks. It makes us pull back from situations or goals that would likely benefit us.

Our brains have been conditioned to respond to fear as a defense mechanism. In prehistoric times, detecting dangerous situations meant the difference between surviving or getting mauled by a tiger.

In modern times, fear comes in many flavors. We fear being alone, getting laid off, losing our savings to a stock market collapse, aging, losing our mental capabilities, and, heaven forbid, losing a loved one. We often cling to the status quo at the expense of change, even if we're not happy where we are. We overrate the known at the expense of the unknown.

Some of our fears are invisible to others; we hold these fears deep inside our souls. Rejection, failure, disappointment, and vulnerability, aren't emotions we tend to enjoy acknowledging, let alone sharing with others.

You would think that you no longer carry these internal fears as you enter your fifties or sixties, but you'd be wrong. Our beliefs form over our lifetimes and are often subconscious. For example, many retirees struggle with the fear of change and the unknown. These fears often reflect the belief that coping with new situations and unpredictable events will be more than we can handle.

Like a physical disability, fear can become overwhelming and crippling. Left unchecked, it can seriously harm the quality of our lives, causing physical and mental damage.

Research has shown that a key determinant of our happiness isn't *what* happens to us but how we react. Learning how to deal with our fears is a life skill we can cultivate. How we deal with fear is a choice. Ignoring fear isn't a long-term strategy, nor is continually adopting a sunny attitude, regardless of what may be going on in our lives.

In her book *Feel the Fear and Do It Anyway*, on page twenty-two, Susan Jeffers presents these five truths about fear:

1. The fear will never go away as long as you continue to grow.
2. The only way to get rid of the fear of doing something is to go out and do it.
3. The only way to feel better about yourself is to get out and do it.
4. Not only are you going to experience fear whenever you're on unfamiliar ground, but so is everyone else.
5. Pushing through fear is less frightening than living with the underlying fear that comes from a feeling of helplessness.

I couldn't have said it any better. As a matter of fact, I keep a copy of these five truths within view of my desk. Re-reading these truths every day allows me to move ahead in my life.

Dealing with your fears. As you retire, you're bound to feel apprehensive about the future. What you've known for three or four decades no longer applies. You're in a new phase of life now. What will it bring?

Retirement is a massive transition for most people, involving heightened levels of fear: fear of the unknown, our mortality, financial security, the loss of social connections, what our purpose in life is, what we are good at, etc.

Here are some insights that could help you assuage your fears.

Become aware of how you've dealt with fear throughout your life. Have these tendencies served you well or hurt you? What's your typical response to coping with stressful situations? Are you composed, or do you fly off the handle?

Avoid extrapolating. So many of our fears are imaginary. Our brains usually go to worst-case outcomes. Am I wrong? There are many aspects of our lives over which we have no control, so why spend energy slaying imaginary dragons rather than dealing with issues where our actions and behavior can make a difference?

Keep in mind that luck has an equal chance of being good or bad. The fear of something terrible happening to us pales by comparison to the upside of living a life of fulfillment. Focusing too much on what can go wrong will keep you from enjoying your retirement years. When you become too risk-averse, you pay in lost opportunities.

The probability of most of your fears coming true is usually much smaller than the room they take up in your head. Pay attention to your fears, but don't catastrophize everything. Your worst fears will likely not become a reality. Allow room in your life for good things to happen.

How we deal with fear is critical to our long-term wellness. As people age, they often become more frightened about what could happen. What if we get sick? What if we run out of money? What if we become invisible to society and possibly even our own families? What if we get stuck paralyzed by helplessness and depression?

It's natural, at times, to feel anxious, nervous, and frightened. We might become paralyzed by our fears, lose energy, and feel like crawling into a hole. Should we accept that our lives will zig-zag depending on how fearful we feel, or should we take charge and seek ways to transform the fear into something more beneficial to our well-being?

CONSIDERATIONS FOR YOUR FUTURE SELF

Working on your emotional energy is not a trendy action. It's a necessity for leading a life of joy and fulfillment. It's as important as keeping physically and mentally fit. Your emotional energy comprises a vital part of your overall **NET WEALTH**.

People in retirement need to become emotionally intelligent. As you age, it's inevitable—you won't feel as physically and mentally strong as you once did. Some of that loss can be replenished by your emotional energy level.

Daily actions drive your emotional makeup. By learning to manage and interpret your emotions daily, you'll increase your odds of becoming the Future Self you imagined.

By harnessing your emotional energy, you will:

- Offset some of the loss of physical and mental capabilities that come naturally with aging
- Understand that your responses and behaviors are your choices, not biologically pre-determined
- Better understand the meaning of your emotions and how they affect you physically
- Respond in more appropriate ways to negative emotions by allowing some space and time
- Get more in tune with the emotions of others and improve your relationships
- Become more optimistic about the future
- Be more resilient in the face of challenges
- Become more creative and flexible in your thinking
- Improve your ability to deal with change and uncertainty

CHAPTER 8
ACHIEVEMENTS

"Some people want it to happen, some wish it would happen, others make it happen."

~MICHAEL JORDAN, NBA PLAYER

AFTER DEDICATING THREE OR FOUR DECADES TO YOUR CAREER, you're probably looking forward to a break. The last thing you're probably interested in is jumping into yet another big project with objectives, key performance metrics, deliverables, and timelines. Am I right? You would rather focus on your dreams and fun stuff.

As people retire, there's a sense of finality. There are no more peaks to climb, no more striving for success, no more stretch goals—just time to relax and enjoy life. That's fine for some people who genuinely want to just relax, take it easy, and keep up with the status quo. They may have dreams, but where they are now in life suits them fine too.

However, for some people, retirement represents an opportunity to do something different from what they've done. There's a feeling that there's more out there for them. There's an itch to do something meaningful; to do something exciting; to stretch out of their comfort zone; to achieve something for themselves; to make their dreams reality.

It all boils down to the age-old question: How big of a future do you see for yourself? Are you happy where you are, coasting along day by day? Or do you view retirement as giving you the freedom to explore and tackle your dreams and aspirations?

Or, put another way, as we discussed in chapter two, do you want an easy life or a fulfilling one? It's up to you. Do you want certainty or the possibility of a greater future? The easy life is within reach for most people. You may not have everything you want, but your basic needs are covered.

On the other hand, a fulfilling life requires working on your dreams to become your Future Self. The easy life keeps you in your comfort zone. That's what many people think they want after three or four decades of working. They retire with a sigh of relief that they managed to make it this far, all while raising a family, navigating the ups and downs of work, and saving for retirement. They feel relieved and grateful that those days are behind them, and now it's time to reap the rewards of a job well-done. I don't blame people who think this way. After all, the traditional retirement model spoon-feeds you the idea that your next act is all about harvesting your well-deserved rewards; the time for planting is behind you.

Unfortunately, retirement life isn't always that straightforward for many people. Many people experience a short honeymoon after retirement, but they grow restless and unsure about a lifestyle focused only on comfort and pleasure within a couple of years. The traditional advisors never told them that this would likely happen, but if they'd read the research in positive psychology, they would've learned that happy and fulfilled humans need to keep striving and working on meaningful pursuits, regardless of age. In fact, one of the key ingredients of the PERMA theory of human well-being involves the pursuit of meaningful achievements.

Pursuing meaningful achievements throughout your life is an important driver of your well-being. These achievements don't have to mirror those of Elon Musk or Nelson Mandela. They could be simple things, such as taking care of your grandchildren, planting a new garden, writing a book, or helping young entrepreneurs start a new business. They could involve working on any of the dreams and aspirations you still harbor.

Working on your dreams requires you to stretch. Otherwise, your dreams would've happened already. You get fulfillment from achieving something meaningful that closes the gap with your Future Self.

Humans want to feel relevant, and we keep looking forward. When people retire to a life of comfort and pleasure, they sometimes lose that connection to the world and their future. In comparison, people who also focus on fulfillment behave in ways that keep them vested in the bright future they have envisioned for themselves, a future that involves striving and working toward your dreams and aspirations. They prefer a future striving for greater possibilities rather than certainty based on past achievements.

There's no statute of limitations or age restriction on your dreams. Retirement gives you the freedom to pursue the dreams you've chased forever. You're the boss of your life. You don't need anybody's permission to aspire to a greater future, but you must take action to make your dreams a reality. Otherwise, they remain dreams forever. In this chapter, I teach you how to turn dreams into achievements by following a three-step process:

- Capturing your dreams
- Turning your dreams into tangible goals
- Acting on those goals

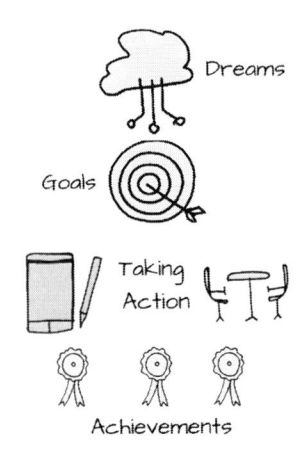

STEP #1: CAPTURING YOUR DREAMS

Many people remain stuck in their parent's retirement model and don't understand why they should pursue any new dreams or goals at this stage in their lives. They have done enough. Their future is capped. But other people need challenges, especially now that they no longer need to work eight to ten hours a day. They want to keep looking forward and working on meaningful projects—just because they no longer earn a paycheck doesn't matter. They still have dreams and aspirations they want to achieve.

Having dreams and goals in life is important, regardless of your age. Too many retirees give up on their dreams. They feel that their time is past and that dreams and goals for the young.

This limiting belief keeps many retirees from enjoying the benefits of working on their dreams and gaining a sense of purpose and structure in their daily lives. Pursuing your dreams keeps you motivated and engaged in the world. It forces you to look ahead rather than dwell on the past. It gives you a feeling of control over your life. Achieving your dreams bolsters your self-esteem, confidence, and sense of fulfillment. You grow closer to becoming your Future Self.

Striving is human, and just as we all need love and health in our lives, we also need to stop letting chronological age keep us from pursuing meaningful pursuits that bring us happiness and fulfillment.

We all have unfulfilled dreams and goals. Retirement presents the perfect opportunity—and potentially your last—to finally make them a reality. It's up to you to pick what you'd like to achieve. You don't get graded by anybody besides yourself on your dreams and goals.

"A dream doesn't become reality through magic: it takes sweat, determination and hard work."

~COLIN POWELL, FORMER US
SECRETARY OF STATE

Even if you don't achieve your ultimate dream or goal exactly, you'll be happy that you tried. The journey will be meaningful, even if the result isn't quite what you'd envisioned. By acting on something meaningful, you gain confidence in your abilities and strengthen your mind to accomplish other goals. The process of planning and acting teaches you important lessons, such as what you're made of and your ability to overcome challenges.

Is there a downside to pursuing your dreams? Well, you could fail. Your achievements might fall short; you could be ridiculed or waste your time.

You could also gain a lot.

Setting goals and taking committed action requires courage and the belief that things will work out. It's not always easy to feel confident doing something new, especially when the path is uncertain. You don't know if you'll succeed, but not doing something meaningful simply because you're hyper-focused on everything that could go wrong isn't a long-term winning strategy.

Playing defense through life might be okay for some, but for people used to thriving and looking forward to joy and fulfillment in retirement, you'll need to play offense, too—that's non-negotiable.

As we discussed in chapter seven, many fear making the wrong move. Fear of the unknown keeps us in our shells, and our long-held dreams and goals become nothing more than a distant memory from youth. Retirement is a chance at a new life; don't let old fears and habits keep you from making it your best life.

When you came up with your Future Self in Chapter two, do you recall your dreams and aspirations? Write them again here:

Future Self Aspiration 1:

Future Self Aspiration 2:

Future Self Aspiration 3:

Future Self Aspiration 4:

Future Self Aspiration 5:

Now that you've had a few more chapters to reflect, are these still the most important aspirations of your Future Self? If not, take this opportunity to revise them. Are there any other dreams you want to add?

If you're having trouble coming up with ideas, here are some techniques to help you narrow your list of key aspirations:

- **Visualization/imagination:** Close your eyes and imagine yourself at your eightieth birthday party. What will guests say about you and your accomplishments? You could also try visualizing what daily living will look like in ten years and ask yourself which of your goals today would allow you to live in such a way. For example, if you see yourself as a prolific *New York Times* best-selling author, your immediate goal should be to write your first book right away.
- **Connecting intellectually and emotionally:** Your "why" needs to be strong to overcome the pull of comfort and certainty. A strong "why" includes meaningful goals, so you become emotionally invested. Many people connect with their goals intellectually, but a positive and empowering emotional connection must be made to make your goals stick. Make your goals personal. Make them an intimate part of your Future Self.
- **Think broadly:** All the components of your **NET WEALTH** are essential. Do you tend to focus your dreams and aspirations on only a couple of areas in your life? It might be worthwhile throwing a wider net to address an issue that's holding you back from achieving the type of life you want for your Future Self. We tend to spend our time on areas we find easier to tackle, ignoring pesky issues that hold us back. For example, I have a friend who, for the longest time, focused obsessively on finding a new career and making more money side issues that weren't really important because the root causes of his unhappiness were his failing relationships and poor health. By ignoring her "sore" spots, my friend set herself up for failure. She might have been better off addressing some of her problem areas first. Ask yourself which

goals would make the biggest difference to your life now *and* in the future. Work on those first!

It's okay to have many dreams, but I recommend you limit your attention to your top five aspirations of your Future Self in the beginning. More than five can overwhelm you fast!

Look at your top five aspirations as the start of your journey toward your Future Self. Once you accomplish some of those dreams, you'll be ready for the next batch. It's good to have something to look forward to!

STEP #2: TURNING DREAMS INTO TANGIBLE GOALS

Our dreams are like a fantasy. We get to make them up. But we can't stop at wishing and hoping; we must take action. Dreams are something to aspire to, but they aren't reality—yet. A dream without a plan and action will just remain a wish.

The first step in achieving a dream is to set a clear goal.

Dreams are often general and abstract. The broad outline is visible, but there's a lot of white on the page. Goals are concrete and specific.

Please don't confuse dreams with goals. You need to act to achieve your goals. To achieve your goals, you pay in blood, sweat, and tears (plus time and sometimes money). Dreaming is always free; you can dream as much as you want, but only goals and actions will change your life and allow you to become your Future Self. Martin Luther King Jr. had a dream, but setting clear goals and acting was what led to change.

Turning dreams into goals requires introspection. It requires intellectual and emotional honesty. It also requires a system for going from an abstract wish to a tangible goal.

One such system is the SMART approach. Over the years, people have come up with their variations of this methodology, but one that I find useful for retirees adds two additional ideas, making it "SMARTER," and is composed of the following elements:

- **Specific**: The clearer you are about the outcome you seek, the better. Clarity results in efficiency and a higher probability of reaching your goal. You have no chance if you're unclear about what you want to achieve. I believe this is the most important step in the process.
- **Measurable**: Ideally, your goal should be quantifiable. It doesn't have to be precise, but some quantitative sense of success helps you measure your progress. If you can't measure your progress, how will you know how far you've come or how far you need to go? How will you know when you've achieved the goal?
- **Actionable**: There's nothing worse than taking something and not having the faintest idea how to execute it. If you don't know what action steps to take because you don't have the skills or general know-how, you need to go back to the drawing board. When setting goals, you must see how actions translate into results.
- **Rewarding**: Change involves work, so why would you go through the messy middle of uncertainty if the outcome won't help you get to your Future Self? The goals with the greatest rewards are usually those that are internally motivated. You don't need to rely on willpower or external measures of success to push yourself forward.
- **Time-bound**: Goals without a deadline are wishes. You must put your stake in the ground. We're really good at postponing taking action, so make deadlines realistic, not open-ended. Most likely, some of your goals will be short-term (such as my ninety days), and others will require a multi-year commitment (your big goals usually take three to five years to achieve). Whether you have short or long-term goals, you need deadlines.
- **Emotional** – The goal must have emotional significance. Day in and day out, your behavior is driven by your emotions. Goals that evoke a positive emotion when visualized are easier to achieve than goals that don't make us feel anything. By analyzing the emotional intensity of your goal, you can determine how badly you want to achieve it. Listen to your emotions to make your goals as tangible as possible.
- **Reinforcing**: Your goals should be internally consistent with the vision of your Future Self. They should support your journey

toward your Future Self rather than impose additional hurdles. Achieving one goal should make it even more worthwhile to achieve the next one. Your goals need to align. Look at the fit of your goals wholly rather than just individually.

Using this framework, take a stab at turning the dreams and aspirations of your Future Self into SMARTER goals.

Future Self Aspiration 1 SMARTER Goal 1:

Future Self Aspiration 2 SMARTER Goal 2:

Future Self Aspiration 3 SMARTER Goal 3:

Future Self Aspiration 4 SMARTER Goal 4:

Future Self Aspiration 5 SMARTER Goal 5:

Let's go through a couple of examples.

Aspiration: I want to be healthy.
Goal: I want to lose weight to become healthier.
Smarter Goal: I want to lose twenty pounds over the next twelve months to feel more energized and attractive.

That's specific. The next step is figuring out how to lose that weight. Will it be a combination of nutrition and exercise? Will you hire a personal trainer?

Aspiration: I want to have more fun.
Goal: I want to be able to dance to salsa music.
Smarter Goal: I want to take weekly salsa lessons with my partner for the next six months to enjoy an activity that will bring us closer together.

That's specific. I'm assuming that your partner finds salsa dancing fun, too. Now you have to book lessons for the next six months at a local dance studio.

> **Aspiration:** I want to have enough money to sustain my lifestyle.
> **Goal:** I want my money to last for the rest of my life.
> **Smarter Goal:** I want to be able to spend twenty-five thousand dollars a year for the next thirty years.

That's getting specific. You still need to develop a plan for generating twenty-five thousand dollars a year from your investment assets, but your goal is clear. Implementing a plan or hiring an advisor isn't important at this stage. That's part of the next step—taking action.

I hope these examples have helped.

As you refine your vision of your Future Self and your **NET WEALTH**, you'll likely go through multiple iterations of this exercise. You'll probably start broad, and over several iterations, drill down to clear and concise goals. It might take you five to ten tries. Each iteration gets you closer to your definition of the goal. Be patient but precise—the more specific the goal, the better.

Ask for feedback. Our big-thinking mistakes are often spotted easily by other people. Are your goals clear to them? Can you describe how you translated your dreams into measurable goals easily? Can you describe easily why these goals are important to you?

I suggest limiting your goals to between three and five. About half should be short-term goals (three months to one year), and the rest should be longer-term (three to five years). As you achieve your short-term goals, you can add new ones. The long-term goals are usually those most transformational in terms of becoming your Future Self.

> *"It's not always that we need to do more, but rather that we need to focus on less."*
>
> ~NATHAN W. MORRIS, AUTHOR OF *YOUR 33 DAY MONEY ACTION PLAN*

Take your cue from the top performers. For example, world-class athletes usually pick one or two things to work on simultaneously and have a single long-term goal. For tennis player Andy Murray that single goal was to become the number one player in the world. Instead of working on all aspects of his game equally, he focused on improving his fitness and becoming more aggressive to finish points faster (i.e., hitting with more power). His focus resulted in a number-one world ranking (November 2016), three Grand Slams, and two Olympic gold medals—not a bad haul!

STEP #3: TURNING GOALS INTO ACTION STEPS

Understand the difference between planning and doing. Anything worth pursuing requires upfront planning and action, but don't confuse the two steps. Figuring out how to make your goals happen is a vital step in the process, but it only provides the blueprints for your goal. You must also execute the plan, and you'll likely have to adapt your plans as circumstances change.

Executive coach Marshall Goldsmith has said, "People are much better planners than doers." From my own experience, I know this is true. Many people love to plan—not many like to execute.

Planning is often more fun than enduring the discomfort of doing the work. We sometimes even believe that we'll achieve the goal by simply planning. Visualizing the end goal feels great, but your goal will remain nothing but a dream without taking the required action steps.

Dreams become goals, and goals become achievements through commitment, hard work, focus, and perseverance. What are ways we can increase our odds of doing the necessary work? Here are some ideas.

Favoring progress over perfection. Everyone would like to have achieved their goals yesterday. We've probably had these goals for a while but remain frustrated that we haven't achieved them yet.

In some cases, the problem is that we expect too much from ourselves. We think because we really want something to happen, it must happen, or it's not in the cards. We have this all-or-nothing mentality about goals: If it's meant to be, we will achieve our goals, and if the goal remains elusive, then it's probably not meant to happen—not the most beneficial thinking for getting things done!

What we forget is that goals require action. There won't be a magical sign that leads us effortlessly to our destination. Action requires effort, and for our actions to bear fruit, we must show persistence. Those first few steps may get us closer to our goals, but they'll compound over time if done consistently and intentionally.

Noted business coach Dan Sullivan writes about the idea of the "Gap versus Gain." In this approach, he warns people against focusing too much on the end destination—the gap between where they are now and where they want to be. Instead, he thinks people should focus on taking one step closer to the goal and measure their progress relative to their starting point—in other words, how much they gain. With this approach, big goals get broken into small incremental gains that aren't as difficult to implement.

Writers have a similar approach. Instead of sitting down in one sitting and banging out a book, most writing coaches suggest focusing on writing a minimum number of words per day consistently. Breaking the goal down into smaller tasks makes the bigger goal look more feasible.

If we focus only on the end destination, we'll get easily discouraged as we encounter hurdles. Sometimes, we just need to take it step-by-step—one, two, three, and repeat. Measure your progress at the end of each day by how much progress you've made, not how far you have to go.

I'm not a mountain climber, but I have friends who have scaled some of the most prominent peaks in the world. I'm told that getting to the peak often boils down to putting your head down and taking the next step forward—

nothing more. Maybe we all need to be more like mountain climbers when tackling our goals.

Lesson: Focus on the progress you've made between where you started and where you are now instead of how much further you need to go. If in doubt, keep going.

Anticipating and preparing for obstacles. When was the last time you set out to do something, and nothing went wrong along the way? Never, right?

There's always something or somebody keeping you from achieving your goals.

You'd think we'd be used to overcoming obstacles by now, but it's surprising how many people assume nothing will go wrong. We expect a linear path to reaching our goals. Unfortunately, that's not how the world works.

In psychology, there is a term called "implementation intentions" that prepares you for dealing with obstacles. It works like this:

Visualize what likely hurdles you'll encounter. Assume you'll meet these hurdles. Decide beforehand your response to the situation. How will you deal with setbacks mentally? Will you fly off the handle and give up on your goal? Or will you take a step back and figure out how to proceed? Making these mid-course adjustments is much easier when you've anticipated them ahead of time.

Knowing you'll feel resistance and confusion at times is natural. Planning for challenges should be a requirement for any well-designed plan.

Lesson: Come up with "what-if" responses to potential hurdles to achieving your goals. Focus on the obstacles you'll likely encounter and design your response ahead of time. Write them down.

Setting up an environment that supports your goals. You're smart and dedicated? You have a solid plan. Yet, you may lack follow-through and fail to turn your goals into reality. Don't believe me? Try using willpower to accomplish your goals. You might have already tried this, and the results were probably disappointing.

Willpower alone isn't enough to achieve your goals. To make success more likely, one science-based hack that psychologists such as Roy Baumeister and Benjamin Hardy have found effective is designing your environment to support your goals.

"Environment is the invisible hand that shapes human behavior."

~JAMES CLEAR, AUTHOR OF *ATOMIC HABITS*

Think of your environment as everything that surrounds you:

- Your physical location
- Your shelter
- Social settings
- The information you consume
- The music you listen to
- Your environment's cultural backdrop

Have you ever noticed the subtle influence your peers and family play in encouraging or discouraging you from pursuing your dreams? A peer group that sticks to conventional wisdom and plays life small might try to sway you toward their standards. Conversely, a peer group open to new possibilities and supportive of your personal growth will likely push and energize you to pursue your goal.

Cut out toxic influences in your peer groups and seek alliances with people who have similar growth mindsets. Who you surround yourself with is important.

Your physical environment is equally important. Have you ever worked in a cluttered office and wondered why you couldn't focus? Or sat at a desk that didn't fit right because it was too small? Maybe your current work environment is surrounded by noise and chatter, making it almost impossible to concentrate? Wouldn't it make sense to design an environment that encouraged you to be more efficient and focused?

Think about your living situation. If your main goal is to get healthier by abstaining from alcohol and exercising daily, would living in a town with umpteen bars and nightspots be helpful? Probably not. The temptation to join in for one or two drinks would be constant.

If your goal is to live healthier, consider a living situation where nature trails and bike paths surround you. Wouldn't those trails and bike paths constantly remind you to exercise and enjoy nature?

Lesson: Choose an environment with an ideal, built-in peer group and physical surroundings to support your goals. Put yourself in situations that demand the type of behavior congruent with your goals, making you less reliant on willpower.

Dealing with the silent spoiler: procrastination. Are you having trouble following up on your good intentions? Do you feel stuck? Do you know what you need to do, but you can't get yourself going?

These are signs of the worst type of avoidance: procrastination. You feel you should be successful, but you can't seem to get moving. You might have had a promising start and were excited, but now the motivation is gone. Yet, deep inside, you still value your goals and want nothing more than to get past the finish line.

Why is this happening again? I'm sure it's not the first time you have struggled to finish something.

Unfortunately, procrastination is very common. Everybody has procrastinated at one time.

Many times, we know what to do. For example, I knew I needed to write at least five hundred words a day to finish this book. I know I should refrain from bingeing on ice cream or oatmeal raisin cookies if I'm serious about losing the extra pounds around my waist. I know it's best to deal with a vexing business matter as soon as possible and not let it fester.

But do we always do what we know we need to do? I don't know about you, but my batting average in this area could use a lot of improvement.

Dealing with procrastination is a daily challenge for many people.

Here are some tips that have helped me become less prone to putting things off.

Tactic #1: Schedule the task you find difficult to follow through. Create time slots in your calendar for the task. For example, you only focus on learning Italian from 9:00 a.m. to 10:30 a.m. on Monday, Wednesday, and Friday. You won't do anything else: no email, no picking up your phone, and no discussions with your spouse about what you're having for dinner.

Stick to your schedule and refuse to do anything else, even if the task gets difficult or boring. Don't let your mind drift. Pretend you're one of those soldiers protecting a national monument. Blink at your own risk.

Tactic #2: List activities you won't do. This tactic works in tandem with scheduling. Create a list of things you absolutely won't do during your focus time. Here are some things on my list when I'm supposed to be working on my goals: Facebook, LinkedIn, CNN, ESPN, email, and phone calls.

Breaking the rule is a no-no. Much research has shown that multitasking costs too much in starting time and focus. Don't get distracted by a moment of relief from the present task. It might feel good, but your productivity will suffer.

Some suggest using computer apps like FocusMe, BlockApp, Cold Turkey, and Offtime. I prefer an old-school method called the Pomodoro technique. It works as follows: Take twenty-five minutes to focus one hundred percent on whatever you're doing. Then take five minutes to recover. I have a Pomodoro timer, but you could also use your phone's timer.

Margaret Atwood, the author of *The Handmaid's Tale,* uses a "to-don't list" to beat her procrastination. I think others can benefit from this practice because of how prolific she's been over her career.

Tactic #3: Stop believing that leaving something for tomorrow is fine. It's extremely tempting to do this. You might feel tired or unmotivated today and convince yourself that working on your goal can wait until tomorrow. You're still hyper-committed to your goal, but not today.

Does this sound familiar? I think I have a PhD in this form of procrastination. You convince yourself there will always be enough time to complete your goal in the future. Yet, as Harold Hills says in Meredith Willson's *The Music Man*, "You pile up enough tomorrows, and you'll find you are left with nothing but a lot of empty yesterdays."

Getting results requires action. If you have the time today, do it today. You don't know what tomorrow will bring.

Will everything fall in place tomorrow? Most likely not, so why not get ahead of the game by doing something today?

Tactic #4: Get yourself a "tough no-bs" accountability partner. Are you still having trouble getting things done? Well, maybe it's time to get some tough love from an accountability partner. Not any partner, mind you, but somebody who's been around the block a few times and has a nose for detecting BS. Somebody who doesn't have a vested interest in your reasons and only cares about helping you ditch the litany of excuses we've become experts at doling out: versions of "the dog ate my homework," I don't feel well, my biorhythms are off, my partner is the warpath regarding my messy desk, my sister wouldn't get off the phone, it rained, it is too hot, too cold, too difficult. You get my point.

An accountability partner checks in on your performance and doesn't let you get away with procrastination. A good accountability partner calls out your excuses and sets you on the right path toward success.

An accountability partner doesn't need to make you feel warm and fuzzy. Instead, they should leave you feeling like you better deliver next time, or you might face embarrassment and tough love again.

Fun? Not really, but it's effective, especially if procrastination is your thing. For most of us, it is.

Tactic #5: Identify what's holding you back. Fear usually holds people back. It could be fear of screwing up, failing, or looking foolish to your peers. It could be the fear of not knowing the next steps involved with certainty.

Take the time to identify the emotion you're feeling. Is it legitimate? Are the consequences of not fighting through the fear worth leaving your goal unfinished?

You might have to just deal with it. Harvard Medical School psychologist Susan David suggests becoming aware of emotional messages to move forward. Not all negative emotions are avoidable. Some are meant to be dealt with, confronted, and understood.

Everybody feels fear and dislikes uncertainty. All major accomplishments require faith because there are always unknown outcomes. Are you willing to face your fears to fulfill your dreams? Are the fears insurmountable or just a hurdle to clear?

Tactic #6: Do something each day, even if it's a little step. Progress builds confidence, not the other way around. By doing something each day that gets you closer to your goals, your mindset will gradually improve, and the task will become easier.

Daily effort doesn't have to be monumental to matter. Like in financial markets, compound interest applies to your daily actions. Even minuscule actions can compound to a large effect if done consistently and over time.

Business coach Darren Hardy talks in length about this idea in his book *The Compound Effect*. He points out that your small actions will hardly be noticeable in the short term, but eventually, you'll reach an inflection point beyond which your progress will grow exponentially. Best-selling author and blogger James Altucher asks: What would happen if you got 1 percent better each day? I'm going to guess a lot of good things. I think that you would agree, wouldn't you?

The key to any of this is to have faith that your actions will lead you to your desired result. Small, daily actions are often imperceptible to the naked eye but cumulate to something significant if done consistently over a long time.

Rome wasn't built in a day, and neither is the goal you're pursuing.

Tactic #7: Remind yourself why your goal is important to you. We often lose track of why we do things in life because we do them out of habit or because others expect something from us. Most of our behavior is driven by subconscious thinking.

To beat procrastination, sometimes we need to remind ourselves why the goal is important to us in the first place; this is why internally motivated goals are so important. It doesn't matter what the goal is, as long as you know why it's important to you.

When things get messy in the middle, and you're tempted to chuck it all, take a moment to remind yourself why you pursued the goal in the first place. Close your eyes and visualize the finish line.

Is the goal worth the effort required? Artist Paul Thorn reminds us, "Everybody looks good at the starting line." Execution is much tougher than planning, and your commitment may waver as the going gets tough.

I've faced this hurdle many times while writing this book. I started with a grand vision of what I wanted to accomplish. I drafted up an outline and started writing with great enthusiasm. But as I got further, I started questioning where I was going with the message, and my writing stalled.

There were many weeks when I couldn't bear to put pen to paper, but that little devil in my head kept reminding me why this book was important to *me*. I didn't care that many people fantasize about writing a book. I cared about writing about my experiences and those of my clients in designing a retirement full of possibilities. Writing a book was my way of sharing those experiences and life lessons.

Are you pursuing your goals because they will bring *you* great satisfaction and fulfillment? Get in touch with your "why" and stay committed to your goals.

CONSIDERATIONS FOR YOUR FUTURE SELF

Have you decided if your life in retirement will be about pursuing the easy life, or are you willing to stretch to seek a life of fulfillment?

Dreaming is good for you, but only if you turn those dreams into actions. Your dreams are those of your Future Self; they'll remain dreams unless you turn them into clear goals and commit to doing the necessary work.

Having dreams allows you to look forward to something, but dreams that remain unfulfilled create stress, and you feel like you're settling for less than you're capable of receiving.

Turning your dreams into goals requires understanding what you want to achieve. You must be crystal clear. You must be emotionally invested in your goals. Making your goals specific and as measurable as possible is the first step. All your goals must sync with each other. Together, they represent the mosaic of your Future Self and what you aspire to become.

Turning goals into reality requires work. The path from idea (or plan) to goal achievement is never linear. You will have to overcome many hurdles along the way. Preparing yourself for the obstacles will help you persevere and move closer to achieving your dreams.

CHAPTER 9
LEARNING

"Anyone who stops learning is old, whether at twenty or eighty. Anyone who keeps learning stays young. The greatest thing in life is to keep your mind young."

~HENRY FORD, INDUSTRIALIST AND INVENTOR

When I was in college, I went to Costa Rica to visit my aunt, who had recently retired. My aunt had always been very involved in learning new things, but she seemed particularly busy this time. I asked her what she was doing to occupy her time, expecting to hear the usual assortment of relaxation-oriented activities. But I didn't hear that at all. Instead, she told me about her courses under the *Educación de la Tercera Edad* program, or in English, Education for the Third Age.

I'd never heard the term third age before, so I asked what it was. It turns out that third age refers to the stage of life after your career and raising a family. Personal freedom and fulfillment are the new priorities of the third age.

These third-age programs were designed to keep the senior population engaged in everyday life, and what better way to do so than by inviting third-agers to campus to participate in academics.

My aunt explained that the program went one step further, making it fun and mentally stimulating for retirees. She told me how excited she was to go on a bird-watching tour the following week with another group of third-agers. The opportunity to keep learning kept my aunt engaged in society while providing a healthy dose of mental stimulation.

Learning is hardly ever mentioned in the context of retirement—society associates retirement with leisure and comfort. Education is often difficult, costly, and time-consuming, so why would retirees bother, right?

Our grandparents' and parents' retirements didn't involve much learning. After all, weren't people supposed to cruise during their golden years?

What's different today is that people aren't only living longer; they also want more out of life. Retirees (whether baby boomers or members of the F.I.R.E movement) appreciate the gift of a longer life, but they want to remain engaged in society and live fulfilling lives.

Many people think that once you retire, you're done learning. Yet, retirement is the perfect time to learn whatever you want because you have the time. Many people feel like a weight has been lifted, giving them the freedom to pursue new knowledge and skills in areas that interest them. How much better can it get?

Learning is key to living a happy and fulfilled life in retirement. You must be nurtured and nourished in your retirement life along with the other elements of your **NET WEALTH**.

Lifelong learning isn't something to pass the time; to keep learning is essential for your well-being.

As people live longer, a critical skill is adapting to and learning new societal norms and practices. Mastering new ways of communicating and behaving in everyday life is part of fitting into society. Research by Professor Valeri Helterbran at Duquesne University concluded that "People over the age of fifty who said they continued to learn about topics that interested them were 18 percent more likely to feel satisfied with their lives and 43 percent more likely to feel vital."

One of my favorite places is the public library because it's multigenerational learning at its finest. You have young children with their caretakers participating in story time, the after-school crowd (mostly teenagers and often loud), and the seniors. I especially love seeing the senior "regulars"—most of them immersed in stacks of papers and books. Some sit at the study tables while others type away at computer keys. What I love the most is that everybody is doing their own thing, enjoying the stimulation of a good story or researching a topic of interest. All that matters is what's going on in their heads. Together the collective vibe of the library is one of quiet empowerment, reflection, and brighter futures.

That's what I feel about true learning; it's empowering, inner-focused, and leads to greater possibilities. I believe that everybody, regardless of age, can benefit from this feeling, but there are also proven benefits to learning that significantly enhance people's lives.

LEARNING HELPS YOU MAINTAIN BRAIN HEALTH

Learning has one significant role in maintaining people's well-being, supporting brain health. Retirees often have a deep fear of losing their mental functions. Learning is one way to offset the normal age-related deterioration in mental capacity.

Your brain is like a muscle. It needs exercise, or it will atrophy through lack of use. Learning forces the brain to develop new neural connections, impacting memory, attention, language, and reasoning skills. We now know the brain continues to evolve and can create new connections. This trait is called neuroplasticity, and it doesn't disappear with age.

Learning something new is a great way to maintain brain health. The brain does well when faced with challenges. Doing the same things over and over won't generate new neural connections. The connections will be reinforced and strengthened, but learning something new that is also challenging offers the most benefits to brain health.

Can you think of something you've always wanted to learn that's also challenging? The brain thrives on new experiences. Anytime we do something that the brain hasn't processed before, it creates new dendrites, synapses, and neural pathways that enhance mental health. While many people think crossword puzzles improve brain health, it's the more complex activities like learning a new language or how to play an instrument that offers the most benefits.

Do you think that it's too late for you? Think again. Your brain improves with use, regardless of age. Think of your brain the same way you think of your muscles. You can always get fitter if you go to the gym and train hard enough. The same applies to your brain.

"The human brain can do far more than anyone ever thought. Contrary to outworn beliefs, its limitations are imposed by us, not by its physical shortcomings."

~DEEPAK CHOPRA AND RUDOLPH TANZI, CO-AUTHORS OF *SUPER BRAIN: UNLEASHING THE EXPLOSIVE POWER OF YOUR MIND TO MAXIMIZE HEALTH, HAPPINESS, AND SPIRITUAL WELL-BEING*

Are you ready to give your brain some exercise? How about learning to play an instrument, speak a new language, perform computer coding, or acquire a skill that has eluded you?

Learning should be fun but learning something new and mentally challenging boosts your mental health the most over the long term.

What are three new things you'd love to learn that are also challenging?

Activity 1:

Activity 2:

Activity 3:

LEARNING CAN BE FUN AND A GREAT WAY TO SOCIALIZE

The benefits of learning go beyond simply attaining more skills and challenging your brain. Learning is also a great way to socialize.

When people retire, they often find they have more time on their hands. What will they do with all this time? Learning something new is a great way to fill the void. For example, my mother signed up for painting lessons. She enjoyed learning basic drawing techniques and meeting other fellow art lovers.

Learning in a group setting can be enjoyable for retirees who often feel socially isolated. Attending class is a great excuse to get out of the house and mingle with like-minded individuals. Sometimes, it's less about the subject matter than it is about the social interaction.

Can you think of any activities that would be fun to do with a group? Activities like group golf lessons, salsa dancing, bird watching, or photography are often more enjoyable when doing them with others.

LEARNING HELPS YOU STAY RELEVANT IN THE WORKFORCE

Whether you get paid, learning allows you to remain relevant in today's labor force. Very few jobs in today's economy won't change over time. Keeping up with these changes by learning new skills and methods is necessary.

You'll probably require some retooling and skill updates even if you work part-time. Our work tools are constantly evolving. Even tools like Excel or Outlook have received significant updates over the years. Maybe you've always been reluctant to become a spreadsheet expert, but you'll be expected to do more than simply add and divide columns in today's work world. A little training can help you keep your skills fresh.

What about learning how to post to social media? Not a skill that many baby boomers or Gen Xers grew up with, but it's necessary now if you want to understand how your company is positioned from a marketing standpoint. Again, you don't need a PhD in social media, but learning some of the basics is only one YouTube video away.

You'll also need to learn the basics if you join a new industry. At first, it will be like drinking water from a fire hose, but little by little, you'll start making the connections, and soon you'll be fluent in "industry speak."

Acquiring new knowledge and skills is only part of the retooling process. Turning them into context-appropriate wisdom is where you get the biggest bang for your buck. Let's be honest—young people are often much better at certain tasks. Rather than hide behind our seniority, a more fruitful approach might be to figure out where our skills, experiences, and perspectives could yield additional value to our contributions.

What do you think you need to know to stay competitive in the workforce? Come up with some skills or tools you need to learn?

LEARNING ALLOWS YOU TO MASTER NEW TECHNOLOGIES

Mastering technology has become an essential life skill. Technology can either be a barrier to communication or a great help. Consider Facebook. It can help you keep up with your loved ones or be a source of frustration if you can't figure out how to use the new features when they're released.

Today's fast-moving economy is fueled by technological innovation and rapid societal changes. Technology is used increasingly to communicate across geographical locations and time zones. Keeping up with technological changes is a lifelong skill that enables people to live independently for longer.

There are many ways that using technology makes retirement lives easier, but you must view technology as a helpful tool. Here are some ways technology can benefit you:

- Do you need a ride to your doctor's appointment? You can call a cab and wait or schedule an Uber or Lyft that will show up when you need the ride.
- Do you want to get directions to a new restaurant? Use Waze or Google Maps to get customized directions from wherever you are.

And, if you don't know where to park, you can use a parking app such as ParkWhiz to book a parking spot in a garage.
- Does it take you long to drive to a doctor's office? See if you can instead use a TeleMed service such as Teledoc Health.
- Do you need to have your medications delivered to your house? You can simply open your computer's browser, order your prescriptions online, and have them delivered to your home exactly when needed.
- Are you stuck at home and unable to go to a yoga class? Well, YouTube may not be a perfect substitute, but it has a lot of classes you can watch to enhance your practice.
- Do you want to participate in your granddaughter's first birthday but can't make the trip? Facetime or Zoom are great alternatives. Learn how to log on and communicate using these video apps.

All these situations require technology. Companies are increasingly relying on internet-based storefronts. To live independently, you'll need to master new technologies because technology will keep evolving. A few years ago, the cheapest way to communicate with people abroad was to use Skype. Now, WhatsApp and Zoom make it even easier and cheaper to communicate. Staying current is staying relevant.

"Change is the end result of all true learning."

~LEO BUSCAGLIA, AUTHOR AND MOTIVATIONAL SPEAKER

With families scattered worldwide, sometimes the only way to stay in touch is to use technology. I recently had a Zoom call with my sisters, who live in the UK, and my 93-year-old uncle, who lives in Costa Rica. My uncle had never used Zoom, but he figured it out with the help of my cousin's daughter. We were all on camera at the scheduled time, and while being together in person would've been better, my uncle now knows we can see each other on camera whenever he wants. A little knowledge goes a long way to keeping family bonds alive.

LEARNING TEACHES YOU ABOUT YOURSELF

Sometimes learning isn't about acquiring new hobbies, skills, or knowledge but about better understanding yourself.

You are more than the facts and figures in your head and your physical profile. We have many emotions and thoughts that help us cope with daily living and, at other times, get our way.

Chip Conley, the founder of the Modern Elder Academy, talks about the concept of "long life learning," which focuses on developing a sense of purpose.

Last year, I enrolled in one of Chip's courses. Instead of learning something that's already been defined (such as a new skill or method), we focused on inward learning. It felt like self-learning, meaning that the answer or life lesson is already inside you, but you're learning how to bring it out from the subconscious to the conscious.

In their excellent book, *The 100-Year Life*, researchers Gratton and Scott write about the concept of "transformational assets." These assets help you cope with transitions and change, such as self-awareness and adopting a growth mindset. They believe that the skills needed to help us adapt to life's transitions must be learned and nurtured like any other skill, such as controlling one's mindset and emotions, developing resilience, and setting routines and habits to accomplish one's goals.

"Our world is awash in knowledge but often wanting in wisdom."

~CHIP CONLEY, FOUNDER OF THE
MODERN ELDER ACADEMY

LEARNING CAN TAKE MANY SHAPES AND FORMS

If you want to learn something new, you can; whether from in-class lessons or remote video-based learning. The 2020 global pandemic accelerated the use of online teaching platforms. Many traditional programs adapted and continue to offer lectures online; some include real-time classroom learning and discussion, making previously inaccessible learning opportunities available to a broader audience.

Online university education has been around for over thirty years and is offered through commercial institutions, such as the University of Phoenix and Southern New Hampshire University. You can also find accredited local or private universities near you that offer online courses. Other online learning platforms include Udemy and Coursera.

> *"Tell me and I forget, teach me and I may remember, involve me and I learn."*
>
> ~BENJAMIN FRANKLIN, INVENTOR

The number of institutions offering online and in-class learning to retirees is vast and growing. Here are some learning resources to start with:

Formal/Classroom:

- Local libraries
- Community adult education programs, such as the Third Age Program in Costa Rica
- Local colleges
- Osher Lifelong Learning Institute works with over 250 colleges to provide non-credit courses to seasoned adults
- Age-Friendly University (AFU) network of universities
- Fordham University College at Sixty Program, which serves people fifty years or older

- Stanford Distinguished Careers Institute (DCI) focused on purpose, wellness, and community
- Notre Dame Inspired Leadership Initiative (ILI) focused on life design
- University of Minnesota Advanced Careers (UMAC)
- University of Texas Tower Fellows Program

Online:

- Platforms (Udemy, Coursera, Lynda)
- Specific Online Courses (AMP (Ben Hardy), Freedom Machine (Jon Morrow), MEA Online (Chip Conley), …
- YouTube
- TED Talks and TEDx Talks

Informal/Social:

- Rhodes Scholar (learn about the world through travel)
- One Day University
- Modern Elder Academy (MEA), focused on mindset
- Elevation Barn, focused on purpose

Work-related:

- Encore.org
- Harvard Advanced Leadership Institute (ALI), designed to help successful leaders become "change agents for society."

"Research shows that you begin learning in the womb and go right on learning until the moment you pass on. Your brain has a capacity for learning that is virtually limitless, which makes every human a potential genius."

~MICHAEL J. GELB, AUTHOR AND MOTIVATIONAL SPEAKER

CREATE A SMORGASBORD CURRICULUM

Retirement gives you the freedom to learn whatever you want. Learning can be fun and intellectually stimulating, which is key to maintaining your mental health. Even if you haven't been an active learner up to now, it's never too late. Your brain will thank you.

You don't have to learn things that don't interest you. Rather than following the usual recipe of brain exercises, create your own collection of fun and challenge. My suggestion is to mix it up. Don't just learn the easy stuff. Commit to learning something challenging.

After earning my MBA, my first job was leading a group of research analysts. One of the best pieces of advice my boss gave me was to allow each person the flexibility and time (one day a week) to learn something new of their choosing. I agreed to the plan, my only stipulation being that they chose to learn something related to their current job. At the end of the year, we discussed what they learned and their progress. As you can expect, some people chose to learn something easy, while others pushed themselves to focus on a skill that would significantly enhance their career long term. Guess which group went on to greater success in their careers and life?

While the focus during retirement may no longer be job-related, I don't think you should ever stop investing in yourself to create a brighter future. Learning involves investing your time and mental energy in activities that, hopefully, give you joy and get you closer to your Future Self.

Like you would do when investing in any other area of your life, you must formulate learning plan. Here's how this plan might look. The first step is to figure out what you want to learn the most. Is it a new hobby? Is it something creative? Is it a job-related skill you lack? I recommend picking at most two or three new things to learn at once. Maybe choose a few fun things that you can learn quickly and one area that's a bit more challenging and might take you longer to master.

NET WEALTH	Rank Your Interests	Is It Fun?	Is It Challenging?	Examples
LEARNING	10=Most, 1=Least	Y=Yes, N=No	Y=Yes, N=No	
Existing Hobby				
New Hobby				
Spiritual				
Technology Application				
Sports/Fitness				
Creative				
Cultural				
Culinary				
New Job Skill				
Health Related				

Do any of these areas interest you? Are you willing to commit to learning one or two new things over the next few months? What is one thing that would make a big difference to your life if you become proficient at it?

> *"Even the greatest was once a beginner. Don't be afraid to take that first step."*
>
> ~MUHAMMAD ALI, FORMER BOXER

Even if you take baby steps, you'll become a lifelong learner from the moment you begin. I get excited when I look at my list, which includes refining my gardening skills, learning to play pickleball, and taking an analytics software course. Many days, I lose track of time because I'm immersed in learning something new. I want you to have the same excitement and satisfaction as you master whatever you have chosen to learn. For those who haven't been lifelong learners up to this point, let the discovery of new knowledge and skills be one of those unexpected bonuses that bring great joy and fulfillment to your third age.

WARNING: DON'T LET THESE THINGS STAND IN YOUR WAY

Fear of looking dumb. Professor Carol Dweck popularized the idea of having a growth mindset instead of a fixed mindset. People with fixed mindsets don't believe they can learn anything new or improve their skills.

Those with a growth mindset look at every opportunity as a way to improve. Being a beginner in any field is awkward. You'll feel dumb and make mistakes anytime you're learning something new, but eventually the learning curve ramps up.

Unfamiliarity with online learning. Most of us grew up going to class. Many of us are often still more comfortable in physical settings. However, a larger proportion of classes are taught online now. To be an effective online learner, you need to get comfortable with a computer. Tasks that seem simple to youngsters may terrify us. Thankfully, there are umpteen free resources that can teach you new skills.

Lack of friends with similar interests. Remember when you were a kid, and your mom enrolled you in a new class? Your first question was probably: Will my friends be with me? We still have these questions as adults. We like doing things with people we like and know. But what if your friends can't or won't join you in taking a class? Do you forget about it, or do you take a chance and take the class anyway? Chances are if you take the class you'll meet new people with similar interests to yours, and who knows, you might actually become friends with them.

CONSIDERATIONS FOR YOUR FUTURE SELF

I believe we learn something new every year. I believed that when I mentored teams of analysts and portfolio managers. I'm an even bigger believer in continued learning while in retirement. I've seen people who love learning live happier and more fulfilling lives than people who view learning as something they might have done in the past but not in retirement.

I don't think learning should be viewed as a chore to keep your brain fit. I don't think you need to push yourself constantly, but I believe learning can be fun and should be an integral part of your day. The most-alive retirees that I've come across are lifelong learners. They are constantly reading, researching, taking classes, and talking to people knowledgeable on topics of interest to them. They do it because they love learning. They love using their brains and staying engaged. They keep earning because they want to gain all the benefits of an active mind, such as mental health, engagement, and self-determination.

Learning new things keeps your brain working. If you learn something that interests you, you'll have fun. Learning is often done with other people, forcing you to expand your social circles. Learning is also necessary to keep your job skills fresh if you return to the workforce.

Maybe you've wanted to learn something for a long time, but didn't have the time. Or maybe it was fear of the unknown and your ego that got in your way. Your Future Self requires courage and action. Take the first step and invest in yourself. You won't be sorry you did.

There are so many new ways of learning in today's hyper-connected world. If you can google it, you can find it. Retirement has given you the freedom to learn whatever you're interested in learning. For many retirees, it's a gift they never anticipated.

CHAPTER 10
TRIBE

"Taking care of your body is important, but tending to your relationships is a form of self-care, too. Those with strong social support experienced less mental deterioration as they aged. Good relationships don't just protect our bodies; they protect our brains."

~ROBERT WALDINGER, DIRECTOR OF THE HARVARD STUDY OF ADULT DEVELOPMENT

Humans are social animals. All humans need for physical and emotional connection. Maslow's hierarchy of needs places belonging right after our need for food, water, and a safe place to live. Studies show that humans with high-quality social connections tend to be happier and healthier.

Many people are so busy during their working lives that they ignore social connections outside of the office. When they retire, they find themselves in a vacuum as they lose their built-in social network at work.

Scottish writer Andrew Chalmers once said that to be happy, you need three things, "Something to do, someone to love, and something to hope for." In most cases, when you do something, there are other people involved. Love, after all, requires another person, and when you hope for something, it often entails people. Our existence revolves around other people.

According to Dan Buettner, the author of *Blue Zones*, social connections are the most important factor determining personal happiness. That is true regardless of wealth or socio-economic status. The people living in the happiest communities worldwide all have strong social ties to family and community.

Many people fail to plan well when it comes to retirement. They focus on the financial side and ignore the rest. They assume that everything else will remain the same or figure itself out.

My parents fit this profile. When my parents retired, they didn't really plan for how they would live in retirement. They had the financial side figured out, but when it came to where they were going to live, the decisions were pretty much made by my father. They agreed to retire in Costa Rica, but for my father, that meant living in a country-club setting near a swimming pool and tennis courts. For my mother, who had grown up in Costa Rica, that meant being close to her ancestral family.

My parents ended up building a house in a newly developed country-club community about an hour from where my mother's family lived. My dad was happy as a clam, but my mother, the more social of the two, felt isolated and unable to see her family and friends as much as she would like. Even though the house and community were beautiful, the lack of socialization opportunities proved difficult, so much so that several years later, they ended up moving away to be closer to family.

My parents' predicament taught me a couple of things. One, plan for the non-financial aspects of retirement. Two, work it out with your partner or spouse beforehand (compromising is much better than a winner-take-all strategy). Three (and this is the topic of this chapter), you must understand how important it is to have a solid network of family and friends around you.

Research has shown that as people age, their social circles narrow. Many retirees no longer view making new friends as something they want to invest in. Moreover, many friendships fall by the wayside as more people in your network retire or move away. Many find their social circles become significantly smaller when social interaction is most needed.

Another issue afflicting many retirees, especially as they enter their eighties or nineties, is the gradual dismantling of their social circles because of health issues. A common complaint among senior citizens is so many of their friends and relatives have died. Even my uncle, who, at the time of this writing, is nearing ninety-three and has always had many friends, recently complained to me about feeling like the last man standing.

My observation is that people often underestimate the value of their social circle until it's almost too late. They assume people will be around when they need help or that they'll be fine alone.

In reality, friendships and family connections must be tended to over time. As people prepare to retire, many assume their social networks will remain intact forever, but the truth is that you constantly have to nurture and nourish all your relationships, new and old, to keep your social circle from shrinking like a violet.

This chapter introduces the idea of viewing your relationships and assessing the health of your social network as investing in an emotional bank account. By focusing on the positive emotions of your interactions with other people, you begin to think of your relationships in terms of quality over quantity.

While many relationships throughout the years evolved seemingly by accident, as you enter your retirement years, it becomes more important to nourish and nurture your relationships consciously, especially when the built-in socialization network of a full-time job no longer exists.

YOUR EMOTIONAL BANK ACCOUNT

Today, many relationships are transactional (our hairdresser or financial advisor, for example) and vanish the minute we no longer need each other's service or product. Other relationships last longer, but they're still casual. Deeper relationships require a commitment. They require an investment in time and give and take.

Think about your closest friendships. What makes them special? What makes them endure the usual ups and downs of relationships?

Award-winning author Steven Covey created the concept of an Emotional Bank Account (EBA) to illustrate the give-and-take nature of relationships. EBAs use emotional energy rather than money as the unit of measurement. Deposits of emotional energy, such as keeping promises, being respectful, and listening, increase your EBA. On the other hand, withdrawals, such as resentfulness, not listening, and making it all about yourself, deplete your EBA.

Your Emotional Bank Account

Deposits	Withdrawals
Keeping Promises	Uncommitted
Kind and Courteous	Resentful
Respectful	Confrontational
Attentive Listening	Self-Centered
Helpful	Defensiveness

Your Social Wealth
Family + Friends + Secondary Relationships

I never thought of my social circle in this way until I got divorced and was forced out of my job as an investment manager during the Great Recession. I lost a ton of relationships in both instances. As in all divorces, people take sides, and while you may eventually renew the relationship, it's never quite the same. Even if you've been lucky to be in a stable marriage, you've probably faced similar situations where you thought you had a deep friendship only to find out later the relationship was based on situational factors, such as you had kids on the same soccer team or you worked for the same company. We've all been there. Have you ever wondered why you're no longer close friends with people that you really liked and had many interests in common?

I don't like to admit this often, but in many cases, my friendships evaporated because of a mutual lack of nurturing and nourishing. Sometimes it was my fault; other times, it was theirs. In hindsight, I wish I'd been a little wiser; I realize now the incredible importance of having a supportive, fun, and emotionally engaging tribe around me.

I love the concept of an EBA because it makes you think about your interactions with your social circle. It reframes how you view your social circle, focusing less on the number of relationships and more on the quality. It measures the quality of the emotional connection instead of the number of social media followers you have.

When we're young, we rate our social network by how many friends and social connections we have—the more, the better. As we get older, we realize our social wealth is more about the depth and quality of our relationships. We understand intrinsically that good relationships with family and close friends have a meaningful impact on our sense of happiness and fulfillment.

"Having more close friendships was associated with a 19 percent greater life satisfaction and a 23 percent greater sense of optimism."

~MATT RICHBURG, AMPERSAND LEADERSHIP GROUP

Have you ever thought of your social circle in terms of emotional give and take?

What would your EBA look like with your friends and family? Would your EBA balance be positive, barely above water, or sinking fast?

More importantly, is your EBA in sync with others? Relationships only work when both parties find them mutually beneficial.

Think of your EBA in the same way as an investment account. Are you investing emotionally in your relationships? Are your investments reciprocated with similar emotional energy investments by the other person?

How many of your relationships with family and friends make you feel good? How many of these positive emotions could you check off when thinking of your relationships?

- Love
- Joy
- Grateful
- Fun
- Inspiring
- Interesting

The list isn't exhaustive. Relationships evoke a range of feelings. Close your eyes and think of each of your key relationships. Ask yourself three questions:

Question #1: What emotion comes to mind?

Question #2: What emotion do you think the other person feels when they think of you?

Question #3: Are these emotions aligned with positive energy?

Putting yourself in another person's shoes is hard, but not doing so is often at the root of relationship mismatches. You'll never know exactly what another person is feeling, but if you're open and honest with yourself, you'll empathize with them better. Or do it the old-fashioned way and ask them what they're feeling. We know deep inside ourselves if we're being good to family or friends. It takes a little more introspection sometimes to get at the heart of the matter.

Your goal should be to maintain a positive balance of emotional energy in your relationships. There will be times when you're in a deficit, but over the long term, relationships must be mutually beneficial, a win-win situation for all. Your relationships should make you feel good, but you also have a responsibility to nurture and nourish the relationships to make the feeling mutual.

Friendships aren't always in sync. You need to draw down your balances sometimes when you need some support, and, at other times, you'll be the giver and deplete your EBA balance.

Friendships can also be one-sided. Your EBA might be full, but your friend's EBA might be negative. Like a bank account with a negative balance, something must change.

As you think about your EBA, ask yourself these questions:

- What two or three things could you do to improve your relationships?
- Do you have any relationships in the red?
- Are these relationships toxic, or are they going through an adjustment period?
- Are you treating your relationships with friends and family the same way your Future Self would?

When you start adding up all your relationships in the context of an emotional bank account, you arrive at your social wealth. Your social wealth is comprised of family members, close friends, and a group of secondary relationships.

Let's transition from looking at your relationships in terms of one-on-one emotional balance accounts and discuss them in terms of social wealth.

HOW SIGNIFICANT IS YOUR SOCIAL WEALTH?

Research done in the early 1990s by Robin Dunbar at Oxford University showed that humans usually have deep relationships with an average of five people. In Dunbar's research, this tight circle of deep relationships typically included two family members, two friends, and one hybrid member. That is typically the size of your inner core.

The next layer of relationships usually includes fifteen people. The bonds aren't as deep, but the relationships are mutually beneficial. As with your inner core, some of these relationships are with family, but this secondary core includes colleagues, neighbors, and people with similar interests.

For the sake of argument, let's say your core social network consists of twenty people. Some of these people will come and go. Not all these relationships will have emotional balance accounts that are in sync.

Your gender also makes a difference. Women tend to be better at maintaining social relationships than men, especially as people retire from their full-time careers. Many men find their social networks significantly reduced when they leave the workforce because they are often more transactional and situational in their relationships. Their relationships were centered around a common theme; once that commonality loses relevance, the relationship tends to fizzle.

Ask yourself:

- Which family members are you close with?
- Who are your closest friends?
- Who is in your secondary core of friendships?
- Is anybody missing from this list?
- Is anybody on this list an obligation, not a positive connection?
- Are you happy with your tribe?

Look at the worksheet below. How would you rate your current relationships with these groups of people?

NET WEALTH	Current Rating (A)	Target Rating (B)	Desired Change (B-A)	Immediate Priority	90-Day Goals
TRIBE	10=Best, 1=Worst	10=Best, 1=Worst		10=Most, 1=Least	Be as specific as possible.
Spouse/Partner					
Children					
Siblings					
Parents					
Extended Family					
Personal Friends					
Couple Friends					
Work-Related Friends					
Professional Network					
Hobby Friends					

If you have any relationships you'd like to improve, set actionable SMARTER goals to start adding to your EBA.

A good idea is to pick a couple of relationships and be specific. For example, if you want to improve your relationship with your best friend from college, don't send them a text message asking how they're doing. Instead, pick up the phone and schedule a time to meet face-to-face over coffee or lunch. Even better, schedule a fun activity to do together. Relationships need nourishing and nurturing.

Relationships are all about the emotional energy they generate. It's better to have a small but high-quality tribe than a collection of relationships with low emotional connection. Quality trumps quantity when it comes to your social wealth. Think of your tribe as the people you want to bring along with you on your journey toward becoming your Future Self.

"Surround yourself with people who remind you more of your future than your past."

~DAN SULLIVAN, MOTIVATIONAL BUSINESS COACH

INVESTING IN THE QUALITY OF YOUR SOCIAL WEALTH

Did your mother use to warn you about who you were hanging out with? She would love some of your friends, and then there would be those friends (usually the ones who were the most fun) that she didn't entirely trust.

Mothers know who their kids keep company with influences their behavior. According to author, entrepreneur, motivational speaker, and prominent management consultant Jim Rohn, you're the average of the five people you spend most of your time with, and these people shape your outlook in life.

Athletes understand the notion of training in an environment where the competitive bar is set high. When Andre Agassi was a young tennis prodigy in

Las Vegas, his father made him go to the Bollettieri Academy in Florida. He hated being away from home, but he was forced to compete daily against older and more skilled players. To become the Grand Slam winner he always envisioned, he had to learn how to compete against formidable opposition. His environment forced him to upgrade his skills and expectations of himself.

There's a psychological concept called the Pygmalion effect, which describes how the expectations of those around you influence your rules and expectations. Surround yourself with ambitious people who work hard to reach their goals, and you have no choice but to push yourself. Do the opposite and accept a happy-go-lucky attitude, and you're not likely to improve much.

The point? Choose your friends wisely.

Are your current relationships strong enough to allow you to become your Future Self?

DIVERSIFYING YOUR SOCIAL WEALTH

Your social capital depends on the quality and the depth of your relationships. Your most meaningful relationships are probably with your family. Other relationships are based on business or professional connections and might be more transitory. Others are based on friendship and a shared interest.

You want real connections, not necessarily with people who look, think, and behave like you. Diversity in your relationships helps you see things differently and explore new paths.

Look around at your social group and ask yourself: Do all your friends fit the same profile? Do they all think and behave the same? Are you following the herd?

Similarity breeds comfort, so until you venture from your typical social circles, your outlook on life and perspectives will remain static. Sometimes you need a friendly nudge to shift your mindset; other times, you need a jolt. Relationships are about more than familiarity and comfort. Having somebody in your social circle who brings an alternative perspective to situations is highly beneficial.

Diversity comes in many forms, including upbringing, belief system, professional experience, interests, age, race, or culture.

As people get older, forming relationships with younger people becomes more important. They are your connection to society in many ways. Society is often viewed through the lens of how young people operate. What young people see and view as important may not align with your views, but instead of resisting the evolution of ideas, wouldn't it be better to understand and adapt? You can teach younger generations something, too. Through your openness to younger generations, they'll be more receptive to your influence.

The natural place to start with intergenerational relationships is with family. Grandkids often serve in this role. They can teach you about the world as they see it, and you can share your own stories and perspectives that benefit them.

Another way to develop these intergenerational relationships is by mentoring younger people. Mentoring benefits everyone. If you decide to mentor somebody younger than you, you'll probably encounter what Chip Conley, founder of the Modern Elder Academy, found when he joined the executive ranks at Airbnb in its early days. On some issues, such as leadership, Chip served more as a mentor, but the younger co-CEOs became Chip's technology mentors. Multigenerational friendships are a clear win-win when approached from a growth perspective.

GROWING YOUR SOCIAL WEALTH

There are many ways to improve your social network's reach and quality. Sometimes, you'll need to reinforce your current networks, and other times you'll need to explore new relationships entirely.

You already know your inner core well. It's your spouse/partner, kids, your siblings, or a couple of close friends. These are the "A" players in your life. You want to nurture your inner core because they're your primary source of support, companionship, and joy.

When people retire from their full-time careers, they often find their relationships become unbalanced. Relationships, especially among spouses/partners, get out of sync. Some areas that involve the greatest initial stress include:

- Change in financial situation. How will you finance retirement without going broke while understanding the different financial values and mindsets of your spouse/partner?
- How much time to spend together versus how much time to spend apart.
- Where to live. Will you stay put, and move closer to adult children or move to a golf course and near other outdoor activities?
- Will you continue supporting adult children and relatives, or is it time to cut the cord?
- What will you do with all your freedom? Will you try something new or stick to the old routine?
- How will you structure your daily activities? Or will you simply go with the flow?

These are important conversations to have with your inner core. They are worth having *before* you take the plunge and retire. There's usually a give and take (also known as the we-need-to-talk chat) required between spouses/partners before you reach a consensus.

Your social capital depends on having good relationships with your inner core relationship group. Retirement can be stressful, and relationships can easily fray while adjusting to your new phase in life. Don't assume that things won't change; they almost certainly will.

Your inner social core is most important to your well-being, but don't dismiss your secondary relationship group. These relationships also need nurturing; in many cases, especially for men in retirement, they develop and grow.

Here are some ideas for doing so:

- **Volunteer for a cause you care about.** Actively participate, don't just donate some money. The chances are that you'll bond with like-minded volunteers. Even if you don't end up making lasting friends, you've helped a cause you care about. So, how can you lose?

- **Mentor the younger generation.** Remember the movie *The Intern* with Anne Hathaway and Robert De Niro that I mentioned earlier in this book? In this movie, De Niro plays an elder intern out of place in a youth-oriented company. At first, Anne Hathaway's character dismisses the intern as hopelessly out of touch, but little by little, she values the intern's wisdom, and they enjoy a friendship based on support and guidance. You could do the same.
- **Find a person-facing job.** Most jobs these days are collaborative. The simple act of dealing with many people will force you out of your shell, and chances are you'll bond with some of your co-workers, maybe even some of your clients. Years ago, one of my retired neighbors worked as a crossing guard at the local junior high. He told me that he'd made hundreds of "little friends."
- **Take a class.** My mom took lots of art classes. My aunt preferred travel-related courses. You could pick ballroom dancing or woodworking. The point is to do something fun in a group setting.
- **Join a gym and take group lessons.** Don't just hang out by the treadmills or weights. Take one of the many group classes most gyms offer—the more interactive, the better.
- **Take an organized trip**. Elder Hostel is well known, but I see similar offerings from my alumni office and organizations such as the Sierra Club. There's also a growing trend of grandparent/grandkid trips. Imagine the bonding opportunities such a trip affords.
- **Re-connect with long-lost friends**. Go on Facebook and search for old acquaintances. I worked with an older gentleman once who'd recently divorced. Distraught, and at his granddaughter's insistence, he decided to check out Facebook and look for long-lost friends. He found one of his former high school friends who'd recently lost her husband. They re-connected when she came to

New York with a friend for a brief holiday, and the rest, as they say, is history—a happy ending!
- **Use technology to connect emotionally**. Schedule a Zoom call or use Facetime to connect. Seeing somebody's face is much better than just listening to a voice, even if the person is far away. Schedule frequent calls with people. My sister scheduled a Zoom call every Friday afternoon during the early months of COVID-19. We had people from England, Scotland, the US, and Costa Rica on the call. Ask your grandkids for help. They know how to use the latest technology.
- **Live in a multigenerational community.** One of the easiest ways to develop close ties with the younger generation is to be their neighbor. Multigenerational communities often have minimal space between residences and incorporate common structures such as a dining hall, an events center, and recreation facilities. The presence of young families creates a certain energy that's often lacking in adult-only communities. Children don't have the inhibitions common in many adults. They'll talk to anyone! Just being around kids brings a smile to my face. How about you?

"Loneliness kills. It's as powerful as smoking or alcoholism."

~ROBERT WALDINGER, PROFESSOR OF PSYCHIATRY AT HARVARD MEDICAL SCHOOL

CONSIDERATIONS FOR YOUR FUTURE SELF

Social connections are key to well-being, but we often assume that loved ones and close friends will always surround us. We assume that nothing will change, but relationships are like garden plants. They need nourishment and nurturing to thrive. Otherwise, they'll wilt and decay. New plants need to be watered and fertilized to grow. A well-tended garden also requires trimming or disposing of established plants to make room for new plants.

Have any of these everyday situations damaged an important relationship in your life?

- **Holding a grudge for something that happened a long time ago.** As we get older and hopefully wiser, we tend to have a more sympathetic worldview. You may want to ask yourself: How many of my relationships ended because I couldn't let go of a perceived affront or because we had a different point of view? Would you do things differently today?
- **Feeling lonely and retreating into a shell**. Have you noticed when people have problems, they often compound their losses by withdrawing from the world? Loneliness can turn into depression and shame, worsening the cycle of isolation worse. According to the *Journal of Geriatric Psychiatry*, loneliness affects between 25 percent and 60 percent of all older adults. Researchers have even correlated loneliness with health problems like hyper-inflammation, decreased immune response, and trouble sleeping. Relying on your friends and family during difficult times shouldn't be viewed as a burden. As long as you've made enough deposits into your EBA, feel free to take some withdrawals when you really need a boost.
- **Letting distance dictate the frequency of interaction**. Sure, it's much easier to have a close relationship with somebody who lives nearby and whom you see daily. Given today's transitory nature, it's not surprising that many friendships die when people move away. Friendships worth keeping require commitment. Letting a relationship wilt because of distance isn't a good excuse. It doesn't cost anything to call someone (at least nationally), and if you really miss seeing someone's face, you can use Facetime or Zoom. There aren't any excuses.
- **Feeling like there is nothing in common anymore.** Many friendships start with a common interest. It could be that your kids play on the same soccer team, you've taken a class together, or you both enjoy the same hobby. But how often have these friendships stalled when that common bond was no longer at the center of your friendship? Probably all too often. You miss your old friend,

but somehow you feel like the relationship was based on a common interest that no longer applies (for example, the kids have all grown up or you stopped going to the same tennis club). How often do we assume that friendships work this way without really stopping and thinking about the actual value of the relationship?

Hopefully, now you realize the importance your tribe plays in shaping your **NET WEALTH**. Your tribe is the people you're traveling with on your journey toward becoming your Future Self. They are vested in your future, and you in theirs. Relationships, whether with family, close friends, or a secondary group, must align and have an emotional connection. Pick your tribe wisely, and your journey in life will be much more enjoyable.

CHAPTER 11
HEALTH

> *"I think that age as a number is not nearly as important as health. You can be in poor health and be pretty miserable at 40 or 50. If you're in good health, you can enjoy things into your 80s."*
>
> ~BOB BARKER, GAME SHOW HOST

I'M NOT TELLING YOU ANYTHING YOU DON'T ALREADY KNOW when I say that your health influences everything you do and how you feel about your life. When people enter retirement, many have already crossed paths with a significant health scare. If not themselves, someone in their peer group has had a scare. Maybe it was cancer, a broken hip, or the onset of diabetes. When faced with a major health care issue, everything in your life seems to stop, doesn't it?

Our health is everything when we don't have it, but we often ignore it until we face an issue that seriously derails our daily life.

In the western world, we've grown accustomed to an unhealthy lifestyle of sedentary living, poor diet, and excessive food consumption. Consequently, today the average male in the US is, on average, ten pounds heavier than a couple of decades ago without being any taller. Thirty percent of US adults over the age of sixty-five are considered medically obese.

The net result is that we're working against ourselves. Health care technology has improved dramatically over the last few decades, but technology and medication only correct what's gone wrong. The health care system of westernized countries is set up to remedy what we've done to our bodies due to our lifestyle choices. Our health care system isn't set up to teach us healthy practices and disease-prevention tactics required to live longer and better than previous generations.

The average person's approach to their health care is to play defense. Medical technology and medications help you keep diseases at bay, but we all know that no game in life is won by defense alone. You must also learn to play offense and be proactive about making lifestyle choices that promote and maintain good health.

According to the World Health Organization (WHO), the average life expectancy for somebody living in the US is seventy-eight-and-a-half years old. The average person can expect to enjoy sixty-eight-and-a-half years of good health. That leaves the average person in poor health for the last ten years of their lives. Is that living well? Wouldn't you rather compress your morbidity (the time in poor health) as short as possible?

This chapter focuses on taking an offensive approach to your health. It's about doing everything possible to be in the best shape for as long as possible to live your life well. None of us knows when our number will be called, but we can make sure our equipment (physical and mental) stays in the best possible shape.

"It is health that is the real wealth, and not pieces of gold and silver."

~MAHATMA GANDHI

There's a good chance we'll live two or three decades in retirement. The longevity bonus gifted to us by medical advances won't matter much if we spend much of the time in ill-health and can't participate in the lifestyle we anticipated.

You might not want to live past one hundred, but you probably want to do everything you can to feel healthy (physically and mentally) for as long as possible. Do you agree?

It's never too late to get proactive about your health. You can influence the rate of aging by leading a healthy lifestyle, but first, let's clear up some widely held misconceptions.

MISCONCEPTION #1: YOUR HEALTH IS ALL ABOUT YOUR GENES

How often have you heard people justify their lifestyle, nutrition, and exercise habits based on their ancestor's genes? They might say, There is no point in eating healthy since I have bad genes, or everybody in my family has died young, so why should I kill myself exercising? Then there's the other extreme: my parents each lived to ninety-five years old and they never exercised! Luckily, I have a good gene pool.

Even among highly educated people, there's a myth that our genes determine our longevity. I held this view for a long time, too. My dad lived to eighty-eight years old, and my mom lived to age ninety-two. Some people have even lived past one hundred on my mom's side of the family. For many years, I held onto the belief that I had good genes and would live into my nineties.

What I didn't know is that genes only account for about 30 percent of a person's longevity—our environment and lifestyle choices account for the other 70 percent. Where we live, what we eat, how we handle stress, our general fitness, and our mental outlook are more important than our genetic makeup.

The gene-pool myth is an excuse without merit. We all have good and bad genes, but our genes aren't preventing us from eating well, exercising, maintaining a healthy body weight, and managing stress. We're in charge of our health choices, which in the long run have a much greater influence on determining our health than our genes.

MISCONCEPTION #2: EVERYBODY AGES AT THE SAME RATE

We like to lump people into age groups and assume that everybody is the same. For example, a person older than sixty-five is placed in the retired bucket. Anyone in their eighties is decrepit, needing daily assistance, and on the verge of death.

Reality is much different because people age differently; the divergence is wide. And, I'm not talking about physical appearance, although, some people age better than others. But what if we looked under the hood? Different body parts age at different rates within each of us. Medical research on identical twins has found that the older we get, the more different we become from a health perspective. Identical twins with different lifestyles and environments have varying health profiles, dispelling the notion that your genes are your destiny. Research, interestingly enough, has shown the same age-related variation within your body parts. Believe it or not, parts of you are younger than you think!

According to medical researchers, there's a difference between our chronological and biological age. Your chronological age is determined by your birthday. Your biological age depends on how healthy you are, not how many candles are on your cake. The wear and tear on your body parts, as determined by your age biomarkers, is how your biological age gets calculated. Biomarkers are metrics. They're based on a large sample of individuals of similar chronological age and correlate to various aspects of one's health.

Everybody ages, but we do it at significantly different rates depending on our environment and lifestyle choices. The point of differentiation often starts much earlier than most people realize. For example, Dr. Dan Belsky of Duke University found evidence of significant differences in biological age in a sample of men of similar chronological age. In his research of midlife male participants clustered around thirty-eight years of age, he found a range of biological ages from thirty to sixty years old. While the study didn't explain why such variations in biological age occurred, Dr. Belsky concluded that environmental influence affects how we age.

Some medical researchers even believe we can reverse the aging process. Let me warn you that this research is in its infancy, but it appears incredibly promising. In a recent small pilot study by Dr. Kara Fitzgerald of the Sandy Hook Clinic, participants lowered their biological age by 3.23 years, on average. How? They followed a diet and lifestyle regimen over two months and abstained from special injections or prescriptions. Dr. Fitzgerald's new book, *Younger You,* details the specifics. Nobody promises eternal youth, but the effect of diet and lifestyle on our health is undeniable.

MISCONCEPTION #3: RELAXING WILL PROLONG YOUR LIFE

There is something to be said about leading a stress-free lifestyle, but is that even possible these days? Life isn't linear, and we all experience ups and downs. As you get older, unexpected health issues have a way of creeping in.

Our parents and grandparents aspired to a life of leisure in retirement, moving to a retirement community in Florida to play endless rounds of shuffleboard and bingo, and attend ice cream socials. After a hectic thirty-year career, this scenario might appear lovely, but do you think packing it in will give you enough out of life for the next twenty or thirty years?

Research in psychology points to humans' inherent need to keep striving. Just because you don't have to go to a job every day doesn't mean you should never exert yourself. If anything, the biggest danger in retirement is becoming even more sedentary than before. Taking it easy may be the worst possible thing for your health.

The tool protecting your health is exercise. You need to keep on moving. You also need to stay engaged mentally. You've heard the saying "use it or lose it," right? Well, it applies to your physical health, too.

A life of leisure might sound great in theory but try doing the same thing every day. I'm pretty sure you'll start dreading your days. You need to keep moving. In the end, your body and mind will pay the price if all you seek is comfort.

MISCONCEPTION #4: I CAN'T DO ANYTHING AT THIS STAGE TO MAKE A DIFFERENCE

Many people admit defeat before even trying. They've led a sedentary lifestyle for so long that they're comfortable with it, and they don't want to change. While we're all experts at rationalizing our behavior, improving your lifestyle and health choices is always beneficial. Clearly, the older you are, the less beneficial these changes will be to your overall health. Still, studies have shown that even individuals in their sixties and seventies significantly improve their overall health after participating in wellness programs that emphasizing diet, stress management, and exercise.

Changing your habits to adopt a healthier lifestyle, such as getting adequate nutrition, better sleep, and more exercise, won't be easy—at first. Developing a new habit takes a long time until it becomes automated, but the benefits of a healthier lifestyle won't take long to kick in. It doesn't take long for your energy levels to rise and for you to feel better.

With these misconceptions out of the way, what does science tell us about how we actually age?

WHAT REALLY HAPPENS TO YOU AS YOU AGE?

Does this sound like a painful section to read? Who wants to be reminded of their flabby abs, lined foreheads, or gray hair? We look at pictures of ourselves from twenty or thirty years ago and are amazed at how good-looking we were—slim bodies, nice smiles, no wrinkles.

Time takes a toll on our appearances. Not to say we're not happy with ourselves, but let's be honest, most people prefer the vibrant, youthful-looking version of themselves.

Aging brings many changes. Some changes are visible, and some are subtle. Some are more obvious, and some remain hidden from us but are more visible to others. Aging isn't something that happens overnight or when you sail past some magical chronological age.

The human body starts aging when we reach our maximum reproductive capacity. We may not have noticed it initially, but the signs were there.

Think about all those world-class athletes who suddenly seem to lose their ability to perform at the highest level. Sometimes you'll hear commentators say the athletes have lost a step or two, or they must rely on their veteran moves to offset their physical decline.

Have you noticed any of the following physical changes to your body over the last twenty years?

- You look shorter in the mirror. Did you know that, on average, people lose about two inches of height by the time they reach age eighty? No wonder we looked so good in our thirties when we were at our tallest. It's not just you. We all shrink.
- You have gained weight in all the wrong places. News flash: your body composition changes with age. You lose muscle mass, and the percentage of your body mass composed of fat increases with age.
- You notice wrinkles on your face and hands and some dark spots on your skin. As we age, our skin loses elasticity, and we become more susceptible to bruising. And those dark spots all over your body? Yeah, they'll keep coming.
- Your natural hair (if you have any left, gents) color is gray or white. The texture of your hair may also change. My friend Mark once told me, "It starts growing in all the wrong places!"
- You can't hear people speak, especially in noisy places. Even worse, you can't understand what young toddlers are telling you so excitedly. Our hearing drops off as we age, and we can't hear higher pitches as well.
- Everything seems a bit duller. Not only does your hearing suffer, but so do your other senses.

Unfortunately, that's what's only visible to you. Aging also happens on the inside, such as the loss of bone density and muscle mass. Your major organs don't work as well—your lungs become less efficient at pumping oxygen to your blood, your kidneys don't remove waste as quickly, and your heart becomes less able to combat stress.

WHAT ABOUT THE MENTAL SIDE?

Okay, we have all heard the jokes about becoming senile. Heck, we might have even made the joke ourselves as we struggled to remember where we parked our car or recall an old friend's name we used to hit up for a game of tennis.

We laugh it off, but deep down, we worry that it's the beginning of a long descent into forgetfulness, or even worse. In survey after survey of newly minted retirees, one of the greatest concerns is losing one's mental faculties. Getting Alzheimer's is the worst fear.

But is becoming senile and forgetful our inevitable destiny? Does the natural aging process lead us down this path?

Let's look at what medical research has to say on this topic. Here are some of the summary findings of Dr. Mark Williams, author of *The Art and Science of Aging Well*:

- Normal aging affects the brain through slower processing speeds and some short-term memory loss and retention.
- The ability to interconnect ideas and concepts *improves* with age.
- Your brain health is greatly affected by your overall physical health, interests, and lifestyle.
- Your brain does shrink with age, but most of the loss is due to lower water within the neurons. Your brain regenerates through a process called neuroplasticity.
- As with physical signs of aging, there is tremendous variability from individual to individual. Some people remain sharp as a tack until they die, and others show early signs of mental deterioration.

Our health is a function primarily of our environment and lifestyle choices, but the fact remains that our physical and mental health decline with age. Aging is not optional, but our choices influence the rate of decline. Genes only play a small role.

The goal for most people should be to live longer in good health—to keep the time you spend in bad health at a minimum. When it's time to go, you hope there's not much warning, but as long as you're living, you want to enjoy life to its fullest. You'll need your health for that, but luckily, your actions and behaviors have much to say about that.

CHOOSING TO LIVE LONGER AND BETTER: YOUR AGING PLAN

We all know that we can't postpone getting older. Death is eventual. However, we can live as healthy as possible for a long time and live well along the way.

There's much we can do to tilt the odds in our favor.

We all want to enjoy our retirement years. We want to remain independent as long as possible and not burden our families. We want to do the things we enjoy, even though we realize we'll slow down eventually.

"Take care of your body. It's the only place you have to live."

~JIM ROHN, AUTHOR, ENTREPRENEUR,
AND MOTIVATIONAL SPEAKER

Let's start with the body.

Here are some ideas to live a healthy lifestyle:

Watch your diet. Preferably prepare meals at home, emphasizing a plant-based diet. Dr. Marc Agronin, the author of the book *The Dementia Caregiver*, swears by the MIND diet, which includes generous portions of fruits and vegetables, fish, legumes, chicken, and olive oil while refraining from processed foods, sugar, whole-fat dairy, and red meat. At-home meals typically have 30 percent fewer calories than restaurant meals.

Poor diet is the number one cause of death and long-term disability in the US.

Maintain a healthy body weight. Obesity is linked to many issues, such as diabetes, heart disease, and high blood pressure. Keep your body mass index

(BMI) between nineteen and twenty-five. I know it's not easy to do, and the global trend has seen the average BMI rise. Fight this trend for own survival. Your metabolism slows five percent every decade after the age of thirty. Don't eat like your younger self; you'll only find maintaining a healthy weight harder.

Watch your sweet tooth. Sugar intake is becoming a key public health issue, contributing to major adverse effects. Sugar makes your blood insulin levels spike. High-sugar diets are associated with an increased risk of many diseases, including heart disease, the number one cause of death worldwide. High-sugar diets can also lead to obesity, inflammation, high triglyceride levels, and high blood pressure.

Drink alcohol in moderation. That means drink a lot less than you think. Most doctors prefer you have no more than one drink per day. If you drink, make it red wine (your liver will thank you). Excessive alcohol consumption lowers the body's immunity to disease.

Never smoke. Enough said.

Watch your bedside manner. Get a good night's sleep, and possibly even take some naps. Who doesn't love waking up all refreshed and raring to go? Sleep is essential to your health. Experts recommend between seven to eight hours of sleep a night.

Walk, jog, or run but move. You could even take a spin or Zumba class to get your heart pumping. The optimal aerobic training involves maintaining between 60 and 80 percent of your maximum heart rate for between thirty and forty-five minutes. Your maximum heart rate is calculated as 220 minus your age. I recently turned sixty years old, so my maximum heart rate is 160. Ideally, I should exercise at least three times a week and maintain my heart rate between 96 and 128 beats per minute. Get yourself a heart monitor.

Aerobic exercise has several beneficial effects on your physical health. It has been shown to lower your risk for stroke, diabetes, and certain types of cancer. On top of that, it improves your mental and emotional energy.

Pump up with strength training to build muscle strength. You don't have to be all jacked up, but you should do enough strength training to overcome what doctors refer to as sarcopenia. Sarcopenia is the gradual loss of muscle mass that begins in your mid-thirties.

Both men and women should do strength training. It doesn't have to involve using free weights. You may prefer exercise machines, which are easier for many people to use. Or work out at home using minimal equipment. You can use elastic bands for resistance training or old-fashioned exercises such as planks, pushups, and squats work too. The goal is to reduce your body's frailty. Two or three times a week for between thirty and forty-five minutes should suffice.

Stretch to increase flexibility and build your balance. Muscles stiffen with age, and the risk of falling increases. Dr. Mark Williams' book, *The Art and Science of Aging Well,* recommends doing flexibility and balance training ten to fifteen minutes daily. If you enjoy group lessons, you're in luck; try yoga, Tai Chi, or Barre.

We all know what to do. Living a healthy lifestyle is less about knowledge than a commitment to the health of your Future Self.

DON'T FORGET TO SHARPEN YOUR MENTAL GAME AS WELL

It is important to focus not solely on your physical health. Your body is connected to your mind and brain. A healthy lifestyle should focus the body, mind, and brain.

"Live as if you were to die tomorrow. Learn as if you were to live forever."

~MAHATMA GANDHI, POLITICAL ETHICIST

What are some things you can do to feel good and stay mentally sharp?

Keep learning new things. It might be learning to speak Spanish or learning how to build a rock wall. It might be learning more about the environment or how to salsa dance. As discussed in chapter nine, everybody should embrace becoming a lifelong learner.

It's not true that creativity declines with age. In fact, the ability to connect things and events while interpreting the context at hand increases with life experience and wisdom.

Challenge your brain. Medical researchers have found that the brain thrives on novelty and new challenges. Doing the same things over and over is highly unlikely to challenge your brain. You need to innovate. If you never try anything new, your connections in your brain will atrophy in a process known as synaptic pruning.

Our brains grow (literally) based on our actions and experiences. The brain is constantly being reshaped by a process called brain plasticity. Feed your brain new experiences, and it will keep on building interconnections.

Tackling something new is what's important. As Eleanor Roosevelt once said, "Do one thing every day that scares you."

Going through the same daily routine simply re-enforces existing brain connections, but novelty is necessary to build new connections. Make it part of your daily routine to challenge your brain.

Practice mindfulness. We all need to learn to slow down our thoughts at times. Many of the nitty-gritty issues that annoy us daily will lessen in importance the more we quiet our minds.

Mindfulness, when practiced through meditation, enables us to lower our stress levels and enjoy the present better. Reducing stress in our fast-moving society is becoming increasingly necessary for ensuring a healthy body, mind, and brain.

There are many forms of meditation, and I don't practice any one form. For me, mindful meditation is more about sitting in quiet first thing in the morning and slowing down whatever is going through my head at the moment.

MANAGING STRESS IS A LIFELONG SKILL WORTH CULTIVATING

We all endure difficult periods in our lives. Stress is a part of modern living. Yet, stress left unmanaged over a long period can cause significant health problems. At a minimum, stress robs us of much-needed energy and leaves us feeling exhausted. We may feel burned-out and lack the motivation to enjoy life's things that would typically bring us great pleasure.

Our brains are programmed to deal with stress through the fight or flee response. When we feel stress, our body pumps out increasing amounts of adrenaline and cortisol. Blood gets diverted to our muscles, and our senses are on high alert. None of this is harmful, but chronic stress can result in serious medical issues, such as reduced resistance to infections and illness. In fact, chronic stress acts as an aging accelerator, affecting your physical body and your mindset. Chronic stress can also lead to severe emotional problems such as loneliness, anxiety, and depression.

According to the 2020 American Psychological Association annual stress survey, 80 percent of participants reported at least one physical or emotional symptom of stress. We live in a stressful environment and finding ways to become more resilient and manage the stress has never been more critical.

What if you are suddenly confronted with a stressful situation? Here are some ideas:

- **Write your thoughts down**. Journaling daily is one of the best ways to find clarity and slow our minds down. Once you write something on paper, many of our fears do not look as overwhelming.
- **Visualization is a close cousin of journaling**. The idea is to visualize happy experiences from the past or things that bring you inner peace, which will shift attention away from the source of immediate stress. Maybe it is a memory from growing up, a favorite tree, or a special place in your heart.
- **Go for a walk, preferably surrounded by nature**. Look up, around, and down. Look at the tree leaves swaying in the wind and listen to the sound of birds. If you're lucky enough to live close to a

place with water, look at the rhythm of the water and listen carefully. Close your eyes. Breathe.
- **Breathe.** Celebrity doctor Andrew Weil is a huge fan of breath work for dealing with stress. We often think of breathing as a purely automatic response, but by consciously measuring your breaths in and out, you can gain control over your emotions.
- **Listen to calming music.** This technique works wonders for me. Many years ago, as part of a corporate retreat, I was tested to see what would lower my immediate stress level. For some people, it's moving around. For others, it's breathing; for me, it's listening to music.
- **Think of the worst possible outcome and how likely it really is.** This idea comes from blogger Tim Ferris. Stress is a manifestation of fear. Tim's suggestion is to stop and think about what might actually go wrong, then quantify the likelihood of the worst outcome actually happening. This simple reframing will lower your stress as you realize that our worst fears hardly ever come true.
- **Pray or appeal to a spiritual power.** I'm a bit reluctant to bring this up because many people frown at mentioning religion. But I find slowing down and speaking to a higher power tends to calm me down. I was raised Catholic, but when I pray, I talk to a higher power that doesn't fit any religious belief system. I simply believe that if you really need help, there will be mysterious ways in which assistance will come your way. That belief by itself calms me down.

START WHERE YOU ARE RIGHT NOW

There is no tomorrow if there is not a today. Get going. Investing in your health is analogous to investing in your financial future. Taking that first step is hard, but little steps, taken consistently, yield many benefits.

Many people start small because that's all they can do: walking around the block, saying no to a nightcap, doing three pushups, eating one portion instead of two, going to bed half an hour earlier, or starting a meditation practice. It's never too late to start living a healthier lifestyle.

Stanford University Professor Dr. B.J. Fogg says there are three ways to develop new habits: have an epiphany, change your environment, or start by changing in tiny ways. Having an epiphany is too rare to be useful. That leaves us with two other possibilities.

Changing your environment, your surroundings, and who you associate with most frequently is an excellent strategy for creating lasting lifestyle changes. Want a healthier, more physically active lifestyle? Try living in a community with easy access to nature trails and physical activities, such as swimming and exercise lessons. As psychologist Dr. Benjamin Hardy has said, "While you're in an enriched environment, your desired behavior is automated and outsourced." A healthy environment will almost automatically lead to an upgrade in lifestyle.

A faster, more efficient method for creating change is to seek to implement small changes in the intended direction. That's what Dr. B.J. Fogg recommends in his book, *Tiny Habits*. Start by implementing small steps. It's not necessary to target next year's Boston Marathon. Instead, target walking around the block or refraining from eating a bowl of ice cream after dinner.

Do something easy, but do it consistently. A new habit takes time to form. A friend of mine once told me that (for him) running was as automated as brushing his teeth. That's your goal—start a new behavior that you know will lead to a healthier lifestyle to the point where you continue doing it routinely without even thinking about it.

You may be focused on changing your diet. Or you may want to start strength training to bolster your muscles and bones. You may want to do yoga to increase your flexibility, balance, and mental focus. Whatever your goal is, the key is acting now.

Here are some ideas to make your new behavior stick:

- **Make exercise fun again.** Don't just do one thing over and over. Try several different ways of exercising. For example, intersperse individual workouts with group lessons. Try working out hard one day, followed by a day focused on a more socially oriented activity,

such as participating in a walking group in your neighborhood. Mix cardio with strength and balance training.
- **Start a "quiet" time practice.** I have never been able to get into a meditation practice. Instead, I sit quietly, breathe slowly, and turn my thoughts to a place of peace and gratitude. I only do this for a couple of minutes, but I find that my mindset and emotions are more balanced after doing so.
- **Eat healthier and control your portions.** We've all heard this before, right? We know what to do, but why does that pasta dish and bread look so good? We all need some indulgences in life, but when it comes to your body and energy level, the fuel you put in it determines the quality of your daily experience. The payoff of healthy eating is immediate. Your energy levels go up, and over time, you miss your "favorite" foods less and less.
- **Feed your brain with something fun.** What is something that has always intrigued you? Your brain loves novelty. Learning something for pure joy is a great way to exercise your brain.

CONSIDERATIONS FOR YOUR FUTURE SELF

How do you see yourself aging? Do you have a mental picture of how you will look and feel when you celebrate your eightieth birthday?

Many successful aging practices impact your physical, mental, and emotional health. I'm talking about things exercise, nutrition, sleep, mental challenges, and handling stress.

Research has shown that your genetic makeup is only a part of how well you age. The biggest influence over the aging process is how you choose to live. Luckily your lifestyle is under your control.

Given the focus on disease management in western medical practices rather than preventive health care, it's time to play offense with our bodies, brains, and minds. It's up to each one of us to work proactively on our health by following a lifestyle that, at minimum, has a plan for:

- Diet
- Sleep

- Exercise
- Stress management
- Mental and social stimulation

It's never too late to get started Start with baby steps if you have to; remember, small actions compound big gains over the long term. Your Future Self will thank you.

CHAPTER 12
ACTING ON YOUR PLAN

"Happiness is not something readymade. It comes from your own actions."

~DALAI LAMA, SPIRITUAL LEADER

The key to thriving in retirement is achieving balance and coherence among all aspects of your life. Having a large 401(k) balance doesn't offset the pain and misery of having poor relationships. Having great relationships but chronic health issues that keep you from enjoying them is also a poor tradeoff. Imagine sitting in a large, beautiful home tucked away in the woods with nothing to do. No one wants a retirement like that.

In the end, all areas comprising our **NET WEALTH** are important. You need all areas of your life aligned with your Future Self. Just like championship sports teams must be proficient at offense and defense, you also need to think proactively and reactively to do well in retirement. You need an offense to build a life that you look forward to and leaves you fulfilled, and you need a defense to deal with the inevitable decline that normal aging brings by being proactive about your physical, mental, and emotional health. The future is in our hands, but only if we have a solid game plan and execute it well.

I hope you decide to pursue a retirement full of possibilities. I hope you take up the challenge of designing a life seeking joy and fulfillment in the form of your Future Self. Dreaming and striving to achieve your goals isn't only for young people. Retirement gives you the freedom to spend your time on activities and pursuits you find meaningful, but you'll have to face your journey knowing full well that you'll face roadblocks along the way. I want your vision of your Future Self to be so strong and motivating that you view these challenges as bumps in the road rather than insurmountable roadblocks cutting your journey short.

After reading and doing the work in the previous chapters, you should better understand what areas in your life require your attention and planning. One thing I know for certain is this: Thinking and planning are not enough. You have to take consistent action. In this chapter, we'll add to the foundation you've built to create an action plan, so you know the exact steps you need to take next.

BUILDING YOUR ACTION PLAN

In our action plan, there are four key questions to answer:

- Where are you today?
- Where do you want to be?
- How are you going to get there?
- Are you fully committed to your transformation?

The Transformation Gap

- Where are you today?
- Where do you want to be?
- Are you willing to take Action & get through the "Messy Middle"?

NET WEALTH – HOW?
- Nest
- Earnings
- Time Allocation
- Work
- Emotional Energy
- Achievements
- Learning
- Tribe
- Health

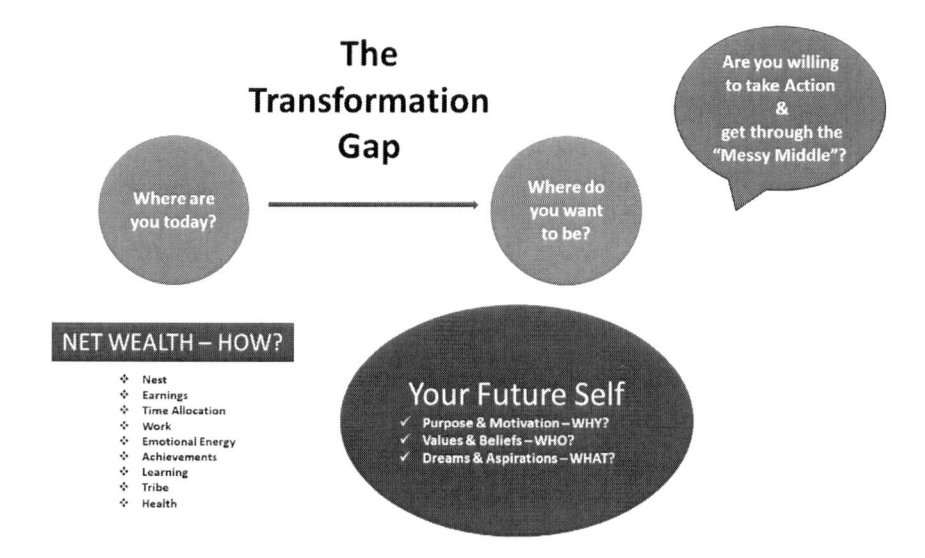

Your Future Self
- ✓ Purpose & Motivation – WHY?
- ✓ Values & Beliefs – WHO?
- ✓ Dreams & Aspirations – WHAT?

QUESTION #1: WHERE ARE YOU TODAY?

Let's recap all the components of your **NET WEALTH** and where you currently stand:

- **NEST**: Are you happy where you live? Do you need to move? Is your environment conducive to the lifestyle you want to lead?
- **EARNINGS**: Do you have enough cash flow to support your desired lifestyle? Do you know how to replace your income with investment and human capital activities?
- **TIME**: Are you consciously allocating your time toward enjoyable and fulfilling activities? Or are you busy for busy's sake—a hamster on a treadmill with no sense of direction?
- **WORK**: How are you using your experience and skills gained over your career to stay engaged in society? The benefits of working go beyond getting paid.
- **EMOTIONAL ENERGY**: You need energy to enjoy life to its fullest. Energy can be physical, mental, or emotional. Ultimately, your emotions drive your behavior. Gaining control over your emotions is a life skill to be cultivated.

- **ACHIEVEMENTS**: We all need to believe that we matter and have something to give. Our achievements represent what we value most. We all have dreams, but we need to turn dreams into goals and goals into tangible action steps.
- **LEARNING**: Learning begins at birth, but many people take a break once they get busy with their careers, families, and other life events. Retirement represents an excellent time to restart your learning.
- **TRIBE**: Your relationships with family and friends give meaning to your life. Are there relationships you need to patch up? Are you investing time and energy into all your most important relationships? Are you cultivating new friendships?
- **HEALTH**: Your health influences everything in your life. Are you doing everything in your power to give yourself the best chance of living a long, productive life? The goal is to live longer and better.

I suggest jotting down your thoughts on paper. To make things easy, rate yourself from one (very unhappy) to ten (very happy) on each component of your **NET WEALTH** in the following table. Be honest with yourself. You're the only one seeing these grades.

	CATEGORY	Your Current Situation — How happy are you with the different areas of your life?	Current Rating 10=Very Happy 1=Very Unhappy
N	NEST	With my current home, lifestyle, and environment?	
E	EARNINGS	With my financial resources and how I am managing them?	
T	TIME	How I am spending my time on the things that matter to me?	
W	WORK	With my work and using all my skills and knowledge?	
E	EMOTIONS	With my level of emotional energy and balance?	
A	ACHIEVEMENTS	With the pursuit of my dreams and meaningful goals?	
L	LEARNING	With my ongoing efforts to continue learning new things?	
T	TRIBE	With my relationships both with family and friends?	
H	HEALTH	With my physical and mental health?	

If you have any areas that are tens, congratulations! You might need some refinements in those categories, but you're mostly set. In my experience, most people rate themselves between a five and an eight. In what areas of your life are you already close to your vision of your Future Self? Maybe it's how you spend your time or the close relationships you have in your life. These areas need nurturing and nourishment like all areas in your life, but probably not a drastic overhaul from your current situation.

On the other hand, if you have some low grades in the mix, you know where you need to focus your attention. Most of us fit this profile. We might have fives or even lower ratings in some areas of our lives. These areas need our attention. Other areas of our lives are great, so it's more about sustaining than improving.

When I rate myself, two areas that I feel need my attention are my emotional energy and my overall level of physical fitness. Being in my sixties, I feel like I need to fortify these two areas to prepare myself for the inevitable bumps in the road as I get older. In the past, I've let my emotions get the best of me, but I know that in the future, I will need to tap into this energy source more to compensate for lower levels of physical and mental energy. Similarly, regarding my fitness, I know that preserving muscle mass will be essential to improved quality of life. I also know that my flexibility needs improvement. I don't enjoy anything about stretching, but I recognize that by waiting, all I'm doing is making it harder for myself down the road.

Most of us have postponed or even ignored some of these areas. It's incredibly easy to assume that everything is fine or that it will all work out. For example, many of my clients have thought about finances and where to live. They might have also spent time thinking about their optimal lifestyle and how to stay healthy. What they often haven't thought about is how they will spend their time in retirement, use their skills, find meaningful experiences or work, what other goals they would like to achieve, and how their emotional makeup may change in retirement.

This might be the first time people are asked to sit down and take the time to think about the entirety of their lives. The retirement industry is, for the most part, focused on finances, housing, and travel. Those are important areas of your life but not the only areas that require attention.

The whole point of these exercises is to go from broad to specific. The goal is to gain clarity and focus on what's important to you. By gaining clarity and focus, you'll take the right actions to progress on your goals. Your journey to your Future Self will go smoother. You won't be as prone to the indecision and uncertainty of the messy middle that we all go through as we transform ourselves. Going through this exercise will bring clarity to your thinking.

As we discussed in chapter two, is your life built on a solid foundation, or do you need to re-examine the three pillars: your values and beliefs, your aspirations, and your purpose?

The whole point of thinking ahead to the next phase in your life is to become crystal clear about the future, which leads us to the next question.

"True success, true happiness lies in freedom and fulfillment."

~DADA VASWANI, SPIRITUAL LEADER

QUESTION #2: WHERE DO YOU WANT TO BE?

Presumably, the previous exercise got you thinking about your life in the future. By evaluating the present, you will inevitably think about how you want your life to look ten, twenty, or thirty years down the road. Life is more than just checking off boxes, living day-to-day, and then declaring victory. A well-lived life requires you to identify what brings you happiness and a sense of fulfillment. It combines comfort, pleasure, freedom, legacy, and meaning. It's up to you to design your vision of your Future Self.

Your current and Future Self are two different versions of YOU. We're never a finished product. We're always striving to reach the best version of ourselves, but first, we need to get clear about where we want to be.

Are the three pillars of our Future Self crystal clear? Your **NET WEALTH** components are built on the foundation of your values and beliefs, your dreams, your purpose, and your motivation in life. If the foundation of your Future Self is shaky, it will be hard to act on the components of your **NET WEALTH** that require your immediate attention.

In chapter two, we built upon the three pillars of your Future Self. Here's a refresher for what the three pillars stand for:

Pillar 1: Your Values and Beliefs (WHO)
Pillar 2: Your Dreams and Aspirations (WHAT)
Pillar 3: Your Purpose and Motivation (WHY)

Are you clear on the who, what, and why of your Future Self? Without these foundational inputs, your attention will be all over the map. You won't have the clarity to narrow your priorities to those that impact your life the most.

Before we move on, I need you to get very specific about your Future Self. When you were going through the exercises in chapter two and designing your Future Self, did you become crystal clear?

What are the values and beliefs of your Future Self?
What are your dreams and goals for the future?
What motivates you and gives your life purpose?

Your Future Self is an idealized version of yourself that draws you forward, removes complexity and distractions from your journey, and empowers you to act.

The **NET WEALTH** system provides structure to your journey. Based on how happy you are in different areas of your life, do you see what three actions you can take starting now that will lead you to your Future Self?

A good starting point might highlighting the areas in question one that you rated less than seven. Next, rank the areas of your life that need your attention in order of importance. What three areas of your life would improve your life significantly?

Priority 1:

Priority 2:

Priority 3:

"If you have more than three priorities, then you don't have any."

~JAMES C. COLLINS, AUTHOR AND MANAGEMENT CONSULTANT

Establishing priorities is never easy, but it's part of good decision-making.

We want it all, don't we? Making progress is about picking our battles wisely. Only you know the areas of your life that need your undivided and immediate attention. Working on those areas of your life will bring the most value to your life. You'll have opportunities later to work on the other areas in your life. Don't expect the work ever be done completely. We're always striving to get to our future selves.

Establishing our top priorities is a huge step, but we can't stop there. We need to turn these priorities into tangible goals and action steps. Action is where the rubber hits the road. It's where dreams become reality, or they die from lack of attention. There is no substitute for taking action on specific goals. That's the focus of the next question.

QUESTION #3: HOW ARE YOU GOING TO GET THERE?

The distance between where you currently stand and where you want to be is called the Freedom Gap. It's the gap we hope to navigate to our Future Self. Sometimes, the gap is small, and sometimes, it's large. It may appear insurmountable, but the key, as executive coach Dan Sullivan says, is to "Focus on the Gain, rather than the Gap." By focusing on your progress instead of how far you have left to go, you'll increase your odds of getting to your Future Self. You'll stay focused on actionable steps.

In this section, the emphasis is on embarking on your journey toward your Future Self in clearly defined, tangible action steps. Remember the SMARTER framework introduced in chapter eight?

The wants you listed in the previous question aren't often specific enough. They are wishes you must refine to become SMARTER goals you can actually work on.

You'll need to translate your wants to be:

- Specific (you know the desired outcome)
- Measurable (you can quantify success)
- Actionable (you can translate the goals into tangible results)
- Rewarding (they will improve your life in a significant way)
- Time-bound (your goals have a deadline)
- Emotional (they have an intrinsic meaning for you)
- Reinforcing (they are in sync with your other goals)

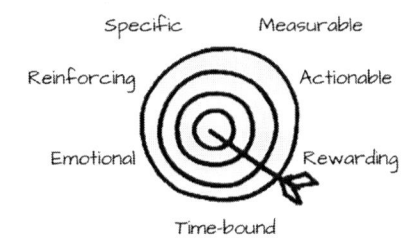

SMARTER GOALS

Specific Measurable
Reinforcing Actionable
Emotional Rewarding
Time-bound

Turning your priorities into SMARTER goals may take a couple of tries. You'll need to refine your thinking until there's no doubt about what you need to do.

For most people, the toughest challenge is being specific enough. It's easy to keep your aspirations high, but that affects your ability to focus and take action. You want to aim for the bullseye, not the entire wall.

Here are a couple of examples of SMARTER goals. Read through them, and then set your goals for each of your top priorities.

SMARTER GOAL EXAMPLES		
CATEGORY	GOAL: Lose Weight	GOAL: Buy a New House
SPECIFIC	10 pounds	Condo in the Mexican Riveria
MEASURABLE	Current weight of 188 pounds	3 bedrooms, min 1400 sq ft, outdoor space
ACTIONABLE	Yes, in the winter go to gym, doctor ok'd	Plenty of supply at reasonable prices
REWARDING	Yes, I feel better when I look better	Yes, will allow me to spend more time in nature
TIME-BOUND	By Dec. 31, 2022	By Dec. 31, 2022
EMOTIONAL	I want to be healthy to play with my grandchildren	I want to be close to my Latin roots
REINFORCING	Being fit improves my mood and mental functioning	Living abroad helps me keep learning
WHY?	To have more energy and remain active	To remain physically active year-round
HOW?	Strength training 2 times/wk, run 4 times/wk	Work with REMAX Mexico and visiting next month

Can you come up with SMARTER goals for each of your priorities?

CATEGORY	Priority 1	Priority 2
SPECIFIC		
MEASURABLE		
ACTIONABLE		
REWARDING		
TIME-BOUND		
EMOTIONAL		
REINFORCING		
WHY?		
HOW?		

Your SMARTER goals are your roadmap. If you're still unsure where to begin, you haven't gotten specific enough. You should be able to share your SMARTER goals with your spouse or a friend, and they should clearly understand what you're trying to do, why, and how. It might take a couple of tries, but it's well worth the time invested in outlining your priorities.

After you outline your SMARTER goals, it's time to take action. Getting started can be difficult, and keeping going can be even harder as roadblocks and detours appear along the way. A big part of you success in becoming your Future Self will depend on your commitment. How much do you value the transformation into your Future Self? Let's go straight to this the next question.

QUESTION #4: ARE YOU FULLY COMMITTED TO YOUR TRANSFORMATION?

Once you know what goals you want to pursue, you need to devise a plan to go from idea to reality. Then you need to act, and that's when it gets tough.

Are you going to follow through with the plan? Are you committed or merely interested in reaching your goals? Commitment requires you to follow a plan, regardless of how many hurdles might get in your way. Being interested gives you an out when the going gets tough. *No one wants to hear —oh well, I tried!*

Many people get so excited about designing a plan that they forget action is required. In most cases, we're talking about a lot of action, doing uncomfortable things, and doing them consistently for a long time. We would've already achieved the goals if the actions weren't uncomfortable and hard.

Marshall Goldsmith, the noted executive coach, talks about people being much better planners than doers. I couldn't agree more. Doing is hard. It requires persevering through adversity. It may involve repetitive tasks that become boring. It may involve being vulnerable. It may involve making invisible progress (to outsiders) for a long time.

Sounds hard, right? Yes, but breaking up the tasks into small actionable chunks is a good start. We go further over time when we focus on the next step or action. Focusing on the enormity of the task can be so daunting that we lose confidence in our ability to get to the finish line.

The SMARTER goals you came up with are your blueprint for success. You must follow the plan to turn what's on paper into reality.

Here are five tools to get you started and, most importantly, keep you going in the face of adversity.

Tool #1: Start today, continue tomorrow. Is there a better time to get started than now? You've done your planning. Now you need to get moving. As simple as that seems, it's a hurdle many people fail to overcome. There is always tomorrow, right? But just like planning to have kids, there will never be an ideal time.

You just have to get started. Don't overthink it. Schedule time in your calendar devoted to your goal and stick to it religiously. What you schedule has a higher chance of getting done. An I'll-get-to-it attitude will most likely lead to fits and starts, culminating in a hard stop. Follow your plan.

After working on your goals for a while, you'll either get bored or face hurdles you'd rather not handle. Now what? You'll be tempted to take a break and look for ways to distract yourself from the hard work.

In your mind, it almost feels like you have already accomplished your goal, but in reality, you still have a way to go. Stopping won't help. Indecision will creep in. Be a pro and keep the streak alive. Star athletes don't wake up in the morning and decide to train. They wake up knowing with certainty that, rain or shine, they will train. It doesn't matter how motivated they feel.

Tool #2: Schedule your action steps. Scheduling is another way to get moving. You might ask yourself: Who needs to schedule something you know you have to do? The reality is that the simple act of writing something down increases the odds of doing it. You may still not act, but you'll be aware of your choice, and the guilt may convince you to take action.

Scheduling time to work on your goals shouldn't be a foreign concept. After all, we schedule a time to wake up, shower, work, have dinner, and go to bed, right? We might not write it down, but we schedule it nevertheless.

If someone else is helping you work on your goals, like a personal trainer or business coach, you likely agree on a schedule, and, in most cases, you pre-pay for the session. Both situations are incentives to get the work done. If you fail to show up, you'll disappoint the other person and forfeit your payment. Not a desirable situation, right? That's why it makes sense to work on goals together. For example, if you and your partner have the same goal of getting fitter, it's much easier to go to the gym together.

On the other hand, if your goals are yours and yours alone, it's important that you schedule your time. When your time is unstructured, it's easy to devise excuses and rationalizations about why you can't get the work done. You'll increase the odds of success by scheduling a day and time dedicated to working on your goals. I like to break up my day in hourly increments, and I always leave at least one day per week for recovery.

Two to three hours of dedicated effort is much better than six to eight hours of unfocused work. So, why not schedule small chunks of time every day and focus on taking small steps forward? Eventually, all those little steps will amount to a marathon, and your goal will be in sight.

"Small deeds done are better than great deeds planned."

~PETER MARSHALL, GAME SHOW HOST

Tools #3: Track your progress. Keep a record of how frequently you work on your goals and the outcome of your efforts. For example, if your goal is to increase your aerobic fitness, you might track how often you exercised, how long you exercised, and the type of activity you did. It doesn't have to be complicated. I track my goals on a piece of paper. You might use your phone or another device. Tracking your efforts ups the ante.

As business strategist Peter Drucker used to say, "What gets measured, gets managed." Tracking is for your benefit only, but you might also want to share your efforts with an accountability partner.

Tracking isn't only good for accountability, but it builds confidence. Even small steps compound into bigger things, giving you more motivation to keep going. Tracking your progress helps you focus on the gains you've made since you committed to your goals.

Tools #4: Stay accountable to a partner. Accountability works similarly, but there's usually a two-way relationship. You are held accountable to a partner, and, in turn, you commit to holding them accountable to their goals. The idea is to share your goals with somebody impartial and report on your progress.

A good accountability partner has a refined BS filter. The BS filter is often on high alert because we lie to ourselves often. We come up with excuses that, on the surface, sound logical, but they're self-imposed. An impartial person can see through our BS and call us out.

Accountability works because we want to be liked, and we don't want to be embarrassed. If you've never had an accountability partner, find somebody who is a good listener and unafraid to ruffle some feathers. They should share your view of personal responsibility and transformation. You want somebody who gives as much as they take in the relationship. Honesty and openness are key attributes to a successful accountability partnership.

Tracking and accountability only work once you've set the direction you want to go. Tracking and accountability aren't meant to bounce ideas around or make you feel better. They are tools to increase your odds of acting and achieving your goals.

Tool #5: Develop your skills or find help. You have two choices if you lack the necessary skills to get the work done. One, develop them yourself by taking a class or finding a mentor. Two, find a way to outsource the activity to an expert.

If you try to tackle a goal that requires expertise outside of your domain, you must allocate more time to the task. You'll have to take the time to learn. If you grow impatient and lose confidence, you'll likely give up.

Rather than giving up, force yourself to learn. You only need to learn the skills required to take action. One way to accelerate your learning is to hire a coach or mentor. Top athletes and CEOs of major corporations do this. If you're having trouble figuring out your life in retirement, why not hire a certified retirement or life coach who can guide you?

Another approach to dealing with a skills gap is outsourcing to an expert who can do the work. Many people outsource a good chunk of their lives to experts, such as doctors, lawyers, and financial advisors. The outsourcing relationship may be long-term or for a couple of years until you acquire the necessary skills.

Execution often stumps people who have well-thought-out goals and the best intentions. If the hurdle is a lack of skills or confidence, don't let that get in the way of taking the time to learn the skill or find an expert.

CONSIDERATIONS FOR YOUR FUTURE SELF

The vision of your Future Self involves deciding who you want to be and where you want to end up—the ideal you aspire to. Where you are today may be a long way from where you want to end up, but acting is the only way to begin your transformation.

Great plans without action remain wishes. People generally like making plans. They can see the possibilities, but where the real progress toward your Future Self takes place is where the rubber meets the road.

Without action, nothing will happen. You can have all the money and time in the world, but if you get discouraged from acting, you'll remain exactly where you are today. Your possibilities will become certainties.

A retirement with possibilities requires work. It requires a vision, a plan, and a system to turn your dedicated efforts from mere dreams into goals and goals into tangible outcomes. Most people get stuck in the middle as they transition from full-time work to their next phase in life. Retirement might be depicted as a piece of cake by the traditional retirement industry, but in reality, it often proves difficult, at least at first, for many people accustomed to the predictability of a structured schedule, as well as an identity cultivated over decades of work that no longer fits. In the next chapter, we will focus on transitioning from working full-time to designing the type of life most suited to your vision of your Future Self.

CHAPTER 13
GETTING UNSTUCK FROM THE MESSY MIDDLE

"The first step towards getting somewhere is to decide that you're not going to stay where you are."

~UNKNOWN

IT'S NORMAL TO FEEL MANY EMOTIONS AT THIS STAGE IN YOUR retirement journey: anxious, worried, and overwhelmed. Most of us have these feelings at different times. We go from elated to worried about the next two or three decades of life, followed by the exact opposite emotions. Hopefully, though, you're also feeling excited about a retirement that's full of possibilities. This is an opportunity to lead the life you want, become the main character in your life movie, and become your Future Self.

Just because you're looking forward to your next phase in life doesn't mean the transition will be straightforward or painless. Transitions are always difficult, even when you have clear priorities and an action plan. They involve external and internal change; most people don't adapt to change overnight. It usually involves fits and starts. Everybody goes through a messy middle" during a transition, but your circumstances and the clarity you have of your vision for your Future Self determines how long you stay stuck in the mud.

You shouldn't expect to find a formula or recipe for whizzing through your transition into retirement. There's no such thing because change is primarily driven internally. You'll go through different levels of grief, awareness, denial, recognition, and excitement—the whole enchilada of human emotions.

In this chapter, I want to forewarn you that the transition into retirement may not be as seamless and effortless as those glossy commercials depict. I want to give you some rope to experiment and, ultimately, arrive at the life that serves the vision of your Future Self in the context of your values, beliefs, dreams, and motivations best. We'll discuss some strategies for dealing with change and getting you unstuck from the uncertainty and indecision of the messy middle.

YOU'RE UNLIKELY TO GET TO YOUR NEW LIFE WITHOUT SOME RESISTANCE

Change is never straightforward. You might be excited to retire, and you might also be feeling some butterflies in your stomach. Retirement represents a significant change, and you don't really know what to expect. You see the positives (primarily more free time), but there's also uncertainty about what it's really like to retire.

Remember the following diagram from chapter one? Can you see yourself somewhere along the continuum of change? Are you fighting the end? Are you stuck in the messy middle? Or are you already at the new beginning in your retirement journey?

Phases of Change

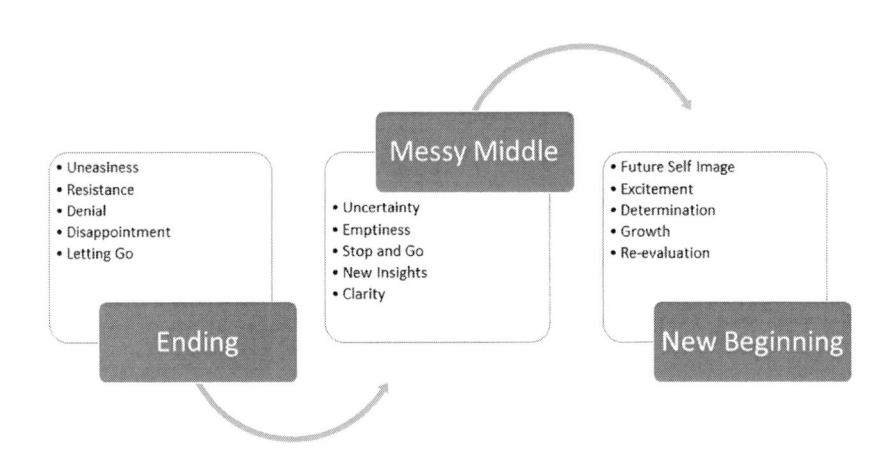

Ending
- Uneasiness
- Resistance
- Denial
- Disappointment
- Letting Go

Messy Middle
- Uncertainty
- Emptiness
- Stop and Go
- New Insights
- Clarity

New Beginning
- Future Self Image
- Excitement
- Determination
- Growth
- Re-evaluation

Most people view retirement as an external event. Your last paycheck was at the end of March, and now you're retired. You need to start drawing down your savings to fund your lifestyle, and your commute time has shrunk to zero. Those are all big changes, but ones you've anticipated. What is discussed less often are the internal changes—what you're feeling inside as you transition through this new phase of life. The internal changes are the ones that cause most people to stumble. Let's review what the change might really involve.

First, there's the recognition that something has ended. That might take time to get used to. You're no longer a player at work. Your job is now being done by somebody else who wants to put their imprint on the position. Ok, you're no longer part of the team. You are no longer Joe or Sally, employed by company XYZ. Many people struggle to admit their career has ended. It can be even more difficult when retirement is forced upon you because of health issues or ageism in the workplace. I certainly struggled to admit that my career as a portfolio manager was over. Eventually, we all realize it's over, and it's time to move on. But the question then becomes: Moving on to what?

That question is usually accompanied by a period of indecision and uncertainty—the messy middle. This is the phase when retirees often find themselves treading water as they struggle to find a new identity and way of being. Who are you now without your career? Is it possible that it's over? Do you have any skills beyond those acquired during your career? What do you even like to do? These questions started bubbling up for me when I went through this stage. I wasn't sure what I wanted to do, and I wasn't sure what I could do. One day I felt optimistic about exploring a new business opportunity, and the next day I questioned whether I had what it took to make the business work. Then it was on to the next idea, and so forth. I went back and forth for a long time, asking myself the same questions repeatedly.

Some people live a long time in the messy middle. They get stuck in the never-ending in-between and may never emerge on the other side. They may never get to a new beginning. They may never be fulfilled, but for those who navigate through the messy middle's ups and downs to find clarity and direction, a new beginning awaits. Clarity and a sense of direction come in the form of their Future Selves. Fortunately, I found my way out of the messy middle, but it took me several years and much introspection. Whenever moving forward proved difficult or uncomfortable, I kept trying to go back to my old life until I recognized I was my worst enemy. I was wasting time acting like a baby (my words). I had to stop feeling ashamed and disappointed. I found a way to replace those negative feelings with excitement when I felt called to start a retirement advisory business; to help people like myself get unstuck and pursue a life of possibilities rather than regrets.

Retirement begins when one's full-time career end, but instead of jumping into a new life, many people get stuck holding onto their work identity. I always thought that I was good at dealing with change, but now I realize that transitioning to a new identity is a really challenging transformation for most people—and one that we all must conquer if we're to truly enjoy our next phase of life. The alternative is to get stuck in the messy middle. I've seen too many people get stuck because they couldn't overcome the fear and uncertainty of not knowing how to overcome the obstacles.

I don't want you to get stuck in the messy middle. You already know what to do. You have a vision for your Future Self, and you understand the areas of your **NET WEALTH** that require your attention. However, change is never easy, and anyone can get stuck. I know you have the best intentions, but we're human. In this chapter, I give you six tools—reminders of what we've already covered in previous chapters so that you can maintain momentum and keep progressing toward your goals.

"Have a bias toward action – let's see something happen now. You can break that big plan into small steps and take the first step right away."

~INDIRA GHANDI, FORMER INDIAN PRIME MINISTER

Tool #1: Have patience. I am not a patient person, and I don't know many people who are. We all want to reach our goals as quickly as possible without much effort. We don't want to hear about hurdles along the way.

However, the real world doesn't work this way. Anything worth achieving requires dedication, effort, and, unfortunately, time. We all know that. Michael Jordan didn't become the greatest basketball player of all time without a considerable investment of time and effort, both physical and mental. Comedian Steve Martin toiled in obscurity for decades before the world was ready to see his genius. The Human Genome Project was conceived in 1988, but the research wasn't finalized until 2001.

Your goals may not be as ambitious or far-reaching as others' goals, but they are monumental to you, nonetheless. When we think of our goals, we often see ourselves at the finish line, but we tend to skip all the intermediate steps that enable us to reach the summit. Invariably, these intermediate steps are the ones that require the most dedication and belief. Nobody needs encouragement at the start or finishing line of a marathon.

Think of reaching a goal like scaling a large mountain. Do you think you can get to the top of K2 in a day? Think again. When we first decide on a goal, we immediately set our eyes on the prize. We look at the mountain top and imagine how nice it would be to be at the top. Soon, we realize that we have a lot of work ahead of us and feel a bit discouraged.

One of the mental tricks used by experienced mountaineers is to focus on one step at a time and set their sights only a short distance ahead. Success becomes taking the next step, followed by many more after that. Rome wasn't built in a day, and neither is your Future Self.

"The journey of a thousand miles begins with one step."

~LAO TZU, CHINESE PHILOSOPHER

Tool #2: Reduce complexity by taking tiny steps. Stanford Professor B.J. Fogg believes the key to sticking to a habit is to start with what he calls "tiny" steps. The example he loves to use is flossing one tooth. Only after flossing one tooth becomes automatic does he recommend flossing all one's teeth.

Similar to flossing your teeth, all goals require work and commitment. By starting in tiny ways, we won't get discouraged by having to go from A to Z in one quick jump. The two keys are: get started and then keep going.

Some tiny habits may appear ridiculously small at first blush.

Say your goal is to write a book. Some writing gurus recommend starting the process of writing a book by writing thirty words a day. That sounds crazy, right? You'll never get it done. But writing just thirty words a day gets you started when resistance is the greatest. Consistently overcoming this hurdle of thirty words a day will give you the confidence to push yourself to do more each day. Maybe your next level goal is three hundred or even five hundred words a day.

Taking tiny steps doesn't mean you can't move faster, eventually. By starting small, you simply get the ball rolling. Progress in the right direction, however small the progress is, builds momentum and increases confidence.

Are you making daily investments in your future no matter how small?

Tool #3: Measure the gain rather than the gap. It's so easy to give up when the task ahead appears monumental. People come up with all sorts of rationalizations: *it's not meant to be. It was a crazy, unrealistic goal. It's not the right time. I don't have the right connections or money.* The list of rationalizations goes on and on. All these excuses seem valid, but are they true deal-breakers or merely hurdles?

We often expect things to happen without us breaking a sweat. We set our eyes on the summit, hoping the trail that gets us there doesn't have ruts, steep hills, or dangerous turns. We want a Disney ride that's over in five minutes, and all we have to do at the end is unstrap ourselves.

Wishing is different from doing. A better approach, advocated by business consultant Dan Sullivan is to focus on measuring how far you've come rather than how far you have yet to go. By focusing on your progress, you'll feel better about yourself and have a greater belief in your actions, getting you the results you want.

Few people can set their sights on their goals, and—*voila*—they happen immediately. Most of us, the mere mortals we are, struggle and feel unmotivated often. One way to overcome the inevitable hurdles we all face is to focus on measuring progress rather than how far we still have to go to reach our goal.

Do you know how far you've come?

"The secret of change is to focus all your energy not on fighting the old, but on building the new."

~SOCRATES, GREEK PHILOSOPHER

Tool #4: Reassess your why. Knowing why your goals are important is key to putting in the work. If we lose sight of this, we lose motivation. Any hurdle then becomes a showstopper.

The fastest way to give up is not having a real reason to keep going. If this happens, you might want to look deep within for answers. Was the goal yours in the first place, or was it something that sounded good? Was it somebody else's idea?

Why is the goal important to you? Drill down and ask yourself this question five times until your why becomes crystal clear. Write it down, and read it every day. We can be quite forgetful.

At some point, you may decide that your why is no longer strong enough or relevant to where you are in life, and that's fine. You don't need to keep working on something that has lost meaning to you.

On the other hand, if you decide that your why is still strong and your goal is worth it, you'll gain motivation to find a way despite the hurdles.

Tool #5: Visualize detours and plan for them. We know that it's unrealistic never to expect complications. To combat our tendency to assume that everything will go smoothly, psychologist Gabriele Oettingen suggests using mental contrasting techniques to increase your odds of achieving your goals. Mental contrasting is the practice of visualizing how good it will feel to reach your goal while visualizing the work you'll have to put in and the potential hurdles you might face.

For example, somebody embarking on a weight loss program will visualize how great it will feel to lose thirty pounds. By visualizing the work involved —grueling sessions on a treadmill and lifting weights to exhaustion—the odds of reaching the goal will increase. Mental contrasting involves thinking about the good (the outcome) and the bad (work involved and overcoming obstacles).

Dr. Oettingen has come up with a practice she calls WOOP to help people increase their chances of reaching their goals. WOOP stands for wish, outcome, obstacles, and planning. For our purposes, let's focus on obstacles and planning.

Thinking ahead of time about obstacles, increases the odds of remaining calm and shifting into constructive problem-solving mode when things don't go as planned.

Let's go back to the weight loss example. You probably wouldn't need to lose weight if maintaining your ideal body weight was easy. You know that losing weight is hard. Why? Well, for many reasons. For example, it's hard to go on a run when the weather outside is gloomy.

The chances of achieving your goals increase when you think about potential obstacles you have the power to overcome. If you can control the situation, you can manage it. Don't waste your time thinking about obstacles you can't control.

Obstacles are often imaginary. Sometimes they are real and insurmountable, but those in our heads can be dealt with by engaging in mental contrasting exercises. Knowing the stories you frequently tell yourself can better prepare you when these thoughts and feelings show up..

The "P" in WOOP involves planning—specifically "if-then" planning, sometimes called setting implementation intentions. This step requires you to devise a response plan before the event happens. For example, if you belong to a busy gym and all the treadmills are taken, instead of pouting and leaving, you might decide that if this happens, you'll use the rowing machine or do squats.

If-then planning is a pre-defined script of how you'll react when obstacles appear. You're removing your emotions from your decision-making.

"If you don't change your environment, it will shape you."

~BENJAMIN HARDY, AUTHOR AND PSYCHOLOGIST

Tool #6: Change the environment. Sometimes we need a change in scenery, a shift in our physical environment to refocus on our goals. It could be something as simple as decluttering your desk or moving your furniture around. Sometimes it's a bit more, such as finding an entirely new place to work on your goals. For example, many writers need to separate work from home to get anything done. I once heard Tim Ferris mention that whenever he writes a book, he rents a hotel suite close to his house to remove all triggers at home.

One simple way to improve our environment is to remove distractions. Some distractions are clearly things that divert our attention, such as piles of dirty laundry scattered around the house; others are more subconscious, such as the ping you hear from your smartphone every time somebody sends you a message. The internet, especially social media, has become a major distraction. Many people don't realize how much of their attention is hijacked from chores, smartphones, and online platforms. If you want to focus, you need to remove distractions. That might mean closing all applications on your computer except for the one required to work on your goal. For me, that means no email, no ESPN, and no streaming stock tickers.

Ideally, we want our environment to trigger us positively to help us accomplish our goals. For example, surrounding ourselves with people who have the high standards we aspire to will no doubt rub off on us. The whole concept of masterminds is built on the idea that surrounding yourself with like-minded people with ambitious goals will create positive energy for everybody in the group. The expectations of high performers will influence your own.

Surrounding yourself with people with high personal standards and ambitions is a great strategy; conversely, sometimes, you need to remove people from your inner circle who bring you down. It's hard enough to face obstacles and detours on your own without hearing the negativity of people around you. For example, if you're trying to live a healthier lifestyle, it's almost impossible to do so if your social circle likes to meet every day for happy hour.

ARE YOU PREPARED TO CHANGE TO BECOME YOUR FUTURE SELF?

Change is difficult. Anybody who tells you otherwise isn't talking about themselves. They're talking about a friend or neighbor. You might be really good at managing external change, but the internal transformation required as you transition away from full-time work to your next phase in life will probably prove more challenging.

As you retire, the transformation required to become your Future Self will be fraught with obstacles and detours. Many people stop at the first sign of uncertainty and settle for the life they know.

You can retire to a life of comfort and pleasure, but if you're the type who seeks to keep growing and evolving, you'll want to live a life focused on long-term joy and fulfillment. You will want to explore a retirement full of possibilities. Getting through the messy middle is the price of admission in your journey toward your Future Self. Don't let fear and uncertainty get in the way of your transformation.

CHAPTER 14
A RETIREMENT FULL OF POSSIBILITIES

"There are three constants in life...change, choice, and principles."

~STEPHEN COVEY

LIFE IS ALL ABOUT MAKING CHOICES: THINKING, PLANNING, AND doing. When things don't go according to plan, we must pivot and find a way around obstacles. A lot of what we face in life is beyond our control, but we can choose how we react to those situations; how we'll influence what we do control through our behavior and actions.

There is a lot of randomness in our lives. You never know how exactly things will turn up, even with the best intentions and planning. That's why I think the best approach to leading a life of fulfillment is to create circumstances and situations whereby the odds of success are in your favor, and if things don't work as expected, you can still recover and choose an attractive alternative.

When I first sat down to think about my retirement from full-time work, I decided that my main goal was to give myself as many options or possibilities as possible to live my life on my terms, focused on the things that matter most to me.

As I have spent countless hours researching and writing this book, it dawned on me that sometimes the best thing we can do to clarify our thoughts is to write down a set of principles to guide our thinking. These principles serve as guidance and summarize, to a large extent, our belief systems.

I encourage everybody to come up with their own, but maybe you'll find my principles of value to you and help you get started.

PRINCIPLE #1: SEEK FULFILLMENT, NOT THE EASY LIFE

I may sometimes come across as an idealist, but at the end of the day, I also like to enjoy a nice lifestyle and not worry endlessly about finances. Unfortunately, we can't spend every second of the day on meaningful activities, and sometimes we need to buckle down to the realities of life. Our material comfort is important. The activities we do for pure pleasure may seem trivial to some, but they sprinkle our lives with joy.

For some people, comfort and pleasure are enough. Life is one extended party. For those people, all that is required is that their finances be in solid shape to support their needs. Most people, however, need a little more from life. Comfort and pleasure reside in the bottom half of Maslow's hierarchy of needs. Putting a roof over your head, having enough food, and access to decent health care and entertainment are the basics. But many people need more than just the basics to feel fulfilled.

Most people need to understand the meaning of their lives. Why are they here on earth? What is their purpose? How can they feel like they are contributing to something bigger than themselves? For some, it's about family. For others, it's about community or a social cause. And yet, for others, it's about being kind and positive in their daily interactions with people they may not even know.

Meaning often morphs into a deeper sense of legacy as we get older. Once we're gone from this earth, what lessons and gifts will we have left behind for future generations? Many people think of legacy as money or material goods, but it's so much more. It's about a life well-lived. It's about setting an example of living with grace and dignity even as the aging process takes its toll. It's about a mentoring relationship that can significantly impact someone. It's about showing striving to learn and improve continuously. Not being forgotten is important to people. Leaving a legacy behind that highlights who you were as a person is one of the best ways to be remembered.

Finally, most people want to live on their terms. Having the freedom to do so for as long as possible becomes immensely important as physical and cognitive decline set in. Feeling like a caged tiger is no way to live.

According to palliative nurse Bronnie Ware, one of the most common deathbed regrets that people have is not having lived a life true to themselves. Freedom means removing the self-imposed and societal shackles that often force us to live below our potential.

Seeking fulfillment does not mean that life will be easy, but rather that it will be worth it to you. You will fight through your obstacles and reap the rewards. You will not always be happy, but in the end, you will lead a life that brings a smile to your face, provides peace of mind, and allows you to feel good about what you are leaving behind.

PRINCIPLE #2: INFLUENCE WHAT'S IN YOUR CONTROL AND WHAT TRULY MATTERS TO YOU AND ACCEPT THE REST

When you're young, you think that the world is fair. If you work hard and are a decent human, you'll sail through life with little trouble, right? Well, eventually, we all find out there's a lot of randomness in the world, and our plans are often thwarted by factors we never saw coming. Best intentions and preparation aren't always rewarded. Life isn't fair or predictable, so should we accept fate and allow ourselves to drift with the wind?

If you have chosen the easy life, just accept where you are and live for the moment. But if you have chosen fulfillment as your ultimate goal, you'll need to figure out what is under your control and focus your actions and behaviors on those things that move you forward.

It takes time and life experience to figure out what you can and can't control. I used to believe that I was in control of most issues affecting my life —where I lived, my health, my career, my savings, my marriage, and my friends.

I learned through experience that a lot in life is out of your control. Many marriages end by a unilateral decision, corporate careers vanish with an economic downturn, cancer unexpectedly rears its ugly head, and a 100-year flood occurs this year rather than in the distant future.

Most people focus on the downside of events beyond their control, but there's another side to the coin. Have you ever been totally surprised by an event that completely changed your life—in a positive way? For example, finding the love of your life after a heart-wrenching breakup. Or losing your high-paying corporate job and (by accident) finding a job much better suited to your skills and interests.

Luck is both good and bad. We can't design for luck, but we can learn to focus on actions and behaviors that do not depend on luck. There will always be people who enjoy a disproportionate amount of luck (both good and bad), but there is always plenty of scope in our lives to shape our destiny.

Think about your happiness. Dr. Sonya Lybordorski of the University of California Riverside found that roughly 50 percent of our happiness is driven by our genes. There's nothing you can do about that, but what about the other 50 percent? Her research attributes 10 percent to your current life circumstances and 40 percent to your actions and behaviors. As with your health, you influence happiness based on your lifestyle, mindset, and behaviors.

Many people wish their current circumstances were better. They wish they were wealthier, more educated, more connected, and better-looking. Yet, the research reveals that ruminating on things beyond our control wastes time. Rather than gripe about what's beyond your immediate control, a healthier approach is to look at your actions and behavior as the lever for your happiness. Your actions and behaviors account for a much larger portion of the happiness pie than the circumstances surrounding you.

You can choose a life of fulfillment by focusing on your behavior and actions, and maybe you'll be lucky enough to change your circumstances positively. Play *your* game, not the game society wants you to play.

PRINCIPLE #3: PAY ATTENTION TO ALL YOUR NET WEALTH COMPONENTS, NOT JUST ONE OR TWO

Most of the retirement industry is focused on helping people figure out where to live, how to manage their money, and what to do with their newfound time. These are all important elements of a good retirement plan, but they're not sufficient anymore.

Today, people need to focus beyond the basic three areas of **NEST**, **EARNINGS**, and **TIME**. If there is one thing that baby boomers have grown accustomed to, it is customization. A cookie-cutter retirement is not a desirable option for people seeking fulfillment.

Baby boomers expect to live a fulfilling life in retirement. They don't expect to retreat from society simply because their hair has turned gray and thinned. They want to experience life to its fullest for however long they have left on earth. For many, that could be thirty or more years after leaving their primary career behind. That's a long time to accept a cookie-cutter retirement.

People want more. They are living longer, and they have more options. It's become necessary to look beyond the basics of home, money, and time. A world of more options implies greater complexity. To deal with the greater complexity, baby boomers need to adopt a system that allows them to think holistically about all aspects of their lives (financial and non-financial).

The **NET WEALTH** framework presented in this book addresses the needs of baby boomers making systematic decisions about:

- Where to live and how (**NEST**).
- How to fund their lifestyle sustainably (**EARNINGS**).
- How to maximize their time by focusing on activities providing joy and meaning.
- How to continue contributing to society by using existing skills and life experiences either for pay or in a volunteer capacity (**WORK**).

- How to emphasize emotions that contribute to higher energy levels, emotional balance, and resilience (**EMOTIONAL ENERGY**).
- Designing goals to create a meaningful improvement in the quality of their lives (**ACHIEVEMENTS**).
- How to continue evolving and staying challenged mentally (**LEARNING**).
- Investing into the quality and breath of their social network, including family and friends (**TRIBE**).
- How to fine-tune the body, brain, and mind to live longer and better (**HEALTH**).

All areas are essential for leading a life of joy and fulfillment. Even if you identified a few high-priority areas that need your attention first, the goal is to bring those into balance with all other areas of your life. You can't be a winner in some categories and a loser in others. The goal is balance and alignment with the vision of your Future Self.

Every component of your **NET WEALTH** needs to be in working order and sync with the rest. Otherwise, the weak link leaves you exposed to disappointment and frustration.

"Growth is painful. Change is painful. But, nothing is as painful as staying stuck where you do not belong."

~N. R. NARAYANA MURTHY, FOUNDER OF INFOSYS

PRINCIPLE # 4: THINKING AND PLANNING ARE NOT ENOUGH; YOU MUST ALSO ACT

Thinking and planning are prerequisites for success, but without action, all you have is a dream that becomes more distant every day, which increases your frustration and disappointment instead of giving you joy.

I deferred dreams to planning for many years and waited for the perfect time to act. But guess what? I ended up with great plans I'm still impressed by to this day, but I'm no closer to reaching my goals. I always felt I needed to learn more, have more money in the bank, have better connections, or the timing wasn't right.

Does this sound familiar?

Doing is much harder than thinking and planning. Doing requires discipline, effort, and a lot of courage. Doing requires you to butt heads with your liabilities and mental blocks. Doing requires you to take a leap of faith and believes things will work out. Doing is up to you, nobody else, and you take all the risks.

Acting on your goals isn't for the meek or those people unwilling to take any risk. We all want a high return with no risk, right? But even in fairy tales, there are valleys and peaks.

Your goals may be languishing for various reasons, but you must find a solution to move from planner to doer if they're important to you.

Here are some tips for doing this:

- **Remove all distractions**. No phone, no internet, no bills to be paid should be in your line of sight. Create an environment that helps you focus on your goals.
- **Schedule dedicated time in your calendar**. I've found that using the Pomodoro technique, setting a timer for typically twenty-five minutes, helps me concentrate. If you can't focus on your goal during your dedicated time slot, the only option is to sit in silence. For most people, silence is scarier than getting things done.
- **Stop waiting for the right time.** I'll never come. Accept that you'll feel resistance at first. Getting started is always the most challenging part.
- **Play a game with yourself by keeping the streak alive**. Mark your calendar with an X every day you've worked on your goals. The goal is to have as many Xs in a row as possible. This technique was good enough to motivate Jerry Seinfeld to write one joke per day.

- **Break your goals into small chunks of time**. Instead of saying you need a minimum of two hours to work on your goals, settle for fifteen-minute chunks of time. Using this method, you'll be less prone to avoid the task at hand. Tiny power moves will turn into massive results if done consistently. We can all find some time to work on our goals.
- **Figure out what you will do ahead of time when the resistance shows up**. If I get derailed by X, I will do Y. This technique is called setting implementation intentions. It allows you to feel in control of your behavior. Figuring out what derails you isn't magic because it's usually the same thing every day.

PRINCIPLE #5: MANAGE YOUR EXPECTATIONS, BUT DON'T EXPECT CLEAR SKIES ONLY; BE READY FOR TURBULENCE AND AIR POCKETS.

A victory lap done at the end. It's good to have a positive mindset and expect favorable results, but is there more to the story than our mind allows us to see?

I don't always say life is hard. I actually don't believe that. I think life can be hard at times, but that's not the same as saying life is mostly struggling. Sure, we all struggle, but we also (hopefully) have plenty of moments of joy.

All I am saying is that one needs to be realistic. Life is never linear. More often, there are a lot of challenges and roadblocks along the way.

A great life in retirement doesn't mean a perfect life. Expecting perfection is the surest way to be frustrated perpetually. It's said that frustration occurs when expectations don't meet reality.

I used to live a life of frustration until I realized two things. The first was that all that frustration was counterproductive. It zapped my energy and created untold stress in my life. The second realization was that a big portion of my frustration was caused by having unrealistic expectations in the first place. I expected everything to happen according to my plan, not realizing that the real world is always changing and temperamental.

When do things go according to plan? Hardly ever. Sure, occasionally, we get surprised, and things go smoothly. But most times, everything has a messy middle.

So how can we minimize the frustration of unmet expectations? It's not easy, but reframing may help.

The following reminders have helped me maintain perspective:

- You can't predict how other people will react, so accept that everybody has their priorities, perspectives, and problems.
- Recognize that things will go wrong at times, and there's nothing you can do about it. It's not personal. You just need to recover.
- Accept that the world is ever-evolving and changing. You will never have enough money, time, looks, or patience to overcome all ills. Adjust to what is, not what was or what should be.
- Nothing is as bad as you think. Most of us catastrophize situations in our heads. We imagine worst-case scenarios that, in hindsight, hardly ever materialize. Take a step back and see how you feel a little later.
- Sometimes, things take longer. We might be great at planning, but we often assume perfect sailing conditions. Your frustration is a function of planning for an ideal world, not one with many moving parts. Give yourself time.
- Don't judge yourself too harshly. You can't expect all your decisions to work out. Nobody is perfect. Remember, great baseball players only hit three balls out of ten.
- Your frustration could result from other things going on in your life. Are you trying to overcompensate for areas in your life where you're feeling stress? What's really bothering you? Your sense of peace and balance in life depends on all areas of your life being in sync. Maybe the pain in your back is all about the stress in your life. Identify the cause of your pain points.

We easily get frustrated because we're comparing ourselves to an ideal that doesn't exist. Move your thinking into the real world. There will be detours and challenges. Some will be expected; some will surprise you. In either case, find a way to move forward if your goals matter to you.

PRINCIPLE #6: BE GRATEFUL AND PAY IT FORWARD

This principle is about the greater good. Plenty of research shows that being grateful does wonders for your mental health. Grateful people tend to lead happier lives.

There will always be people who appear to have more than you. They live in a bigger house, have a beautiful family, drive better cars, are better-looking, smarter, and have more connections, but would you trade your life for theirs without knowing what lurks behind closed doors?

Are you willing to accept that maybe the grass isn't always greener across the fence?

A friend once asked me if I was wealthy. The question gave me pause because compared to many of my friends in the financial industry, I made far less money, but I was considerably wealthier compared to many other people, especially those I grew up with in Latin America.

After I regained my composure, I told him yes; I was wealthy, but not because of money in the bank. I'm wealthy because I have (under most plausible scenarios) more than enough to lead the type of life that brings me joy and fulfillment.

I have my family, friends, health, and things to do with my time that are important and meaningful to me. I have shelter, food, basic care, extra luxuries like my annual trip to the US Open with my son, beach days with my kids and their significant others, handmade Colombian shoes, and bread pudding.

I have peace of mind and an understanding of our insignificance on our own but vitally important to the well-being of our fellow human beings. We only exist because of others, and we only thrive in the company of others.

These things, plus many others, make me grateful for my life. We all have had disappointments and regrets, but at this moment, I'm happy to have had the life I've had.

I also realize that many people aren't where they want to be in their lives, and gratitude may be harder to practice. However, the benefits of expressing gratitude are immense. For example, being grateful for your life makes you more open to forming new social connections. It correlates to better health, physical and mental. It makes you less reactionary and aggressive when you experience stress and more open to helping others.

When grateful, your positive energy has a funny way of manifesting itself in the presence of others. One of my primary beliefs in life is that we owe it to the universe to pass on good vibes and help others who aren't as blessed.

PRINCIPLE #7: REMAIN OPEN TO POSSIBILITIES

A psychological concept popularized by Dr. Daniel Gilbert called the End of History Illusion describes how individuals who've experienced growth and change throughout their lives don't expect much change in the future. Even though they have changed a lot in the past, they expect the status quo to prevail moving forward.

Research confirms that people underestimate how much they'll change in the future. The tendency to underestimate change prevents people from actively changing. The effect is found to be more pronounced as people age.

A willingness to entertain a Future Self and life circumstances different from today is key to fulfillment. Despite the tendency of people to expect that everything will stay the same, we know that change is all around us, and, if anything, the pace of change has accelerated dramatically over the last couple of decades.

If the world is changing, shouldn't we? Are we not changing our thoughts and beliefs along the way? Change is ever-present. Our external world is changing, and so are our internal perspectives.

> *"Change is the law of life. And those who look only to the past or present are certain to miss the future."*
>
> ~JOHN F. KENNEDY, FORMER US PRESIDENT

A LIFE OF POSSIBILITY

The world is full of possibilities. Some are right for you, and some should be shut down permanently. Some possibilities, frankly, may scare you even though they're intriguing. Some of your fears may be imaginary, but they feel real to you. Many times, you'll feel more comfortable staying put where you are. New possibilities always involve uncertainty and risk.

Despite the risk, what new possibilities are you open to taking—a new place to live, a new friendship, a new way of contributing to society, or new growth-oriented behaviors and daily habits?

In turn, what are you shutting down? What are you removing from your life? A soul-sucking job, a toxic group of friends, unhealthy eating habits, or old behavior patterns that no longer fit?

What set of beliefs have been holding you back? Are you stuck in the past, always thinking of the good old days when you were much younger?

Do you wish things would stay the same forever and life was predictable? Unfortunately, there's zero chance that that will happen. Time flies, and it whizzes by like a hurricane as you get older.

A life of possibility doesn't mean that nothing changes once you set the vision of your Future Self. Your journey isn't a straight line from your current self to your Future Self.

As with all journeys, you'll encounter changing weather conditions, roadblocks, and detours that require you to stay mentally strong and resilient. Life will also require you to develop a flexible mindset. At some point, you may realize the best path forward is no longer the one you expected. Maybe you'll see something along the way that intrigues you and pulls you in a new direction. Perhaps your final destination is no longer where you want to end up? If (or when) that happens, it might be time for a new vision!

Like a well-tended garden, you'll always nourish and nurture your vision. Retirement is not a one-and-done deal. In the two or three decades you spend in retirement, things will change, and, more importantly, you'll change, too. What gives your life meaning may vary depending on your experiences and relationships. Your values and beliefs may also grow and evolve with the times. Our lives are not static. It's up to us to design our Future Selves, to evolve and grow. It's better to recognize a world of possibilities than limit ourselves to what is familiar and comfortable. Maximize the return on your time, be grateful for your past, and look forward to your future. I am with you on this wonderful journey! Here is to happiness and fulfillment!

ACKNOWLEDGMENTS

This book could not have been possible without the support of a large number of people.

I am immensely grateful to Jeff Goins and his team at Fresh Complaint LLC especially Sandy Kreps and Ariel Curry for guiding me through the process of becoming a first-time book author. I first met Jeff back in 2018 and his insightful and personal approach has been an unexpected bonus during this creative process. Thanks for sticking with me.

My evolution as a writer has not been easy. While early in my career I spent a considerable amount of time publishing journal articles and "geeky" white papers writing for a broader audience of laypeople is quite different. Luckily, several years back I stumbled across noted blogger Jon Morrow and his right-hand person Marsha Stopa who gently gave me the confidence and frameworks to adopt a friendlier, more interesting way of writing. Without both of you, I would still be writing white papers.

For the last four years, I have been a member of Dr. Benjamin Hardy's AMP mastermind. Ben's program has exposed me to a ton of incredibly relevant guiding principles in the personal growth space. Moreover, Ben's willingness to share his own journey has been inspirational. Two of his most powerful teachings that have stuck with me are everybody's ability to change and the necessity to always look forward and take action. Thanks, Ben, for being such a great example of personal transformation. Your enthusiasm is infectious.

Writing a book requires a ton of commitment and belief. You will not get to the finish line without overcoming a lot of detours and self-doubts. I would have not been able to do it without the support of my accountability group

(Pod#21). We met every Tuesday night for over two years. You kept me going when it would have been easier to declare victory and focus on an easier path. Thanks, Gabriella, Jan, Robin, Emily, Andrew, Mark, Pedja, Michael, Jeff, and Tom. You'll always have a seat on my personal advisory board.

Finally, I have to acknowledge my family as the main source of emotional energy and spiritual support. To my wife, Tricia, who has listened tirelessly to all my ideas and fascination with the topic of retirement and personal growth. Your caring and encouraging nature have kept me grounded. I am lucky to be sharing this journey with you.

I would also like to thank my uncle, Alvaro Chaves who has been a source of inspiration throughout my life. I have never encountered somebody so able to instantly make friends with people across all age groups and circumstances in life. You immediately became "Tio" to them. Your passion for life and especially relationships has been a great source of motivation in my life. You are my role model for how to live a happy and fulfilling life in retirement.

Finally, to my three adult children – Jessica, Gabriela, and Nicholas. My desire to provide you with an example of re-invention and self-improvement is what gives me energy day in and day out to be a better person. You are my true legacy to this world. Thank you for putting up with all my dad jokes and endlessly playing 80's music as you were growing up. You've made my life so much richer.

ABOUT THE AUTHOR

Eric J. Weigel is the founder of Retire With Possibilities, an advisory and retirement coaching firm dedicated to helping people consciously design their own journey into retirement. Eric is a Certified Professional Retirement Coach and University of Chicago MBA with more than 3 decades of experience helping institutions and individuals better align their investments to the outcomes they truly desire.

Eric is a Baby Boomer born in Washington, D.C. to a Costa Rican mother and German father. He has lived in four countries and is fluent in Spanish. His muti-national upbringing has greatly influenced his outlook on life. Around his 50th birthday, it dawned on him that he needed to take greater ownership over his life. He started thinking about having more adventure in his life again. He started thinking seriously about his finances, how to stay in better shape, and hobbies that he once had such as gardening and tennis. He began exploring new lines of work that could bring me more fulfillment.

Rather than just wing it, he started seriously thinking what he needed to do to achieve a happy and fulfilling life in retirement. He knew that a cookie-cutter approach would not work in a world of limitless opportunities and complexity. Rather, Eric went about it in an intentional manner starting with a vision of what he wanted his life to be and then designing the necessary action steps. This book is the outcome of over a decade of research and self-introspection.

Eric splits his time between Boston and Martha's Vineyard. He is still hoping to someday convince his wife to move part-time to either Costa Rica or Mexico, but for now he endures the New England winters visiting his three adult children and granddaughters, watching a healthy dose of English football, and keeping up with the latest developments in the personal growth, financial innovation, and economic development fields.

His current professional activities involve coaching individuals at Retire With Possibilities on the financial and non-financial aspects that make for a happy and fulfilling life. He is also active within the investment industry holding a couple of board level positions, managing portfolios to create an income stream in retirement, and investing in leading edge financial innovations.

BIBLIOGRAPHY

Agronin, Marc E. *Alzheimer's Disease and Other Dementias: A Practical Guide*. Routledge, 2014.
Altucher, James. *Reinvent Yourself*. New York: Choose Yourself Media, 2016.
Bengen, William P. "Determining Withdrawal Rates Using Historical Data." *Journal of Financial Planning* 7.4 (1994): 171-180.
Bridges, William. *Managing Transitions: Making the Most of Change*. Da Capo Press, 2009.
Buettner, Dan. *The Blue Zones: 9 Lessons for Living Longer From the People Who've Lived the Longest*. National Geographic Books, 2012.
Cabral, Stephen. "2201: How to Enjoy Endless Energy." *The Cabral Concept*. February 14, 2022. Podcast, MP3 audio. https://stephencabral.com/podcast/2201.
Conley, Chip, and Ingo Rauth. "The Emergence of Long Life Learning." (2020).
Covey, Stephen R. "Emotional Bank Accounts." *The Journal for Quality and Participation* 17.7 (1994): 36.
David, Susan. *Emotional Agility: Get Unstuck, Embrace Change, and Thrive in Work and Life*. Penguin, 2016.
Dweck, Carol. *Mindset: The New Psychology of Success*. Random House, 2008.
Dychtwald, Ken. *What Retirees Want: A Holistic View of Life's Third Age*. John Wiley, 2020.
Fitzgerald, Kara. *Younger You: Reduce Your Bio Age and Live Longer, Better*. Hachette, 2022.
Fogg, BJ. *Tiny Habits: The Small Changes That Change Everything*. Houghton Mifflin Harcourt, 2020.
Frankl, Viktor E. *Man's Search for Meaning*. Simon and Schuster, 1985.
Fredrickson, Barbara L. "The Role of Positive Emotions in Positive Psychology: The Broaden-And-Build Theory of Positive Emotions." *American Psychologist* 56.3 (2001): 218.
Fredrickson, Barbara. *Positivity*. Harmony, 2009.
Gilbert, Daniel. *Stumbling on Happiness*. Vintage Canada, 2009.
Goldsmith, Marshall. *Triggers: Creating Behavior That Lasts*. Crown, 2015.
Goleman, Daniel. *Emotional Intelligence: Why It Can Matter More Than IQ*. Bloomsbury Publishing, 1996.
Gratton, Lynda, and Andrew J. Scott. *The 100-year life: Living and Working in an Age of Longevity*. Bloomsbury Publishing, 2016.
Hardy, Benjamin. *Personality Isn't Permanent: Break Free From Self-Limiting Beliefs*. Penguin Random House, 2020.
Hardy, Benjamin. *Willpower Doesn't Work: Discover the Hidden Keys to Success*. Hachette, 2018.
Hardy, Darren. *The Compound Effect: Jumpstart Your Income, Your Life, Your Success*. Da Capo, 2010.
Hawkins, David R. *The Map of Consciousness Explained: A Proven Energy Scale to Actualize Your Ultimate Potential*. Hay House, Inc, 2020.
Hawkins, David. *Power vs. Force: The Hidden Determinants of Human Behavior*. Hay House, 2013.
Holmes, Thomas H., and Richard H. Rahe. "The Social Readjustment Rating Scale." *Journal of Psychosomatic Research* 11.2 (1967): 213-218.

Kahneman, Daniel, and Angus Deaton. "High Income Improves Evaluation of Life But Not Emotional Well-Being." *Proceedings of the National Academy of Sciences* 107.38 (2010): 16489-16493.

Kirshenbaum, Mira. *The Emotional Energy Factor: The Secrets High-energy People Use to Beat Emotional Fatigue.* Delta, 2008.

Lyubomirsky, Sonja. *The How of Happiness: A Scientific Approach to Getting the Life You Want.* Penguin, 2008.

McKeown, Greg. *Essentialism: The Disciplined Pursuit of Less.* Currency, 2020.

Oettingen, Gabriele. *Rethinking Positive Thinking: Inside the New Science of Motivation.* Current, 2015.

Peterson, Christopher, and Martin EP Seligman. *Character Strengths and Virtues: A Handbook and Classification. Vol. 1.* Oxford University Press, 2004.

Quoidbach, Jordi, Daniel T. Gilbert, and Timothy D. Wilson. "The End of History Illusion." *Science* 339.6115 (2013): 96-98.

Ryan, Robin. *Retirement Reinvention: Make Your Next Act Your Best Act.* Penguin Book. 2018.

Schwartz, Barry. *The Paradox of Choice: Why More is Less.* ECCo, 2004.

Seligman, Martin EP. *Flourish: A Visionary New Understanding of Happiness and Well-Being.* Simon and Schuster, 2012.

Smith, Emily Esfahani. *The Power of Meaning: Finding Fulfillment in a World Obsessed With Happiness.* Crown, 2017.

Sullivan, Dan, and Benjamin Hardy. *The Gap and The Gain: The High Achievers' Guide to Happiness, Confidence, and Success.* Hay House, Inc, 2021.

Vaillant, George E. "Triumphs of experience." *Triumphs of Experience.* Harvard University Press, 2012.

Waldinger, Robert. "What Makes a Good Life." *Lessons From the Longest Study on Happiness* (2015).

Ware, Bronnie. *The Top Five Regrets of the Dying: A Life Transformed by the Dearly Departing.* Hay House, Inc, 2012.

Williams, Mark. *The Art and Science of Aging Well: A Physicians Guide to a Healthy Body, Mind, and Spirit.* North Carolina Press, 2016